PRAISE FOR *THE WOMAN MAGICIAN*

"Every once in a while a book is published that has the potential to shatter preconceptions and change them forever. Such a book is The Woman Magician. This revolutionary book recognizes the theoretical, literary, and practical advances of the women's movement and women's spirituality that have roiled the world, especially over the last fifty to one-hundred years. It boldly applies them to the archaic conventions of the past, resulting in a form of magick, initiation, and spiritual evolution that will move women to the forefront—in name and in fact—of the ceremonial magick world. Watch out, you old-school guys! The Woman Magician is coming, and we'll all be better for it."

—Donald Michael Kraig, author of *Modern Magick*

"*The Woman Magician* is an amazing and much-needed book. It is a valuable, powerful, and personal yet universal look at our shared 'Magia Traditionis,' and anyone who is a seeker or practitioner will find much here to relate to and learn about. I highly recommend this book to any and all who seek a deep and unique exploration of our shared magical roots from a Woman of Power."

—Denny Sargent, author of *Global Ritualism* and *Your Guardian Angel and You*

D1636398

ABOUT THE AUTHOR

Brandy Williams is a Witch, Ceremonial Magician, and ordained priestess of EGC. Her previous books include *Practical Magic for Beginners*, *Ecstatic Ritual: Practical Sex Magic*, and *Women's Voices in Magic*. She lives in Kitsap County in Washington state, where she is active in the local transition movement. Additional information about Brandy and the Order of the Sisters of Seshat can be found at www.sistersofseshat.com.

THE
WOMAN
MAGICIAN

Revisioning Western Metaphysics from
a Woman's Perspective and Experience

BRANDY WILLIAMS

Llewellyn Publications
Woodbury, Minnesota

FIRST EDITION
First Printing, 2011

Cover art © John William Waterhouse/Bridgeman Art Library, London/SuperStock
Cover design by Adrienne Zimiga
Interior illustrations by the Llewellyn Art Department

Llewellyn Publishing is a registered trademark of Llewellyn Worldwide Ltd.

Library of Congress Cataloging-in-Publication Data
Williams, Brandy, 1956–
 The woman magician : revisioning Western metaphysics from a woman's perspective and experience / Brandy Williams. — 1st ed.
  p. cm.
 Includes bibliographical references (p.   ) and index.
 ISBN 978-0-7387-2724-0
 1. Magic. 2. Women. 3. Feminism. I. Title.
 BF1621.W55 2011
 133.4'3082--dc23

                          2011021127

Llewellyn Publications
A Division of Llewellyn Worldwide Ltd.
2143 Wooddale Drive
Woodbury, MN 55125-2989
www.llewellyn.com

Printed in the United States of America

DEDICATION

To all the sisters of my heart. In particular to Soror Inde Seraphina, who kept asking for this book until I wrote it.

ACKNOWLEDGEMENTS

I am indebted to many generous and thoughtful people in the magical communities, in the Pacific Northwest, and in the contemporary intellectual traditions for their support of the processes that resulted in this book.

Two women provided the quiet spaces into which I retreated, the real physical enclosures that granted me the solitude to hear my own voice during the process of writing this book: Petra Martin and the Whidbey Island Writer's Refuge, and Therese Charvet of Sacred Groves, a ten-acre forest sanctuary and eco-retreat center on Bainbridge Island. I am deeply grateful for their generous hospitality.

The women and men who attended my workshops and lectures contributed interest, energy, and perspective. Chance comments that may seem trivial can have profound effects.

I had the good fortune to speak with Irshad Manji, the woman who wrote *The Trouble with Islam Today*, knowing she'd spend the rest of her life traveling with bodyguards. When I told her of the fear I experienced championing women's concerns in traditionally male-centric communities, she said to me, "In a free society there is no reason for self-censorship." I repeat those words to myself often as I write. I also think about the grand dame of Dianic Witchcraft, Zsuzsanna Budapest, who enjoined me (along with many others) to "Make trouble!"

The *Women's Voices in Magic* project acted as a collective counterpoint to this soliloquy. I am grateful to all the women who contributed to the volume, as well as managing editor Taylor Ellwood, whose belief in the work made it possible.

The women participating in the e-group Magia Femina and the women and men of the Open Source Order of the Golden Dawn have provided ears willing to listen and an extended community. Creative women have always needed a group context to support the work; you have provided mine.

My sisters and brothers in Ordo Templi Orientis lived through numerous iterations of my lecture on feminist Thelema, which prepared the ground for this treatment. I appreciate the opportunity I was given to present that work to the national O.T.O. community at NOTOCON VI.

Special thanks to Richard Kazynski, editor of the volume *Beauty and Strength: Proceedings of the Sixth Biennial National Ordo Templi Orientis Conference*, whose conversations on this topic helped to clarify my thinking.

The readers who took the time to comment on this volume were invaluable: Ted Gill, Kallista, Shellay Lynn Maughan, Renee Randazzo, and Soror Inde Seraphina. I am also grateful to T Polyphilus for references, discussion, and feedback, which made this a better book. Finally, Llewellyn acquisitions editor Elysia Gallo's meticulous review was invaluable and deeply appreciated.

As always, I must thank Alex Williams and Ted Gill, who gave unstintingly of their time, encouraged me in my darkest moments, stood back when the circle closed them out, and stood guard outside that circle to make the work within possible. They are exemplars of brotherhood.

I have spent much of my adult life with my sister Kallista, talking feminism and magic, as well as writing, performing, and critiquing ritual. She spent many hours with me on the ritual section of this book, which is immeasurably improved by her input. Her insights resonate throughout this book.

Finally, I offer my profoundest gratitude to the first Sisters of Seshat: Dana Doerksen, Egypt Rose, Kallista, Kineta Chien, Onyieh Bunnie Jewel, Shellay Lynne Maughan, and Soror Inde Seraphina. Your work has made these rituals sing and has broken the ground for the sisters who come after us.

While this work would not have been possible without aid from the people listed above, all opinions, conclusions, errors, and omissions here are strictly my own.

CONTENTS

PART THREE: The Heart of the Tradition

LIST OF ILLUSTRATIONS

INTRODUCTION

I am a woman magician. By *woman*, I mean that I was born into a culture that recognizes two biologically based sexes and that I was raised in the female sex. I have always been comfortable with my body's sex assignment, but I have not always been comfortable with the assumptions made about me because I am a woman and the way I am expected to behave. Also, I have not always been comfortable in the company of other women, although I have come to understand and cherish women's culture.

By *magician*, I mean that I practice Western Traditional Magic. Magic feels like home to me. I've jumped at every scrap of information I could get about it since I was a little girl. I've spent a lifetime organizing, writing, teaching, and living in the magical communities. Even so, I have often felt as uncomfortable in magic as I have been as a woman, and for many of the same reasons. This sense of *standing outside my home* has led me to spend decades studying religion, history, and philosophy, seeking to understand how magic has come to be what it is today and how it has come to view women and men the way it does. This work is an exploration of the tradition from a woman's point of view. It explores what the tradition gives us, how it fails us, and how we can shape it to serve us better.

Throughout this book, I use my own life as a jumping-off point for discussion. I do this deliberately, as a reflection of women's ways of knowing, which insist on grounding in the historic, the specific, the

1

useful, and the intimate, deriving authority from personal history and embodied experience.

I was not born into the lineage of Western Traditional Magic. I was born a year before the Witchcraft laws were repealed in England, at a time when very few were being raised as Witches. I was raised Catholic but converted to Witchcraft at sixteen.

As a Catholic, I grew up immersed in stately and majestic ritual lofted by music. The priest's robes, the magical language, the gestures all seemed fantastically sacred to me. I looked longingly at the robes of the priest and said, *That's what I want to wear, that's what I want to do.* If I had been a man, I would have said I had a calling and gone into the priesthood. The glitch here, of course, is that I am a woman, and the Church did not then and does not now permit women to enter the priesthood.

I set out to find a religion that accepted the positive contribution of women. In the pre-Internet 1970s, as a minor child, my exploration was limited to what I could read. When I picked up a copy of Sybil Leek's book *The Complete Art of Witchcraft,* I found my religion. This book was written by a woman who modeled a way of being in the world that acknowledged the natural forces and sought to work with them, as well as opening a gate into mystery. As a Witch, a woman could conduct ritual—I could conduct ritual on behalf of my coveners.

Many of us enter the tradition in this way, through books, and now through the Internet. Western Traditional Magic is a literate lineage, recorded and passed through the published text.

I spent a number of years reading the handful of books available and constructing a practice from those. My earliest attempts at ritual taught me the lesson that has been the most important of my magical career. There were a lot of rules to Witchcraft when I first started practicing it, and in my teens I endeavored to follow them all. I ordered a silver cup from a jeweler. I buried a knife in the ground for seven days. I bought a length of red fabric trim for my cord. Following the rules, I used my cord to measure my living room. The circle I was trying to cast was supposed to be nine feet wide, but I discovered I did not quite have nine feet of floor space in the room. Standing up next to my couch holding the end of the cord in my hand, confronted with the choice between sticking with the text and not doing the ritual or going forward, I made my first and most enduring rule: *you can change it so that it works.*

When I entered into the magical communities, the cutting edge of magico-religious thought was centered in the neo-Pagan and women's spirituality movements. The first group I encountered was a Dianic woman-only study group centered on the teachings of Zsuzsanna Budapest. As this study group was also primarily composed of women in the local National Organization for Women chapter, I simultaneously entered the world of feminist discourse and action. We cast circles, ran consciousness-raising groups, and protested injustice, and each action supported both our feminism and our spirituality. Through Z's work I experienced the power of women's magical community.

Through the occult bookstores of the era I encountered Aleister Crowley's work. I had at one point a shelf of his books. As I read his work, I'd occasionally come across a misogynistic passage and throw the book against the wall. There was no entrance for a feminist woman into this work at that time. I gave the books away and turned away from that part of the path for some years.

I was drawn to Crowley because I was reaching for information about sex magic. This was just at the moment when the feminist movement took its sex-negative turn. My Dianic group no longer offered me the experiences I was drawn to explore. As a woman and a heterosexual sex magician, I needed to work magic with men. I undertook an apprenticeship and a first-degree initiation as a traditional Witch.

One characteristic of Western Traditional Magic that all the groups share is that, although you can practice on your own and learn from books, to truly belong to the lineage you need to be initiated. Some person or group must conduct a ritual that, among other things, inducts you into the group.

Initiation is a perilous topic. While initiation confers membership into a group, that group will almost certainly be a subset of the lineage. Initiations are quite emphatically not recognized by other groups, even groups that are quite similar. Witches may be Gardnerian, Alexandrian, Georgian, each of these lines taking its name from its founder, whose ritual or initiatory lineage differed in some way from his predecessors. Today you can be a traditional Witch, eclectic Witch, or Wiccan, each name describing some further subdivision of religious practice. Golden Dawn groups splinter like split firewood. O.T.O. groups are not only mutually exclusive but actively hostile to one another.

Initiation into traditional Witchcraft exposed me to the gender expectations that I had avoided while sheltered in the Dianic woman-only world. As soon as I was initiated, a sexually charged twenty-one-year-old woman, I was hit on by every man in the group, which alarmed and alienated me. As a feminist, I could not help but notice that the High Priestess who was supposed to be in charge of the group was a housewife who deferred to her husband in the day-to-day world. It was less than a year before I left that organization and struck out again to find a way to practice where I was safer from masculine predation.

What I found was a Ceremonial Magician. He provided a door into the world of ritual magic for me. He stood beside me as a man who cared about me, understood me, and who supported my feminist ideals. We married and went on a three-year retreat, living and working in an apple orchard in eastern Washington while devouring works on history, psychology, philosophy, and the new physics. In his company, I started a course of independent study of Golden Dawn and Aurum Solis magical texts.

The path I took into the Ceremonial lodges is not unusual. While some encounter a practicing group and take initiations while studying, others spend years studying the material before seeking out initiation. Also, while some women are drawn to Ceremonial Magic on their own, it is common for a woman to enter into a Ceremonial system through relationship with a man in the system.

During this retreat, I was invited to join a group called the Feminist Qabbalist Collective. It was the mid-1980s, the high-water mark of feminist movement in the twentieth century, when women exuberantly explored many realms previously barred to us. Collective members wrote essays, photocopied them, and sent copies to each other in a pre-Internet discussion group. The stated goal of this group was to write a book to be called *The Feminist Adept*. I was one of the youngest, least experienced, and least well-read members of this group. When the group disbanded a few years later, I was determined to gain the education and experience to be able to write that book.

In the decades since the collective took its first feminist look at Qabbalah, there has been very little feminist or woman-centered work done on Ceremonial Magic. Ellen Cannon Reed, Rachel Pollack, and Judith Laura are the pioneers in this field.

My husband and I moved to an urban area where we quickly connected with the magical communities. I spent the 1990s in community work as a Witch and a Pagan organizer. It was only in 2000 that I returned to the ceremonial lodges to work my way through O.T.O. and Golden Dawn initiations.

As I entered into lodge practice, I laid aside my feminist understandings. There were many places where the metaphors didn't work for me, where the ritual seemed like a coat cut for a man. At one point I acted this out—I went to a Twenties-themed costume party dressed in a man's suit and tie, sporting a fedora. I didn't verbalize this sense of displacement, but I entered into the initiations as a full participant, willing to learn and to experience the tradition on its own terms.

After one of my O.T.O. initiations, my initiators asked me, "Why do people think the O.T.O. isn't feminist?" There it was, the question of my life. Carol Lee Flinders talks about the moment when she felt a conflict between feminism and her spiritual path, and "there was no way in the world I could go on pretending it wasn't there" (Flinders 1998).

I launched into an effort to understand my spiritual path in the light of my feminism. I read, I wrote, I talked to other women. At first I thought it was a work that would be accomplished and then incorporated into my life, that I would move beyond it. I'm not so sure now that this work is ever actually finished, and for most of a decade now this work has been central to my life. There is so much to be done, it is not work that can be done in a short time or by only one woman. It takes much time, study, discussion, experimentation, and the input of many women.

My husband has become more fiercely feminist over the years. He, my inamorato, and other men in our magical family act to support the women around them. I have come to understand how vital it is that men support women in our explorations. They are our allies as well as our fathers, brothers, lovers, sons, and friends. One of our most important works is to revision our relationships with them.

It is also important that women talk and act together. Many women in my Internet-extended magical world are exploring similar questions: Who were the women who came before us? What did they write? How do we adapt these systems to meet our needs? How do we relate to each other as women in the magical world? Our most important work is to revision how magic works for women.

In *Privilege, Power, and Difference*, Allan G. Johnson discusses four axes of privilege. The assumed person is male, white, heterosexual, and able-bodied. I am female and disadvantaged on that axis. I am also white, heterosexual, and able-bodied. The only acceptable use of privilege is to use it to level privilege. On the axes on which I inhabit privilege, I aspire to make a difference and to assist people who challenge the inequality of power.

The issue of the unconscious assumption that magical culture is white has been raised to me in several venues; white leaders in the magical communities must work to identify privilege within ourselves and create opportunities for people of color to do the magical work they wish to do, to create a Magica Humana worthy of the name. Also, many women and men in the magical communities have created family structures that are not officially recognized and do not share the protections granted to heterosexual marriage, placing many of my friends at risks in ways that heterosexual people are not. We create family structures recognized within the communities, such as marriages performed by the Ecclesia Gnostica Catholica (EGC), carving out a humane world inside the dominant culture.

Contemporary Western culture consumes world resources at an astonishing rate and even more shamefully wastes many of those resources. We insist on the best and the perfect, on produce without blemishes and the best cuts of meat, throwing away bruised apples and working appliances that are simply old. We throw away people too, marginalizing those whose faculties are not perfect and warehousing our elderly. As I age, I increasingly encounter derision and dismissal, and increasingly fear the loss of physical capacity. As a person who is not yet old, I encourage elders in the magical communities to tell and record their stories so that their collected wisdom remains available to us. I also spend significant chunks of time sitting beside people in hospitals making sure they are cared for and that they are surrounded by people they love. It is easy to run over the frail and infirm, who cannot protect themselves; each of us who knows an older person can act to make their lives better. Remember too that this is the area in which we will all lose privilege—someday every one of us will need an advocate, so creating a culture of caring now directly benefits us in the future.

As a woman, I have often been aided by men who cleared a path for me to be able to do my work, both in the work world and in the magical communities, and I am grateful to all of them.

This book is really a set of notes about my course of exploration, what I have learned so far, and some ideas about how the work can move forward. Again and again this work challenges me to listen to myself. At its best, this is what all philosophy, theology, spirituality imparts: the importance of really hearing ourselves, finding our own truths, and faithfully clinging to those truths whatever may happen to us. When we touch down to the truth about ourselves, we find the truth of life, the sacred center of the universe. In the words of Doreen Valiente's "Charge of the Goddess," "If that which thou seekest thou findest not within thee, thou wilt never find it without thee" (Valiente 2000).

There are enemies to this voice. The root enemy is the philosophy that gives rise to racism and sexism, to the destruction of the earth's lovely web of life; the philosophy that authorizes war and atrocity, turning people and places into things, taking sacred creation and converting all into objects to be used. Carol Lee Flinders cites the author bell hooks as saying: "There is nothing in you that is of value; everything of value is outside you and must be acquired" (Flinders 1998).

Once we learn to listen to the voice within, to distinguish this voice from all the other voices outside us, it rings clearly, like a bell. It is unmistakable. But it is hard to get to the place where we can hear it. It takes extraordinary measures. This is what magic is about, getting us to that place. The concerns of the world pull us away from that endeavor. Even when we finally hear that voice, it is the easiest thing imaginable to let it go, to drift back into the comfortable place where we do not have to act on what we know. Even when we faithfully cling to that voice, the enemies of that voice strive to drown it out.

But if we let go of that voice, we lose ourselves. As I write, I sit in front of a window looking out on the ocean at Long Beach, Washington, in December. Wind slams rain into the window glass. Later I will bundle up and walk along the beach. It's eleven miles in length and varies in width with the tides. As I walk, I will keep my eyes on the water, wary of sneaker waves, unexpectedly large waves that land much higher on the littoral than the ones before and after. The ocean here isn't safe for swimming, even in summer; vicious rip tides swirl everything out to sea. It is said that once you lose your footing on the beach, you have lost your life.

You have lost your life, that is, unless you are rescued. Again and again I lose my footing, swept away in the tide of voices speaking with the authority of ages, the authority of position, the authority of certainty. It is hard for any woman to speak authentically; I continually lose the thread of my story. Again and again I am rescued by listening to other women's voices: the spiritual women, Sister Prudence Allen, Judith Plaskow, Rita Gross, Irshad Manji; the sociological women, Mary Belenky, Blythe Clinchy, Nancy Goldberger, Jill Tarule; the philosophical women, Andrea Nye, Marilyn Frye, Christine Battersby; the magical women, Vicki Noble, Ellen Cannon Reed, Rachel Pollack, Judith Laura; the historians of magical women, Alex Owen, Mary K. Greer; Carol Lee Flinders, whose voice I return to again and again; and to the magical sisters in my life, Kallista, Shellay, Onyieh, Egypt, Heather, Courtney, Helen, Soror Inde Seraphina. They set me back on my feet. They hold me to my story. They are the sisters of my heart.

PART ONE

MAGIA FEMINA

What some call Ceremonial Magic, meaning magical lodges from lines such as the Golden Dawn, Aurum Solis, Ordo Templi Orientis, Stella Matutina, and the Society of Light, grew out of Freemasonry in the late Victorian era. What we now practice as Witchcraft developed out of the marriage of the forms of Ceremonial Magic with European folk religion. This traditional magic met the challenges of the modern age: the reshaping of the Western spiritual core away from Christianity and toward a more diversified spirituality, the development of science as a legitimate standpoint, and the increasing demands of women to be included in fraternal life.

Western traditional magic has not yet met the challenges of the twenty-first century: the historicizing revision that reframes the universalizing mythologies of the past as responses to their own context; the legacy of the academic frame that negatively contrasted magic with science and religion; contemporary academic colonization of magical groups and texts as material to be analyzed, and often still negatively contrasted with science; the competition of astrophysical cosmology with religious cosmology; the articulation of religious meaning in the context of world religions and the conflicts between them; and the increasing demands of women not just to be included in fraternal life, but to be included on an equal footing with men.

Addressing these challenges will transform Magia Traditionis into Magia Humana. This is an ambitious project that a number of magicians work toward today. As a woman, my own interest has centered on gender analysis and the reform of the magical traditions to fully include women as equal partners. An essential precondition for the development of Magia Humana is the articulation of Magia Femina—traditional magic reshaped around the physical form, emotional center, and spiritual needs of women.

ENCLOSURE, TRANSFORMATION, EMERGENCE

There is a pulse to women's lives, expressed physically in the cycles of menstruation and gestation, and in the grand life arc of fertility, from child to fertile woman to post-fertile and fully mature. This pulse also works in women's spiritual lives. While men's initiations involve isolation, liminality, and reintegration, women undergo a three-step process of enclosure, transformation, and emergence.

What does it mean to be enclosed? Medieval women retreated to small cells walled off from the world, literal enclosures in which they were free to spend their days studying, praying, meditating, contemplating, thinking. I am writing from just such a refuge, a small cabin on Whidbey Island in Washington state. This writer's retreat is a very small cabin with a pocket kitchen, bathroom, one closet, two shelves, and a bed tucked into a curtained alcove. The window beside the desk looks out onto the forest; the whole house is surrounded by trees, which fade into the distance as far as the eye can see, quiet and mysterious.

As I begin this work, it is summer. I wear a denim dress, a costume as unlike my daily wear as possible, a symbol of my dedication to contemplation, my version of the nun's sanctifying habit. I throw a yellow lace shawl on my shoulders and a straw hat on my head to walk in the woods. At night I sometimes sleep on a cot out on the screened porch, listening to several species of owls hooting in the unbroken darkness.

In this refuge, with no distractions, no television or cable channels to watch, no people to talk to, no duties to perform, nothing prevents me from confronting myself. Touching down into the well of the creative, the first thing I encounter is fear. Petra, the woman who has provided this cabin to me for this retreat, reassures me that many other inhabitants of this modern cell have experienced fear here. There is a lot of fear involved in writing, the fear of starting, the fear of not getting it right. This work in particular frightens me because it is so intensely personal that the writing makes me publicly vulnerable. Most of all I am afraid of the world's censure. I am speaking of emotions and stances that many magicians I know, men and women, take personally. I am speaking of change, and change always makes people uncomfortable. I try to be a loving and kind person, a good friend, and confrontation makes me profoundly unhappy.

I reach deep into myself to find the courage to go on with the work, to look without flinching at the heart of gendered magic, to speak my truth gently but clearly. Casting around for a model, an inspiration, I reach out with my entire spiritual self: who will support me in this moment and help me find the courage to speak?

The cabin reminds me of Christine de Pizan's study, particularly the final image reproduced in Susan Groag Bell's essay "Christine de Pizan in Her Study," of Christine sitting at her desk in front of her draped bed (Bell 2008). It occurs to me that Christine must have been afraid too. She was only twenty-five when her husband died, leaving her without a male protector in the world and with a mother and children to support. In 1390, with few options, she turned to writing to support her family.

And what writing! "One day as I was sitting alone in my study," she wrote, she came to wonder "how it happened that so many different men—and learned men among them—have been and are so inclined to express both in speaking and in their treatises and writings so many wicked insults about women and their behavior." In her lament, she called on God to help her understand why a creature he had made, woman, could exhibit such abominations. The spirits who answered her prayer were three ladies, Reason, Rectitude, and Justice. They enjoined Christine to build a City of Ladies to house the memory of women's courage and achievements (de Pizan 1405, 1982).

As a postmodern, feminist, Pagan magician, calling on God doesn't work for me; what makes sense to me is to call on Christine. I summon her memory in my mind's vision and ask her to inspire me, to comfort me, to lend me her strength in the face of my fear.

Christine's prayer was answered by three spirits. I consider invoking those three ladies, but it seems to me that these are not quite the right spirits for my time. I am not sure yet which spirits will guide me. Who should I invoke? Where should I begin my inquiry? First, I reason, I need to look into the heart of the tradition of magic where I have made my home and examine its foundations, to see how it has come to view women in the way that it does.

LADY TRADITION

With Christine's example in front of me, and a little courage borrowed from her in my heart, I turn first to Lady Tradition. I make the invocation: *Come to me, Lady Tradition, and help me to speak of my magic.*

The lady who appears to me has a slender, athletic build. She wears a straight floor-length skirt, a high-necked blouse. With her hair piled on her head, she is the picture of a Victorian aristocrat. She holds herself upright, back arched, eyes straight ahead, clear and intelligent. She is the picture of health, strength, and courtesy. She is neither chilly nor warm—she discourages familiarity, but she is able to be not only severe but also comforting. What she provides, more than anything else, is structure.

I love her. I love everything about her. I love her formality, her discipline, her courage. I have dedicated my life to ensuring that the magical traditions survive intact to pass to generations to come after me. Lady Tradition lives through me.

I say to her, "Why do I have the feeling that I am not at home in the magical traditions into which I have been initiated?"

She answers by pointing to me. Her answer, as always, is that I must understand magic through my own experience.

My spine straightens at the desk and my fingers fly to the keyboard. Under her sturdy gaze, I can begin to tell my story, one story of what it means, in the first decade of the twenty-first century, to be a woman practicing Magia Traditionis.

ENGAGING WESTERN TRADITIONAL MAGIC

I am an initiate of a Golden Dawn lodge, an initiate of Ordo Templi Orientis (O.T.O.), and an initiated traditional Witch. These magical systems are lineally connected in that order through an underlying stratum of shared history and understanding based on late Hellenistic religious-magical theology and ritual practice. Together they form a distinct lineage of Western Traditional Magic. This tradition in turn is the direct lineal predecessor of both the modern neo-Pagan movement and the women's spirituality movements.

A note about the Aurum Solis: because I have not taken an Aurum Solis initiation I do not represent myself as a member of that line, although it has informed my experience of Ceremonial Magic in important ways. I do not discuss this line as a facet of Western Traditional Magic primarily because the only published history available as I write is its official history, so it is difficult for an outsider to assess its relationship to the lineage.

Formal ritual practice is one of the defining characteristics of Western Traditional Magic. Each system (Golden Dawn, Thelema, Witchcraft) has a published set of rituals practiced by its members both alone and in groups, and both before and after initiation.

Ritual descriptions are nearly always given as instructions, directed at the second person, "you" (or in deliberate archaisms, singular "thou"). These instructions are sincerely meant to draw the practitioner into the system, to make it accessible even without a physical teacher. However, that approach masks a number of assumptions about who the practitioner is and where the ritual will take place. It assumes among other things that every practitioner will experience the ritual in the same way. The instructions are written to an imaginary default practitioner.

In reality, these rituals are not performed by a default practitioner, but by real people in real-world situations, which may differ radically from one another. My practice differs from that of my partners and my initiators. This is why each individual story is important, because it illuminates the genuine experience of a real person who is practicing these traditions.

To describe these rituals, I will tell the story of the most recent occasion (at time of writing) that I performed each of these rituals—where I was, what I did, how I understood what had happened, and how I felt when I was done. I take these rituals in the order in which they were created, their lineage order, to make the connections between these rituals clearer. This description will also make clearer how these rituals distinguish between magician and woman.

GOLDEN DAWN:
THE LESSER RITUAL OF THE PENTAGRAM

Preparation

To prepare for this ritual, I make sure I am clean (I take a shower). The appropriate clothing is a white robe, although often (as today) I just wear street clothes.

The Temple

This ritual is performed in my temple. As it happens, this is also my bedroom. The Victorian/Edwardian upper-class people who created the ritual I am about to work had sprawling houses with lots of spare rooms and could dedicate one entire room to this purpose, but I don't have that kind of room in my house.

Performance

Standing in my bedroom in a small area at the foot of the bed, I face east. I lift my hand above my head with an in-breath, and while exhaling bring my fingers down to touch my forehead, visualizing a shaft of white-gold light entering my subtle body through the center above my head and coming down to my third eye. I vibrate "Ateh." Vibration draws on sound techniques imported from several Eastern cultures. It has elements of singing and chanting, but has a more powerful sound, as the note will literally vibrate the body of the practitioner.

I bring my (right/dominant) hand down the front of my body, touching my heart center on the way, to rest on my pubic bone, pointing to the genital center, while visualizing the white-gold column of light extending downward to my feet. I vibrate "Malkuth."

I touch my right shoulder, visualize a spot of light there, and vibrate "V'Geburah." I touch my left shoulder, visualizing the white-gold light forming a cross-shaft along my shoulders, and vibrate "V'Gedulah." I bring the palms of my hands together at chest, pressing my thumbs into the heart center, and say, "Le Olam, Aum," substituting "Aum" for "Amen." The Hebrew words say "Thou art the kingdom, power, glory, forever, amen (aum)."

That's the first gesture, called the Qabbalistic Cross. Next, I move into the second section of the ritual, the Lesser Ritual of the Pentagram.

Still facing east, I trace a pentagram with my hand, imagining a blue line of light as I draw a star with one continuous line. There are a number of ways to draw a star with a continuous line. Depending on which way the line starts, the star is meant to invoke or banish one of the four elements. The pentagram drawn for this ritual is always the banishing earth version, which is why it is sometimes called the Lesser Banishing Ritual. (The Greater Ritual of the Pentagram invokes all the elements.)

I draw my hand back while taking in a breath. Then I step forward, push my hand through the blue light pentagram, and vibrate, "Yod He Vau He." This is the spoken form of YHVH, the Hebrew God.

Turning to the south, I draw a pentagram, pierce it, and vibrate "Adonai," Hebrew for "Lord." To the west, I draw and pierce the pentagram and vibrate "Eheieh," meaning "I am that I am." To the north, I draw and pierce the pentagram and vibrate "AGLA," a notaricon of the sentence "Ateh Gibor Leolam Adonai" meaning "Thou art mighty forever, O Lord."

Facing east again, I lift my arms and visualize a yellow-haired archangel standing in the east dressed in yellow and lavender and surrounded by a gentle breeze. In a normal voice, I say, "Before me" and then vibrate the archangel's name, "Raphael." Without moving, I visualize a white-haired archangel standing in the west, dressed in blue and orange, holding a cup. I say, "Behind me" and vibrate "Gabriel." Next, I visualize a red-haired archangel standing in the south dressed in red and green, holding a sword, say, "On my right hand" and vibrate "Michael." Finally, in the north, I visualize a brown-haired archangel holding a globe, dressed in autumn colors—citrine (yellowish), olive, rust red, and black. I say, "On my left hand" and vibrate "Auriel."

Then I say, "For about me flame the pentagrams, and within me shines the six-rayed star." With this I visualize a Star of David in the heart center. This center is the place in my body where the vertical light column running above my head and through my feet intersects the shaft of energy through my shoulders that links the north and south ends of my circle. I have created a globe of energy reaching from the stars to the center of the earth, and along the horizontal plane of the world and universe, where I stand at the center.

I then repeat the Qabbalistic Cross.

How It Works

This ritual centers me as a magician and creates a space within which I can work other rituals. It does this by making an explicit connection between my body and the sacred universe. No other ritual I do makes this connection in the same way.

First, the universe is imagined as sacred, both filled with God and created by God. The divine force emerges in a series of upwellings that form spheres. Each sphere is associated with many things, including the seven planets known to the ancients. This system is called Qabbalah, and it's old and relatively complex, handed down through time, passed through a succession of religious prisms. We shall investigate this system in more detail later.

The universe can also be described as a cosmic man, the Adam Kadmon. The Hellenistic Jewish philosopher Philo articulated this viewpoint in a synthesis of Jewish religious philosophy with Greek philosophy. The Adam Kadmon, original or heavenly man, is formed by associating astrological signs with the human body.

Qabbalah describes the universe as an outpouring of God in the shape of a tree, while a related tradition describes the universe as a zodiac of astrological signs shaped like a person. The Qabbalistic Cross combines these notions by superimposing the spheres of the tree onto the physical body. Kether is at the crown, Malkuth is at the feet, Geburah is on the right shoulder, Chesed (Gedulah) is on the left shoulder, and Tiphareth is at the chest.

The next movement of the ritual, the Lesser Ritual of the Pentagram, also draws on the mixture of Pagan, Jewish, and Christian elements, which first came together in the Hellenistic world. The quartered circle is a very common ritual form. In use in the Mediterranean world as far back as the Babylonians (who put protection charms at the four corners of their houses), it's so ubiquitous around the world even today that it lends itself well to Pagan adaptation. The archangels were Jewish in origin. They drifted into common magical use in the Hellenistic era and were adopted by the Christian religion while remaining in magical use.

The Star of David, the six-pointed star of the ritual, bears layered neo-platonic, Jewish, and modern magical meanings. In alchemy, the downward triangle represents water and the upright triangle represents fire. Superimposed on each other, these two triangles form a six-pointed star, representing (for Ceremonial Magicians) the union of spirit and matter. The downward triangle represents the soul's journey into matter, while the upward triangle represents the soul's aspiration to return to its home in the stars.

At the conclusion of the Lesser Ritual of the Pentagram, the magician is at the center of the universe, and further stands within a sacred circle guarded by archangels, affirming the sacred nature of the universe and the magician's own divine origin and sacred nature.

Personal Experience

This ritual is grand in scope. It exalts the soul to envision the universe as sacred and the self as identified with the sacred universe. It reconciles the gulf between the seemingly uncaring cosmos and the sense of the life importance of each individual human being. Its history is layered and complex, but it is itself an easily learnable rite. For these reasons, I love this ritual and perform it often. It is fundamental to the practice of traditional magic, and performing this ritual is fundamental to my identity as a traditional magician.

It also makes me profoundly uncomfortable. It is a ritual meant to bring me into alignment with the universe, but while performing the ritual, I feel like an outsider and a pretender.

First, I am Pagan. I am not Christian, and while I respect Christian religion and participate in efforts to end the historical antipathy between Pagan and Christian religion, I explicitly reject the valorization of sacrifice and suffering as meaningful in my own life.

Also, I am not Jewish. I am distressingly aware of the appropriation of Jewish mystical thought by Christian and modern hermeticists. I am also aware that Jewish people object to this, and that they have been objecting to this appropriation since Hellenistic times. I attended a class delivered a few years ago by a Jewish Ceremonialist gently reminding us of this fact, so I know the objection continues to the present day. It is important to me to acknowledge this, to indicate respect for Jewish religion and Jewish Qabbalah, and to work to redress this issue.

Since I am Pagan, calling the universe by the name of the monotheistic deity, Yahweh, Adonai, Lord, God, seems specific to a religion not my own, calling up a wealth of assumptions and history which I do not share. Every time I see or hear the word "God" a small voice at the back of my mind objects, "I don't believe in God, that's not how I experience the universe." The term "God" acts as a placeholder for me for the essential sacrality of the universe for which there is not a good description in English.

Some contemporary hermeticists brush off this objection by saying that the Jewish Yahweh is not what the Ceremonial magician means by using the term YHVH; instead this stands for Yod He Vau He, the magical-philosophical formula describing the nature of the universe. Certainly this is the understanding under which I am able to enter into using this system at all; when I vibrate "Yod He Vau He," I am not visualizing the monotheistic deity. The objection nonetheless stands that underlying this explanation is the history of Jewish religion which Ceremonial Magic has appropriated. The magical-formula defense also accounts only for YHVH, and not the other names used in the ritual. Raphael Patai points out that Yahweh is pronounced "Adonai" and translated "Lord," and Elohim has as its short form El and is translated "God"; so all of these really are variants of the same name, the name for the supreme deity of Judaism (Patai 1967). Also I suspect that those who make this argument are significantly more comfortable with monotheistic deity than I am.

These are the religious reasons I am uncomfortable with the ritual—I stand outside this ritual as a Pagan. I also stand outside this ritual as a woman.

The ritual imagines a universe created by a Lord, a monotheistic male deity. This universe is shaped like a man, Adam Kadmon. The ritual explicitly equates the magician with the sacred shape of the universe, or expands the magician into the entire universe, depending on how you look at it. At the end of the ritual, the sacred man stands in the center of the sacred male-created universe. But I am not a man, I am a woman. This ritual does not acknowledge female deity in any form. This image of the universe does not look like me.

Many women enter into this ritual without grappling with this issue. I once asked a roomful of Golden Dawn woman magicians how they dealt with Adam Kadmon, and they answered me, "By ignoring it." This is an honest answer and at least provides an entry point to the system. However, it seems to me that by ignoring this issue I am just pushing it forward in time. I can pretend Adam Kadmon isn't there, but he is—this is the image authorizing the magician's work, and that image is the image of a man, whatever the gender of the person performing the ritual.

There is a different image of women in the magical systems. The Thelemic magical system makes that image explicit.

THELEMA: THE STAR RUBY

Performance

I prepare for this ritual in the same way as for the Lesser Ritual of the Pentagram and perform it in my temple-bedroom.

Facing east, I breathe in deeply, bring my (right/dominant) hand to my forehead, then sweep it out beside and behind me and say sharply, "Apo pontos kakadaimonos!" (Greek for "away evil demons!").

I then perform the Thelemic version of the Qabbalistic Cross. I make the same visualization of the cross of light as with the Qabbalistic

Cross and make the same set of gestures, but the words are Greek and vary somewhat in meaning from the Lord's Prayer. At the forehead, I vibrate "Soi" (yours); at the genitals, I vibrate "O Phalle" (phallus); at the right shoulder, I vibrate "Ischuros" (strength); at the left shoulder, I vibrate "Eucharistos" (eucharist or grace); and at the chest, I vibrate "Iao," a God name pulled from Gnostic texts and Hellenistic magic.

The next part is the Thelemic version of the Lesser Ritual of the Pentagram. I make the pentagrams by placing my hands at my forehead, visualizing a star of blue light, then throwing my hands out in front of me while visualizing the star flying out into space. I end up in the sign of the Enterer, with both hands stretched out in front of me, similar to the piercing gesture made in the Lesser Ritual.

As in the Lesser Ritual, I make these pentagrams while turning to each of the four directions and invoking a deity name. Instead of vibrating, the ritual calls for a different level of vocal intensity with each invocation. In the east, I shout, "Therion!" Turning north, I say, "Nuit." In the west, I whisper, "Babalon." In the south, I call, "Hadit!"

Turning east again, I make a series of gestures. The first is *puella*, girl. It mimics one of the ancient images of Aphrodite and Venus: I put my left hand over my breasts and my right hand over my genitals, as if shielding them. The second gesture is *puer* (boy). I raise my right arm, bend my elbow and point my fist at the ceiling, bring my left fist to my genitals and point out my thumb. The third gesture is *vir*, man. I put my fists on each side of my head with my thumbs outward, like horns. The fourth gesture is *mulier*, wife. I spread my feet and raise my arms in a crescent. With each of these gestures I chant, "Io Pan."

I then extend my arms out level to the ground, forming a Tau cross with my body, and say, "Pro mou iyunges, opiso mou teletarchai, epi dexia synoches, eparistera daimones, flegei gar peri mou o aster ton pente, kai en thi stelei o aster ton ex esteke." In English this means "Before me iyunges, behind me teletarchai, to my right synoches, to my left daimones, for around me flame the pentagrams, and in the column shines the six-rayed star."

How It Works

This ritual was created by Aleister Crowley as the Thelemic form of the Lesser Ritual of the Pentagram. The usual way people learn these rituals is to do the Lesser Ritual first. Since the Star Ruby is based on the form of the Lesser Pentagram, understanding the Lesser Ritual makes understanding and performing the Star Ruby easier.

There are a number of differences between the rituals. First, the Thelemic version is not based on Jewish deity imagery, but instead invokes Thelemic forms of deity. The ritual calls on two divine couples, Therion and Babalon, and Nuit and Hadit. (An earlier version in *The Book of Lies* used Therion-Babalon and Psyche-Eros). Therion and Babalon refer to Crowley's personal visions valorizing the Beast and the Whore from the biblical book of Revelation. These visions are based in symbols of Christianity, the religion in which Crowley was raised, but which he rejected for (among other things) its sex negativity. Finally, Nuit and Hadit are two of the three deities who speak in *The Book of the Law.*

The sacred language of this ritual is Greek and not Hebrew as in the Lesser Ritual of the Pentagram. In another substitution, Crowley uses neo-Platonic forms of spirits instead of archangels; iyunges, teletarchai, synoches, and daimones are classes of beings rather than individual beings, originating in neo-Platonic philosophy.

Finally, the ritual specifies referring to the genitals as "phalle." In his commentary on the ritual, O.T.O. Grand Master Sabazius noted that Crowley called the phallus the "immortal principle" of either a man or a woman, and that immortal principle refers to the principle of life which renews itself continuously. Many women Thelemites perform this ritual today.

Personal experience

It is vastly comforting to me to conduct a ritual that invokes the divine in feminine and masculine forms. That these divine forms reimagine Christian forms, and derive from Crowley's encounter with Egyptian religion, is also comfortable to me. Nuit as loving star goddess is a powerful and moving image of the universe as female, an image picked up by later neo-Pagan religion as the Star Goddess.

Babalon is a modern aspect of a line of goddesses for whom I have long been priestess, a line that includes Inanna, Ishtar, Aphrodite, Hathor, Qadesh, Asherah, and a number of Semitic desert goddesses, all of whom were worshipped in the Mediterranean region over a span of several thousand years. This line has in common a sense of sacredness and joy in women's sexuality and the connection of sexuality with power. This was the specific line of female sacredness that the author of the Book of Revelation demonized and that was repressed in Europe in the post-Pagan era. In the modern period, Babalon roared back, and Crowley as her priest promoted her power and the power of women's sexuality. This was not only shocking and radical in his time, during the late Victorian-Edwardian era, but remains shocking and radical today, where women's sexuality continues to be repressed rather than celebrated. (You may have seen a naked woman on an altar, but you probably haven't seen a naked woman on an altar on prime time TV, especially as an object of sincere worship.)

In the Star Ruby, four deity forms are invoked at the four quarters, two male and two female. This brings a balance to the gendered universe. It is also polytheistic, recognizing that the divine has multiple forms, which as a Pagan I also find comfortable.

In addition to these deity forms, two other deities are invoked, Iao and Pan. Both are ways of describing all divine things rolled up into one, and both are masculine names. Thelemic religion at times calls on this same ultimate-divine-force as Lord or God. This of course is tremendously disappointing. Although Thelema explicitly differentiates itself as a religion from the monotheistic religions with the veneration of female deity and with polytheism, in the places where religious texts call on Lord and God it seems to me to echo the monotheistic image of the universe as fundamentally masculine.

It also shares the Western philosophical image of the *person* as fundamentally masculine. I am very appreciative that Crowley and prominent contemporary Thelemic theologians include women among the holders of the universal power. This is an innovation in Western philosophy, as we shall see. However, calling the phallus the immortal principle and equating this immortal principle with the renewing principle of life is a male-centric point of view. We shall explore the metaphysical phallus at length with a review of Freudian-Lacanian philosophy.

In the end, I am as uncomfortable performing this ritual as I am performing the Lesser Ritual of the Pentagram. The Star Ruby does not seem to sacralize my experience as a woman, and it does seem to affirm gender assumptions which I challenge. I don't have a problem valorizing my phallus (and I must note that I never say "my phallus" in any other context than this ritual) for the purposes of doing the ritual, but this ritual does not accurately map the root experience of my body. As a woman, I am still not at home in this ritual.

Thelemic religion does have a ritual in which my gender is explicitly valorized. That ritual is the Gnostic Mass.

THELEMA: THE GNOSTIC MASS

This is a big ritual. It takes a team of three to five people an hour to perform, and can take a lifetime to understand. It is far too complicated to fully discuss or reproduce here. The text is available online in many places (search for "Liber XV, the Gnostic Mass").

It is performed by clergy from the Thelemic fraternity O.T.O. for the benefit of congregations across America and around the world, so it is relatively easy to attend a live performance. I recommend this experience very highly for any practitioner of Western Traditional Magic and for any member of the magical-spiritual communities. This ritual is the source of much later material and very completely expresses the Edwardian magical philosophy on which all our work is based.

Only the members of the Sovereign Sanctuary of the Gnosis are fully instructed in the formulae of the Mass. Understanding unfolds through intellectual study, conversation with other practitioners, and experience of the ritual itself. Undertaking the O.T.O. fraternal initiations is another opportunity to experience the Thelemic symbol system and to bring that new understanding back to the Mass.

I am an ordained priestess of O.T.O. in its church the Ecclesia Gnostica Catholica (E.G.C.). As an ordained priestess, I have a level of initiated and consecrated understanding, and I am authorized to perform the Mass, but my understanding is not as complete as that of a bishop or a member of the Sovereign Sanctuary, and I do not wish to assume an authority I do not possess. For that reason, I want to make clear I am discussing my *personal experience* with this ritual. I bring to it my prior experience as a Witch and Pagan priestess as well as my studies in Western Traditional Magic.

Here is a report of my experience of the Mass I performed most recently. It no doubt reveals the deficiencies in my understanding; I hope it also bears some insight.

Performance
The Furnishings of the Temple

The place where I usually perform the Mass is a rented Masonic hall. We set up our equipment in the hall and take it down when Mass is over.

One way to look at this temple is that it is laid out in a Tree of Life pattern. It is supposed to run east to west, although in practice we put the furniture where it fits in the room. At the (virtual) west end of the room is the tomb, in the position of Malkuth. At the beginning of the Mass the priest stands there, hidden behind a cloth curtain. Next comes the font in the position of Yesod, then the small altar in the position of Tiphareth. The deacon stands between these two altars.

The children stand on either side of me in front of two pillars. In the Tree of Life these would be the pillar of mercy and the pillar of severity. I stand between them. The veil hangs in the position of the abyss between the rest of the temple and the high altar. The high altar in the east takes the position of the supernals.

The congregation is positioned on each side of the temple, just outside the line of the pillars. The temple includes them—they create it by their presence.

Officers

There are five officers for the Mass: the priest, priestess, deacon, positive child, and negative child (the role of "child" is usually filled by

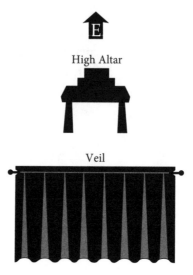

High Altar

Veil

Pillar

Fire Altar

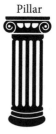 Pillar

Font

Tomb

Illustration 1: The Gnostic Mass

adults). What each of us can wear is specified by the ritual. We can all wear white. Today all the officers except me are wearing white albs. The priest wears a red and gold chasuble, the deacon wears a yellow stole, the negative child wears a black chasuble, the positive child just wears a white alb. The priestess wears blue and a red girdle; I wear a blue skirt and lighter blue shirt, a white shawl, and a red cord which supports my sword.

Ceremony of the Introit

I wait out of sight of the congregation while the deacon brings the congregation into the temple. Usually the waiting place is behind a door, in a hallway, even a closet; sometimes when the altar is big enough and far enough away from the wall we can wait back there. Today, it's behind a door in a kitchen.

I whisper reminder instructions to the children. One stands in front of me, one behind. This varies depending on where we are waiting in relationship to the altar. Today the negative child stands in front of me, holding water and salt, and the positive child stands behind me, holding a censer and a bowl of Abramelin incense.

We listen as the deacon brings *The Book of the Law* into the temple. Then the deacon leads the congregation in the Creed. The children and I whisper it together, a moment of grounding and centering, and our first connection to the energy of the Mass.

The Creed ends with three intonations of "Aum." When the congregation has said the last "Aum," I touch the shoulder of the child in front of me. The child begins to walk, hopefully slowly, while I walk behind, hoping the child behind me is keeping up. I only really know that this has worked out when we turn to face the congregation and they are in their places; today they're where I expect them to be.

I face the congregation, holding the paten with the priest's cake of light. I say, "Greeting of earth and heaven," and wait. The congregation gives me the hailing sign of the magician, putting their right hands on their heart and raising their left hands. I feel a connection with the congregation, which acknowledges me as wearing the power of the priestess and bearing the paten, and I feel authorized by the congregation to perform the Mass in their service. It's a humbling moment—I hope that I bring to them whatever it is that they need and that I perform the service well.

I turn to put the paten on the high altar, and give a sweeping bow in adoration. The deacon has added *The Book of the Law* to the altar. I have added the paten. It is now complete, bearing all the magical tools required to perform the Mass.

I turn and wait while my sound tech turns on the CD with the Turkish dance music. When the beat starts, I sway and begin my serpentine dance, weaving around the altars. The children fall in behind me. The deacon moves to the high altar, leaving the temple free for the dance. I swing my arms wide to include the entire room and the congregation in the movement of the Mass. As I dance past the high altar for the first time, the whole temple seems to spring into existence with a flash of golden light. This light surges throughout my body and knocks my consciousness right to the back of my brain. The form of the Mass carries me along; my job from now on is to steer along the river and keep my own boat upright.

At the end of the dance I am drawn to the tomb. The children stand on either side of me, along the line of the pillars.

I draw my sword, a power that feels solid and familiar in my hand. I use the sword to open the tomb, pulling the veil back. The priest stands there in just a white alb with his eyes closed. He is holding a lance. I say, "By the power of iron, I say unto thee, arise." He opens his eyes. I hold the power of iron in my hand, and as a woman, hold it in my body. With this power I make three crosses on the air before the priest, at his throat, chest, and groin. I call him from the tomb to "administer the virtues to the brethren."

The priest steps forward and asks me a question: "How should I be worthy to administer the virtues to the brethren?" That question had been answered for me when the congregation hailed me.

I don't answer him with words but with gestures. I take water and salt from the negative child. I go to the font, mix the salt in the water, and say, "Mother, be thou adored." In the creed, I said, "I believe in one earth, the mother of us all." Many cultures view the earth as female—

as a Pagan I have sung "the earth is our mother" any number of times. I take the bowl of salted water to the priest, dip my hand in it, and make the three crosses again, saying, "Be the priest pure of body and soul." Water and salt purifies. For this Mass, the office of priest is being filled by my personal working partner, and sometimes I physically touch him with the water because we have that relationship, but today I make the crosses in the air.

I hand the bowl to the negative child. From the positive child I take incense and censer. I take these to the small altar, put incense on the charcoal, and say, "Father, be thou adored." In the creed, I say I believe in "one father of life" and "one air, the nourisher of all that breathes." This gendering of the elements—water and earth female, fire and air male—has been a part of Western Traditional Magic for several thousand years. At this moment, the priestess works with all of the elements. Walking back to the tomb, I make the same three crosses in the air with the censer and say, "Be the priest fervent of body and soul."

In Western Traditional Magic, water purifies and incense consecrates. Consecrations of these elements, and the use of the magical tools such as knife and cup, trace at least as far back as the grimoire *The Key of Solomon*.

The deacon brings me the priest's red and gold chasuble. I slip it onto the priest, saying, "Be the flame of the sun thine ambiance, O thou priest of the sun." The deacon hands me the priest's serpent crown, the crown the pharaohs of Egypt once wore. I say, "Be the serpent thy crown, O thou priest of the Lord."

Then I kneel in front of the priest. I take the shaft of his lance between my two hands and stroke it eleven times. As I stroke the lance, I cannot help but think of the worship of the Shiva Lingam, the male fertile power, as well as all the personal sex magic rituals I have performed. I am swept away into this energy. When I have completed eleven strokes, I say, "Be the lord present among us!"

The deacon gives the hailing sign of the magician and answers, "So mote it be." The congregation does this with him.

Opening of the Veil

The deacon started the Mass activity. The priestess picked it up and moved it forward. Now the priest will be moving the Mass forward.

He says, "Thee therefore whom we adore we also invoke. By the power of the lifted lance," he lifts his lance, "I, priest and king, take thee, virgin, pure without spot. I upraise thee," and he helps me to my feet. "I lead thee to the east." We walk together back toward the high altar. "I set thee upon the summit of the earth." He helps me to sit on the high altar.

The deacon and children have followed us. The children take up their positions in front of the pillars. The deacon stands ready to assist the priest, holding his lance when the priest hands it to him.

I take up *The Book of the Law* and hold it in front of my chest. The priest takes the bowl and sprinkles me with five crosses. He takes up the incense and censes me with the same five crosses at forehead, shoulders, and knees. He kisses *The Book of the Law* three times. Then he kneels at my feet and adores. This is a very intimate moment, so it could be awkward, but I have never found it so, even working for the first time with a priest I don't know well. Partly this is because it isn't me and my guy performing the ritual; it is the priest and the priestess, who are quasi-magical beings in their own right and have specific things to do with each other. Partly this is because the ritual is so solemn and majestic, and the people participating in it are so sincere, that it is sobering and exalting to perform.

While the priest adores, the children take the bowl and incense burner to the font and small altar, and then return to their posts in front of the pillars. At this moment, as in much of the ritual, the priest can only see me but I can see the whole temple. I nod to him just a little when the children are back in position so he can tell it is time to make the next move.

The priest stands and closes the veil. He circles the font and small altar three times with the deacon and children following him. I can't see them, but I know that is what they are doing. I take off all my clothing and stand naked behind the veil.

The priest speaks a long piece addressed to Nuit. It begins, "O circle of stars of whom our father is but the younger brother," and ends, "Let it be ever thus, that men speak not of thee as one, but as none. And let them speak not of thee at all, since thou art continuous."

As a Pagan priestess, I had a lot of experience with having deity invoked on me before I began to perform the Mass. I am familiar with the feeling of channeling. That feeling possesses me now—I feel Nuit at the front of my head.

I say (she says), "But to love me is better than all things." The priestess speaks a whole prayer behind the veil. It is important to me to have this prayer well memorized, so that remembering the words isn't the focus of my work, and I can lose myself in the channel. Nuit speaks through me directly to the congregation. There are times I see in my mind's eye a particular person as she aims a specific phrase at them. She also speaks to the priest who carries the power of Hadit. The prayer ends with her call, "To me, to me."

The priest responds with Hadit's words: "I am the flame that burns in every heart of man, and in the core of every star." I listen to him closely. He ends, "I am alone. There is no god where I am."

The deacon says, "But ye, O my people, rise up and awake." Although I cannot see them through the veil, I know that the deacon, children, and congregation have been kneeling and now stand up. The deacon speaks a piece beginning, "Let the rituals be rightly performed with joy and beauty." Meanwhile, I prepare myself for the veil to open. The priestess can choose not to re-robe and to be naked for the rest of the rite, or can choose to re-robe.

I sit back on the high altar and take up the paten, which I had placed there, and the cup, which was on the altar when the children and I entered the temple. The priest speaks another invocatory piece, "Appear thou glorious upon the throne of the sun," ending with chanted vocals, just as the Egyptian priest-magicians once did.

I reply triumphantly with the Thelemic battle cry, "There is no law beyond do what thou wilt!" At this the priest draws open the veil again. The congregation can see me for the first time since the priest called on Nuit. When the veil opens and the priestess is naked, the congregation often draws in a breath. A naked woman on the high altar is a very powerful statement.

The priest makes a series of adorations, "Io Io Iao Sabao," and says in Greek, "Kaire phalle, kaire panphage, kaire pangenetor," meaning "hail phallus, hail devourer, hail begetter." My partner brings a specific chanting technique to this based on his understanding of plainchant. The priest ends with a long triumphant call, "Hagios Hagios Hagios Iao!"

He hands me his lance. I kiss it eleven times, and then cradle it. The priest kneels at my feet and kisses my knees. This again could be awkward, but in the Mass it is a very moving moment—the priest seems overcome with passionate joy and has fallen to his knees to adore the sacred.

The Collects

The deacon speaks the eleven collects. These function like the collects of some Christian sects. The collects are called Sun, Lord, Moon, Lady, Saints, Earth, Principles, Birth, Marriage, Death, and The End. The saints are a list of male saints who are asked to be present to "perfect this feast," which I understand to mean to enter into communion with the congregation.

The collects end with a set of blessings on birth, marriage, and death. If the Mass is being celebrated for any of these reasons, the deacon may ring a bell at the appropriate collect. Today the Mass has its most usual purpose, being performed for the benefit of the congregation present.

Consecration of the Elements

When the collects are ended, the priest stands. Priest and priestess then perform a series of movements with the lance, paten, and cup. The priest calls on the saints and claims communion with them. He uses the cake to make the same five crosses over the cup he has been making on the priestess.

The consecration ends with the priest holding the cake above the cup. The deacon rings a bell, then the priest chants again, "Hagios Hagios Hagios Iao." The lamen (magical talisman) of the O.T.O. shows a dove descending into a cup, an image which I relate to this moment.

The Anthem

Priest, deacon, and congregation now speak the anthem. I like this section as it has alternating sections for both women and men.

Mystic Marriage and Consummation of the Elements

The priest now takes up the cake on his paten, breaks it, and addresses it in Greek, saying, "This is my seed. The father becomes the son through the holy spirit."

The priest and I put a little bit of the cake on the tip of the spear, tilt the tip over the cup so the cake drops into the cup, and say together, "Hriliu!" Each priest and priestess speaks it differently, an expression of their work together.

The priest turns to the congregation and says, "Do what thou wilt shall be the whole of the law." They reply, "Love is the law, love under will."

I give the priest the cake, which he eats, saying, "In my mouth be the essence of the life of the sun." I give him the cup, and he drinks the wine, saying, "In my mouth be the essence of the joy of the earth."

Then he turns to the congregation, crosses his arms over his chest, and says, "There is no part of me that is not of the gods."

Depending on who the priest is, his preference, or his bishop's direction, the priest goes to different places at this point. The priest I usually work with stands inside the veil, but beside me rather than in front of me. I've seen priests stand in front of the priestess and at the tomb as well.

The deacon now supervises communion. Each congregant approaches the high altar. The children hand the congregant a cake of light and a goblet (usually quite small) of wine. Each congregant eats, drinks, and says, "There is no part of me that is not of the gods."

The priestess remains on the altar throughout. Priestesses of higher degree than mine talk about the energy of the Mass being used up at this point and being lost in contemplation. After one of my higher initiations I definitely felt spacier at this point. I see a lot of floating lights.

As they approach the high altar, some congregants seem very intent on worshipping Nuit in a personal sense. Sometimes I hear Nuit in the back of my mind saying things to each person as they come up. Other priestesses report this to me as well. The ritual does not call for the priestess to talk at this point, so after the Mass I sometimes go up to the person and tell them what I was hearing. Generally they are not surprised by this. "That's what she's been saying to me" is the most common response I get.

Once the last congregant has taken communion, the priest closes the veil. I've seen priestesses slump at this point. I definitely feel a release of energy—this is where the Mass is over for me.

The priest gives a final blessing to the congregation, "The lord bring you to the accomplishment of your true wills, the great work, the Summum Bonum, true wisdom and perfect happiness." He then leads the deacon and the children into the tomb. The Mass is over.

Personal experience

I love this ritual and perform it as often as I can. It's an astonishing accomplishment on so many levels. First, this ritual was written nearly a hundred years ago and is still being performed today. Since it is preserved by a church that takes its magic very seriously, it is performed using pretty much the same script Crowley wrote, and (with some regional variations in bits of business) is performed pretty much the same way around the world. On any given day, someone somewhere is likely to be performing the Mass.

Also, it takes quite a bit of preparation to pull off. The minimum number of people required to do the ritual is four: priest, priestess, deacon, and one congregant (in a pinch the priestess and priest can do without the children). This isn't a solo effort. The Mass also requires all that equipment—tomb, high altar, small altar and font, bowl and salt and censer and incense, crown and lance and sword, and color-coded clothing. I've seen everything from small home-based Mass sets that used a table and a shelf on the wall to elaborate high altars draped with velvet. Even at its minimum, though, it uses a lot of physical stuff.

It also takes some time to learn how to do it. The priest has quite a bit of memorizing to do, although the priestess has lines as well, and it's nice when the deacon is entirely off the written page. My account of the ritual elided a whole series of magical actions the priest and priestess perform together that take some rehearsing to get right.

In this ritual, a woman (naked if she chooses) sits on the altar and is the focus of adoration. It seems to me that the physical priestess is the visible manifestation of the female power of reproduction, and the Mass valorizes the tender power of sexuality to create the magic of life.

This extraordinary ritual is a very early example of the veneration of the divine feminine which developed in the modern era. It is the first moment that a priestess appears in the context of a church. In E.G.C., the priestess holds exactly the same power as a priest—she can conduct baptisms and confirmations, marriages and funerals, and she can ordain deacons with the dispensation of a bishop. As bishops, women also hold the same power as the men, to ordain priests and priestesses. This church quietly and without fuss levels the playing field for women in a way that monotheistic religions still struggle to attain. While there are women rabbis, priests, and bishops, and even a few imams, there are branches of Jewish and Christian religion that refuse women the right to administer sacraments, and the few women imams practice secretly. Women who move into positions of authority in the monotheistic religions routinely receive death threats. In E.G.C., these positions are normative.

This ritual includes gendered parts, with a male priest and a female priestess. This gendering acknowledges the lived experience of the body, although, as is common, this comes with a cost. The gendering of elements here allots to women the earth-water-passive-body-intuition side of creation. Men occupy the air-fire-active-intellect-passion side of creation. That may sound as if it is balanced, with male and female occupying separate but equal spheres, but Western metaphysics nearly always weights one side of a polarity with greater value than the other, justifying the dominance of that side over the subordinate other. In the male/female, white/black, rich/poor, healthy/disabled, young/

old polarities, Western culture favors the male, white, rich, healthy, and young. Western occult metaphysics subordinates emotion to reason, receptivity to action, body to mind, and female to male.

We can trace the subtle valuation of the male again in the deities of the systems. Nuit and Hadit form a triad with the child Ra-Hoor-Khuit. The father-mother-son triad is commonplace in Egyptian mythology, and Thelemic theology is unexceptional in this. In this system, the woman can embody the priestess, speak as Nuit, and represent Babalon, the mother-lover goddesses, the queen and bride. But the child of Nuit and Hadit is a male child, Ra-Hoor-Khuit, and Babalon is not equivalent to that child.

This is the first ritual in the modern era which a woman could perform as a woman. It is a great joy to participate in religious ritual as a woman. It is majestic and moving. It is not, however, a woman *magician's* ritual. For most of the ritual, the priest is the active, directing principle. The Mass team acts in service to the congregation, and the entire congregation benefits from the ritual—women as well as men take communion with no gendered distinction. However, while the priest takes communion, the priestess, deacon, and children do not. The priestess does not stand at the center of the work or direct the work. The priest says, "The father becomes the son through the holy spirit." The priestess does not say, "The mother becomes the daughter through the holy spirit." The priestess is not the magician, she is the *soror mysticae*, the magician's mystical sister.

This ritual is the first we have studied that sacralizes my experience as a woman. However, it does not yet valorize the woman as a magician. It also still understands the sacred universe through a dominantly male lens. The religion that came after it, Witchcraft, finally moves beyond God into natively Pagan theology.

WITCHCRAFT: THE CIRCLE

Performance: Coven Circle

I work with more than one coven. One of them is a traditional coven in which I am the high priestess and my working partner is the high priest. Covens meet to celebrate sabbats and full moons, to conduct spell craft, and to initiate. My last traditional Witchcraft circle was held for the same purpose as my private circle, to reconnect with the God and Goddess, and to re-strengthen the group's egregore (magical existence).

We meet in my partner's temple, a room dedicated to magic. He has a number of altars. The one we use for this circle is the altar on the north wall. Above this altar hang two carved stone faces, one a maiden surrounded by flowers and one a green man, the faces of the God and Goddess in the springtime. We also use a pentacle, a cup, a bowl, and a censer.

I wear a black robe embroidered for me by my coven sister with twining vines and wildly colorful flowers. I also wear my initiation cords, an amber and jet necklace, and my knife. My partner wears a black robe and his cords.

When we cast a circle together, my partner and I generally split up the movements. I sweep and asperge, he censes, in line with the traditional association of female with water and male with fire.

We evenly split up the quarter calls. To the east, I make an invoking earth pentacle with my knife, pierce it, and say, "Hail to thee, guardian of the watchtower of the east. Notus, guardian of the eastern portal, I do summon, stir and call you up, to witness this rite and guard the circle." In the south we call on Euros, in the west we call on Zephyros, and in the north we call on Boreas.

I draw the circle with my knife while he speaks the invoking prayer: "I conjure thee, O circle of power, that thou become a boundary between the human world and the realm of the mighty ones. Whereby I call thee in the names of Aradia and Cernunnos."

Back at the altar, he lights the goddess candle and says, "Aradia, be here now." I light the god candle and say, "Cernunnos, be here now."

When we invoke the deities, we sometimes invoke them into each other—I invoke Cernunnos into him, he invokes Aradia into me. When we invoke them into each other, they generally speak, first to each other, then to the coveners. In initiations, we always invoke into each other, and both of the deities speak to the initiate.

On this occasion, we bring out the coven stone and drop a little wine onto the stone, acknowledging the God and Goddess, and infusing the stone and the coven egregore with power.

Then we consecrate wine and cakes, in this case our usual red wine and shortbread cookies. While my partner holds the chalice, I dip a knife into it, saying, "As the knife is to the male, so the cup is to the female, and conjoined they bring blessedness." Then we sit, eat the cakes, pass the wine cup, and send the energy of the circle out into the world. As usual, we have a string of wishes others have asked us to make on their behalf, mostly for physical healing or to resolve a highly stressful situation. We have promised to remember them in circle, and we do.

When we have finished the circle, we thank the God and Goddess and the quarter guardians for their presence. We cut across the circle and say, "The circle is open but unbroken. Merry meet, merry part, and merry meet again, and may the gods preserve the Craft!"

How It Works

The magic circle is the most ancient of protective rituals. Although many forms exist around the world, and many forms exist in neo-Pagan practice, this particular form is based on material in *The Greater Key of Solomon*, as are the Lesser Ritual of the Pentagram and parts of the Gnostic Mass. The circle is specifically created to form a protective boundary in which magical work can take place, calling some spirits into the circle and keeping some out. Water and incense function here just as they do in the Key and in the Mass. The magical tools, knife and cup, also derive from the Key, and the runes specified by the Key to be inscribed on those tools are the ones inscribed on my knife.

The quarter invocations call on the guardians of the watchtowers. The four-pillared universe guarded by watchtowers derives from Enochian magic, the Renaissance magical system developed through scrying sessions conducted by John Dee with the medium Edward Kelly in which angels taught the men their language.

Although the form of this ritual is recognizable within the forms of Western Traditional Magic, the ritual departs markedly in theology. There is no monotheistic God here; the deity forms are Pagan. In the

Witchcraft circle, the names called at the four quarters are not the titles of the Hebrew God, or the four Qabbalistic archangels, but four of the eight winds of the classical Mediterranean world. The deities themselves, the God and Goddess of the Craft, evolved from bits and pieces of folklore. The names Aradia and Cernunnos surface in Gardner's earliest rituals.

My personal altar holds candlesticks carved with the images of the God and Goddess of the Craft as they are understood by practitioners today. The goddess candlestick features three figures: a young woman, a pregnant woman, and a hag. The god candlestick shows two figures: the green man and a horned hunter with hound.

The circle constructs the immediate situation of the practitioner. The Witch is a child of the Goddess and God, paired and equal deities of earth, moon and sun, greenery and animals, life and death. Commanding the elements and guided by deity, the Witch keeps pace with the seasons and acts magically on behalf of herself and of others who have requested her aid.

Personal experience

Monotheistic religion envisions deity in male terms. The divine feminine requires polytheism—there must be at least two aspects to deity. Witchcraft accomplishes this. There are two deities in the universe, one male and one female. For this reason, I am most comfortable with this ritual. It is the place I feel most at home in all the religious places I have been offered in my life.

That said, I turn the goddess candlestick looking for an image that corresponds to my experience, and I do not find it. This image represents female power in terms of human fertility: pre-fertile, pregnant, post-fertile. As a childless mature woman, neither young, old, nor mother, I do not find my place here. The goddess Babalon, the unbridled lover, fits me more accurately. When I think of myself in terms of any goddess, she is that goddess.

While the four winds replacing the archangels come from the Pagan tradition, these winds are all male forms, again reflecting a male-by-default image of the universe.

The circle functions as the expression of a religion. It does not, however, create me as an instance of the sacred universe. The system of Witchcraft does not yet possess a personal exploration and development such as the initiatory magical systems offer. There is a primary emphasis on experience, with a concomitant de-emphasis on study and intellectual pursuit.

Witchcraft places me at the center of the circle with full power to wield it and change it. Witchcraft creates me as a priestess and Witch. But it does not create me as a magician.

EVALUATING THE TRADITION

When we look at each of these rituals in sequence, their lineal connection becomes clearer. Each of these rituals evolved out of components of their early modern predecessors, especially *The Greater Key of Solomon* and Eliphas Lévi's work. They resemble each other in some ways and differ in others.

The rituals I have described are routinely performed by women today and have been since they were developed. None were created by women, but were developed in the context of groups that included women. That they exist for me to perform a hundred years after their development is a tribute to Lady Tradition. Her formality provides continuity—she acts to preserve those in her care. I have dedicated my life to her work, and I will not forsake her.

Her virtue is also her obvious flaw: she is rigid. Alteration means loss. Any addition or omission dilutes and distorts her inheritance. In fragmentary traditions like Witchcraft, passed from mouth to mouth or through books copied by hand, a single misheard word or miscopied line resonates through decades of changed ritual. Any Ceremonial Magician who has struggled to compare different versions of the same text understands the benefits of strict transmission. So Lady Tradition fiercely resists any change in the tradition, whatever its motivation or effect.

Although Lady Tradition lives through me, I cannot live only in her. The Victorian cut of her clothes has not changed in a hundred years.

Just as we have abandoned petticoats and corsets, women's lives have opened up, moving out of the drawing room and into the world.

While I am a woman, and I am a magician, in these rituals I do not experience myself as a woman and also as a magician at the same time. Western Traditional Magic has not opened to me a path in which I can authentically develop spiritually while grounded in my embodied experience.

I say to the lady, *How can I experience myself as a woman magician?* She does not have an answer for me, and fades away, leaving me alone again at my desk. Where can I find the answer to that question? Perhaps it would be helpful to look at the past, to examine who developed the magical rituals I perform today, and how those people understood women and magic. I turn next to my most faithful informant, the lady who has led me again and again to understand the origins of the forces that shape my life.

LADY HISTORY

I make the invocation: *Come to me, Lady History, and show me the origins of my magic.*

My writer's enclosure, the little cabin in the woods, vanishes. I find myself in a magnificent library, a vast hall carpeted with massive red shelves on every side lifting far above my head to the vaulted ceiling painted as a sky—on one end the sunny blue of the day sky with white clouds, on the other the dark blue of the night sky spangled with stars. The little wooden desk where I sit is worn with centuries of study.

Through an arched door at one end of the hall, the spirit who answers my call hurries into sight. She is much less formal than Lady Tradition, clearly paying less attention to her own appearance than her work; she has tucked a white shirt into her tailored black trousers, and wisps of hair fall into her face.

I say to her, "How did Western Traditional Magic come to understand women in the way that it does?"

She turns to a shelf and pulls down a heavy book, a huge leather-bound volume glinting with gilt edges. It is The Book, the one that *has to* exist and for which many have searched all their lives, the book that contains the secret keys, the proper incantations, the genuine rituals, the deepest and most hidden names.

I have followed this lady on her haphazard race through the stacks of the library many days and nights of my life. Often, she leads me down a path that glitters with interest but takes me away from the central thread of my inquiry. As always, I am desperate to have a look at the book in her hands. She drops it on the desk before me and flips it open for me to read.

WESTERN MAGIC TIMELINE

Western Traditional Magic comprises a distinct body of work in the modern period. This lineage developed out of its historical predecessors, natural philosophy, medieval magic, and hermetic magic, and gave rise in turn to the magical movements that developed in the postmodern period.

There are two defining characteristics that set Western Traditional Magic apart from its predecessors. The first is the reinterpretation of magical philosophy to incorporate insights from psychology, casting magic less as a set of formulas or interaction with divinely controlled spirits and more as a personal development system. The second is the deliberate incorporation of the divine feminine in magical philosophy and women in magical groups, in sharp contrast to Freemasonry and the magical texts of previous eras. Lady History's book traces this lineage back in time at least two thousand years, to the Hellenistic period.

Hellenistic Period: Hermetica

This is also called the late classical or antique period. Roman civilization connected Europe, the near East, and north Africa, including Egypt, in a single political empire maintained by military might. Its urban centers mixed the languages, religion, and sciences of the world's peoples in a way very similar to today's one-world cultural fusion. In many ways, our world is a direct descendant of the late Roman world.

Just as Romans conquered the Celtic and Egyptian worlds, writing their own versions of the histories of those peoples, modern scholars write the history of the Western world from the perspective of privilege. In *Black Athena*, Martin Bernal pointed to the unconscious assumption made by white scholars that Egyptian history is white history, and noted that Egypt is an African country, which in its long history has often been governed by blacks. While European historians valorize Greek (read: Indo-European) culture as the wellspring of Western civilization, Bernal makes the point that Egyptian culture was already ancient by the time Greece developed a coherent culture (Bernal 2006). Historian Gloria Harper Dickinson notes that while ancient Greek writers acknowledge their debt to Egypt (ancient Kemet), nineteenth-century ethnocentric and racist scholars minimized the contributions of Egyptian, African, and Semitic peoples to Western culture. Dickinson calls Egypt a prime cradle of human development (Dickinson nd).

Nineteenth-century esotericists drew heavily on Celtic and Egyptian sources to create their rituals. Contemporary esotericists, including myself, continue to draw on these sources, precisely because Egyptian magic sidesteps many issues inherent in Indo-European magic, including but not limited to racism, sexism, the mind/body split in Greek philosophy, and the marginalization of magic in the ancient and modern worlds.

Our magic directly descends from Hellenistic magic. Rituals preserved in the Greek Magical Papyri can be performed by the educated magician today. These magical texts blended Egyptian and Greek magic with bits of surviving Babylonian lore and early alchemy, and Gnostic insights combined with neo-Platonic philosophy and Hellenized Judaism. A number of magical and philosophical texts were assembled in a collection called the *Corpus Hermeticum*, named for Hermes Trismegistsus, the Greek-Egyptian sage or god attributed with authorship of the texts, translated most recently by Brian Copenhaver (Copenhaver 1995).

Today, we still use the Greek words describing magic: "magi" gives us "magic", and "goes" gives us "goetia." This magic was concerned with names of power, sacred sounds, and the precise use of correct magical knowledge. It is a mechanical system: perform an action, get a result. The people who used and preserved the magical texts held the spoken and written words as magical in their own right. An act as simple to us today as reading the right book or speaking the right spell could perform an initiation and confer a power.

Middle Ages: Grimoires

This period covers the fall of the Roman empire to the modern period, spanning a thousand years. The political landscape shifted a great deal during this time period. The rise of Christianity resulted in the suppression of Pagan religion, although Paganism survived in many areas through preservation of local customs. This was especially true in Eastern Europe where there was no definitive showdown between Christianity and Paganism. European folk religion remains alive in pockets of many countries.

In the medieval period, monasteries served as the centers of learning and culture. These were segregated by gender. The monasteries provided woman-only communities which were sometimes placed under the supervision of male clerics, and sometimes were led entirely by women. In the monastic system, women had the chance to study with women theologians and philosophers, and sometimes engaged in lively discussion with men also in the monastic system. Monasteries also kept libraries, and monks earned a living copying and illustrating books for the libraries of the aristocracy—not just bibles and religious books, but also philosophy, history, romances, and fables.

Tucked away among those books were the medieval grimoires, including *The Greater Key of Solomon* and *The Lesser Key of Solomon*. Arguably the noblest of their kind, these texts dealt with the magus's power over angels and demons to provide secret knowledge, power over others, and wealth.

Early Modern Period: Natural Philosophy

This era, from 1500 to the mid-1800s, spans the development of science, the secularization of politics, the rise of nation states, and technological progress that resulted in increased communication and ease of travel.

Magicians practicing astrology and alchemy were attached to courts and wealthy families. Scholars were employed at court also, translating late antique philosophical and magical texts into Western languages from Greek and Islamic sources. For example, Cosimo de Medici commissioned Marsilio Ficino to translate the *Corpus Hermeticum*, one of the first works to be printed and distributed in Europe.

This influx of antique thought gave rise to natural philosophy, the study of spiritualized nature. The church objected to this Pagan-influenced approach to science and enforced its spiritual monopoly by imprisoning and killing the new philosophers. A compromise permitted natural philosophers to keep their lives. The Church alone would remain in charge of spiritual matters, while philosophers could investigate the mechanical workings of the world. This mechanical philosophy developed into modern science. The split between spiritual life and scientific inquiry continues to have grave consequences today.

In this period, the centers of learning shifted from the monasteries to academies located in major cities. While women participated in the monastic system, only a few academies opened their doors to a handful of women. The development of women's theology and philosophy closed down for a period of centuries. This continues to have grave consequences today.

MODERN PERIOD:
WESTERN TRADITIONAL MAGIC

The modern period began in the late 1800s and ended with World War II in the mid-twentieth century. The Enlightenment completed the secularization of politics, emphasizing progress and the development of human knowledge. Magic in this period incorporated scientific insight into the occult worldview.

The Enlightenment re-evaluation of the status of women created a climate in which women slowly moved back into the public sphere, in particular entering academia. Enlightenment-era attitudes toward women also encouraged the inclusion of women in magical lodges.

The modern period in which the Golden Dawn and Thelema developed also encompassed the development of psychology. The magical systems that preceded the modern era sought to explain the world and to give the magician control over the world. Western Traditional Magic sought to explain not only the world, but also the magician, and to give the magician control over the personal psyche. These systems are among the first self-help systems. The psychological theories of Freud, Jung, Adler, and others are embedded in the explanations of magical practice.

Lévi

Eliphas Lévi bridged the early modern and modern eras. He wrote in the language of early modernism, exteriorizing magical experience in dealings with angels and demons, valorizing the male Christian god, and drawing on medieval grimoires for ritual practice. His works also outline the basis of later ritual magic, discussing Qabbalah, astrology, alchemy, the use of the magical will, sex magic, and initiation to achieve the great work. Lévi's work served as the foundation for turn-of-the-century esotericism.

The Golden Dawn

The new magicians who succeeded Lévi and built on his work translated ritual into modern psychologized terms and opened the imagery of the divine to the feminine. First and foremost among the lodges was the Golden Dawn, founded by three Freemasons: Dr. William Robert Woodman, Dr. William Wynn Westcott, and Samuel Liddell Mac-Gregor Mathers.

Mathers wrote a great deal. Born in 1854, he died in 1918 in the great influenza epidemic. Mathers was familiar with Eliphas Lévi's works; his translation of the *Key of Solomon the King* marks the beginning of the literate lineage of Western Traditional Magic. In this medieval grimoire we find the magical tools, knife and cup; the elemental conjurations of water and incense; and the appeal to the world of spirits. Here Christian philosophy rests on Jewish and Pagan predecessors, with an unacknowledged debt to Islam, in the religio-philosophical mixture that characterizes the lineage.

The three men who founded the Golden Dawn had received a charter from beings they referred to as the Secret Chiefs, in particular Anna Sprengel. They contacted Sprengel through an address attached to a manuscript Westcott acquired called the Cipher Manuscript (Greer 1995). Many now believe Sprengel to be a fictitious creation. Alex Owen notes that prior to founding the Golden Dawn Westcott and Mathers had attended Anna Kingsford's Hermetic Society meetings (Owen 2004). Kingsford may have served as the inspiration for Anna Sprengel. In her 1926 preface to Mathers's translation of early Qabbalistic texts, *The Kabbalah Unveiled*, Moina Mathers noted her husband's friendship with Anna Kingsford and his sympathy with Kingsford's advocacy of women's rights.

Eventually the Golden Dawn fractured through personal conflict. A late initiate of the splinter group Stella Matutina, Israel Regardie, published the Golden Dawn rituals and many of their internal teachings after World War II, permitting them to be more widely disseminated.

Thelema

Two Freemasons and sex magicians, Theodore Reuss and Karl Kellner, broke with the Freemasonic tradition that excluded women to establish their own lodge, Ordo Templi Orientis, which they designed partly in order to include women in its membership. Reuss had additionally developed the Ecclesia Gnostica Catholica as an offshoot of l'Église Gnostique de France, the Gnostic Church informed by Jules Doinel's visions in the salon of Marie, Countess of Caithness. Reuss wrote for the Church a version of the sacramental Gnostic Mass which included the actions of a priest and a priestess.

One of the initiates of the Golden Dawn was Freemason Aleister Crowley (1875–1947). He took part in the disputes that fragmented the Golden Dawn and along with many others ultimately left the order. An English gentleman of means, Crowley married Rose Kelly (a marvelously magical name!) and together they traveled the world. In 1904, Crowley spent three successive days in a trance recording *The Book of the Law*, a revealed text with three chapters, each spoken by an Egyptian deity.

Reuss and Kellner approached Crowley to join O.T.O. When Crowley became head of O.T.O., he rewrote the order's initiation rituals. As Patriarch of the E.G.C., he also wrote a Gnostic Mass ritual, that Mass in which I participate today as priestess.

The E.G.C. broke from Christian tradition, converting to the religion founded on *The Book of the Law*, Thelema. *The Book of the Law* among other things spoke to Crowley as the priest and scribe, and also referred to a female counterpart to the priest, the Scarlet Woman. Throughout his life Crowley sought a physical Scarlet Woman to partner with him in his magical explorations. To name only a few: in addition to his wife, Rose Kelly, there was Mary Desti, friend and biographer of Isadora Duncan, who co-wrote parts of *Book 4*; Leah Hirsig, who co-founded the Abbey of

Thelema; and violinist Leila Waddell, who co-produced the earliest staging of Crowley's Rites of Eleusis.

Crowley's magick demanded not only intellect, determination, and strict freedom ("do what thou wilt shall be the whole of the law") but also love ("love is the law, love under will"). Crowley taught, worked with, and loved a succession of women and men. He married, had affairs, fathered children. He touched hundreds of people in the course of his life.

Witchcraft

One of those people was the Freemason Gerald Brousseau Gardner (1884–1964). After the repeal of the anti-Witchcraft laws in England in 1957, Gardner revealed that he had been initiated in 1939 by Dorothy Clutterbuck into a surviving Witchcraft group in the New Forest. Subsequently Gardner rewrote the rituals he had been given by that group and published several books, sparking the Witchcraft revival.

Gardner was familiar with Ceremonial Magic. He met Aleister Crowley and had a charter from him (Heselton 2001). Julia Phillips notes Gardner's connection with the Rosicrucian Order Crotona Fellowship at the time he said he received his Witchcraft initiation (Phillips 2004). Gardner himself noted that he owned a copy of Mathers's translation of The Key of Solomon and numerous magical manuscripts.

His familiarity with the magical orders and the traceable elements from those orders in his rituals has led some to claim that Witchcraft derives entirely from those lodges. This turns up in Internet memes, such as the claim that Crowley "wrote" the Gardnerian rituals. This is as silly as the claim that Witchcraft had nothing to do with its predecessors. Gardner drew on the content of European folk religion and the structure of Ceremonial ritual to shape the form of Witchcraft we know as Gardnerian. Gardner's version of Witchcraft placed the High Priestess as well as the High Priest at the head of the coven.

Gerald Gardner published the first book on modern Witchcraft (a novel, High Magic's Aid). Following in his footsteps, Alex and Maxine Sanders and Stewart and Janet Farrar, along with a number of other Craft elders, made public appearances, taught and initiated, and wrote books. Witches today trace initiatory lineages in Gardnerian and Alexandrian lines along with many other lines, and many groups have formed inspired by their books. Although traditional covens continue to meet, and new books and stories about Witchcraft's debutante days continue to surface, the development of traditional Witchcraft marked the final development of the literate lineage of Western Traditional Magic.

The Magician's Body of Knowledge

The primary accomplishment of this lineage, and its legacy to its successors, was the assemblage of the Magician's Body of Knowledge. The writers and artists who joined these groups and participated in the formation of their rituals and philosophies were classically educated and well traveled. They combed the writings of the ancients and the grimoires of the Middle Ages for any useful scraps of philosophy, ritual, and magic. They then categorized and assembled these disparate sources into a coherent system. The body of knowledge covers the planets and their associations; planetary squares; Tarot and astrology; the elements and their powers; the seasons of the year and their qualities; information imported from Eastern systems, notably the Tattvic tides and the chakra system; and mastery of basic psychic skills.

Assembling the body of knowledge was a group effort. Writers contributed both book-length public works and smaller privately distributed works, such as the Flying Roll essays of the Golden Dawn. The development of this collection of data continued throughout the modern period. The body of knowledge is shared by all the systems in the tradition. It became the common occult substratum which all subsequent systems take for granted.

Each of the three systems in Western Traditional Magic also has a unique set of knowledge. Ceremonial Magicians learn the Hebrew alphabet, Qabbalah, the names of the archangels, and techniques such as assuming god-forms. Ceremonial Magic also incorporates knowledge and practices from older traditions such as Enochian magic, alchemy, and Goetia. Thelemites additionally learn yoga, Thelemic theology, and general philosophy. Witches learn energy work, including grounding and centering, and raising and sending energy, as well as techniques for channeling deity, which differ from the Ceremonial assumption of god-forms. Witches learn the eight sabbats of the yearly round, and practice and preserve folk magic customs that have survived from European folk religion.

POST-MODERN MAGIC
Neo-Paganism and Women's Spirituality

The postmodern philosophical and cultural movement developed in the postwar era as a reaction against the modernist principles of progress and hierarchy, which were viewed as having led to totalitarianism. Postmodern philosophy and culture emphasize diversity, ambiguity, and singularity.

The postmodern emphasis on individuality led to a widespread rejection of organized religion. Traditional religions continued to exist, but new movements developed that encouraged individual approaches to spirituality. Individuals felt greater freedom to shop in the marketplace of ideas for a compatible religion or to combine pieces of religions in ways that fit their own worldviews.

This tendency also affected the magical communities. Traditional magical lodges and covens continued to exist and exist today. Branches of the magical lodges that had gone dormant or disbanded during the war were revived in the postwar years. Traditional Golden Dawn groups practice today, along with Crowley's O.T.O. (and many other Thelemic organizations).

Along with these survivors of modern magic, new magical movements developed along postmodern lines which rejected the vision of a singular truth, magical oaths of secrecy, and hierarchical authority. The rejection of tradition in magic led to the formation of the neo-Pagan movement and the women's spirituality movement. These movements emphasize personal spirituality and individually created theology and philosophy. Each person is his or her own priest or priestess, having a direct and unmediated relationship with divinity.

These movements remain active today. Neo-Pagan revivalists reconstruct Celtic, Norse, Egyptian, Greek, and other pre-Christian religions.

Neo-Pagan experimenters create entirely new forms of Pagan spirituality, and neo-Pagans of all kinds enter into dialogue with other faiths, create membership organizations, and conduct educational and public awareness campaigns.

The women's spirituality movement overlaps the neo-Pagan movement, but particularly emphasizes the study of goddesses and of historical women. Groups often limit membership to women only. Studies and practices coming from women's spirituality groups have deeply affected academic research into goddesses and into the lives of ancient women, and have also affected theologians in all religions, who struggle with the revival of feminine aspects of deity.

Although these movements have affected the academy, the reverse is less true. The new movements shared an understandable mistrust of intellectualism and academic scholarship. In the modern period, academic discussion contrasted magic negatively with science and religion, terming magic a pseudo-science or a primitive precursor to religion, and postmodern academic studies continue to take a debunking tone toward the analysis of magical texts. Neo-Pagans do make use of academic research in religious reconstruction, approaching academic data as raw material for ritual use. This tendency to disembed and make use of information is not always welcome to the academics who may feel that this process does not respect the terms under which they conduct their life work.

While the new spiritual movements are based partly on folk religion, personal insight, and academic research, the neo-Pagan and women's spirituality movements imported the Magician's Body of Knowledge in its entirety as a structuring framework. Since these movements resist academic thought-tools and privilege individual experience, the body of knowledge was not subjected to any systematic analysis or rethinking. As a result, while feminism married postmodernism and set about to reform philosophy, Western magic has been left with a largely modern metaphysic.

Post-Post-Modernism: Collectives

The post-postmodernism movement is so new that its name has not yet solidified and its principles have not yet been clearly articulated. This philosophical and cultural development is emerging to counter the paralysis caused by the postmodern emphasis on ambiguity and the fragmentation of continual deconstruction. Post-postmodernism, or after-postmodernism, developed in the late 1990s. It is characterized by the instantaneous communication of the Internet, which encourages the formation of interest-based communities. There is a renewed emphasis on gestalt, accountability, and grounding of experience in embodiment.

Although no clear magical direction has yet developed, virtual magical collectives have formed around the exploration of a synthesis of academic and scientific worldviews with traditional magic. The new movements re-engage the tradition, reassessing the Magician's Body of Knowledge in the light of both postmodern analytical tools and emergent values. This present work is one such effort.

WOMEN IN MAGIA TRADITIONIS

Lady History's *True and Complete Book of Magical Ritual and Secrets* contains this narrative. There she keeps copies of the Greek Magical Papyri, the *Corpus Hermeticum*, *The Greater Key of Solomon* and *The Lesser Key of Solomon*. This is the work that allows the continual development and preservation of the Magician's Body of Knowledge.

This is an important thread, and it is essential to answering the question I asked. I have fiercely resisted Lady History's invitations to dig deeper into many of these fascinating stories, keeping our focus on the main inquiry. Still, this history has not yet explained to me how Western Traditional Magic has come to understand women the way in which it does. I demand of the spirit, "Show me the women's stories."

Lady History picks up the heavy tome and strides purposefully away, filing it on the shelf. She hurries to one end of the library, plucks a book off the shelf, and brings it back to place it reverently in front of me. This is not bound in leather, but has been recently printed and is much smaller than the first. Nonetheless it is clear it is precious to her, as it is shortly to become precious to me.

Women's History

We are very lucky to have the history that we do. Historian Gerda Lerner famously said, "Everything that explains the world has in fact explained a world that does not exist, a world in which men are at the center of the human enterprise and women are at the margin 'helping' them" (Berkenwald 2010).

The corollary observation is what Carol Lee Flinders calls the First Law of Lerner: "Women's history is essential to women's emancipation." Christine de Pizan turned to history, the stories of women, to mount her spirited defense of women's character in *City of Ladies*. Flinders elaborates, "When a woman is about to break away from the cultural norms for women—to build a house, run for president, break a horse—learning that even one other woman has done it successfully brings that act into the realm of possibility after all; it has, indeed, what economists call a multiplier effect that she'll actually do it" (Flinders 1998).

When I first studied Western Traditional Magic as a young woman, women's magical history was difficult to trace. Even now it is normative to write about the lineage as a succession of central male figures, Mathers—Crowley—Gardner. These men wrote (in Crowley's case enormously, prolifically) and have been the continuing focus of interest of both insider and outsider histories, which consider their work as central while treating the women in their lives as contributing tangentially, helpers on the margin.

History that treats the women as central figures in their own lives is only now being written. For the women of the Golden Dawn, we owe a debt to Mary K. Greer and Alex Owen. Greer undertook to bring the women's biographies to light. She noted that Moina Mathers did not intend her work to be remembered—she wanted to erase traces of herself in the magical record. Without Greer's intervention, we might never have known of Mathers's important contributions (Greer 1995).

Owen placed the women's work in the context of the time in which they lived, and in particular noted the key position Anna Kingsford held in the development of the magical lodges. Owen's work sheds significant insight into the relationship the women of these movements had with each other (Owen 2004).

Works on Thelema continue to treat Crowley as the only important figure, with women figuring in his biographies as his Scarlet Women, lovers, muses, and victims. There is one insider biography, Phyllis Seckler's *Jane Wolfe, Her Life with Aleister Crowley*, which was published by the Thelemic journal Red Flame (Seckler 2003). *Jane Wolfe: The Cefalu Diaries 1920–1923* was published in 2008, edited by David Shoemaker (Wolfe 2008). Historic work comparable to Mary Greer's or Alex Owen's, treating the lives of women in early Thelema as central subjects, remains to be done.

These new histories have recalibrated our understanding of the roles women played in the development of Magia Traditionis. Their lives and contributions are embedded in the tradition.

Spiritualism

Today we have largely forgotten how widespread spiritualism was. This decentralized religious movement spanned the early modern and modern periods, flourishing from the mid-1800s to the 1920s. Many prominent intellectuals held séances and sought to commune with the dead, and by the 1870s few households were untouched by its influence. Alex Owen makes the point that this movement cohered around the work of women mediums who used the gender assumption that women are intuitive as a springboard to speak with authority and ultimately to challenge traditional notions of femininity (Owen 1989). Many prominent spiritualist women were involved with social movements, working for women's rights, the abolition of slavery, the dissemination of birth control information, and the humane treatment of animals, the poor, and the ill.

Women developed the mediumistic skill more easily than men. The Victorian gender narrative stressed the refinement of upper-class women; genteel women embodied delicacy and intuition. Being central to the spiritualist experience, upper-class women moved into leadership positions in the movement, and from there into leadership in various esoteric societies (Owen 1989, 2004). This context is important to understand why women in esoteric circles often acted as mediums. A sensitive woman often worked with a male scribe or questioner, sometimes her husband and sometimes not.

Theosophy

World traveler Helena Petrovna Blavatsky drew on Hindu and Buddhist spiritual concepts to formulate her understanding of the "perennial philosophy," Theosophy, which taught, among other things, that all religions have a piece of the Truth. Blavatsky (among others) brought the concepts of karma and reincarnation into Western occultism. Theosophy attracted social reformers and spiritualists, including Annie Besant, Anna Kingsford, and Marie, Countess of Caithness and Duchess de Pomar.

The Theosophical Society in Britain leaned toward the mystic, preferring meditation and contemplation to active ritual. Theosophist Anna Kingsford's preference for ritual over meditation led her to leave the Theosophical Society and form the Hermetic Society, whose meetings attracted, among many others, Samuel Liddell MacGregor Mathers and Wynn Westcott (Owen 2004). Anna Kingsford lived apart from her husband and worked with amanuensis Edward Maitland, who published some of her mediumistic visions after her death in *Clothed with the Sun* (Kingsford 1937).

Kingsford's friend Marie, Countess of Caithness, formed the Parisian branch of the Theosophical Society, where she engaged in séances with the Gnostic Jules Doinel. In these séances female deity demanded recognition. Doinel "gradually developed the conviction that his destiny involved his participation in the restoration of the feminine aspect of divinity to its proper place in religion" (Apiryon 1995).

Victorian Mythologizing

The Victorian-Edwardian women and men in the Victorian magical lodges shaped their ritual from material provided by their classical educations and a sensibility informed by a new sympathy for Pagan ritual.

These women and men did not reject their Christian and Jewish roots, but grafted a Celtic and Egyptian Pagan sensibility onto that stock.

In her book *Persephone Rising,* Margot Louis argued that the nineteenth century marked a shift away from the Christian mythos as the imaginative core of Western culture. The new center of spiritual life shifted toward the study of the mystery rituals of the Pagan world (Louis 2009). Late nineteenth-century classical scholars studied European myths for remnants of ancient rituals. The scholars of the Cambridge-based Myth and Ritual school, which included Jane Harrison and J. G. Frazer, were fascinated to find the origins of the idea of religion. They extensively explored the theory that religious ideas begin as explanations of natural phenomena (Ackerman 1991). Frazer's multivolume work *The Golden Bough,* first published in 1890, traced the roots of the Christian mythos of the dying and reborn god in older traditions of the vegetative god who married the Earth Mother, died, and was reborn each year (Frazer 1922).

Late nineteenth-century esotericists incorporated the study of ancient myth and ritual into their work, but took that work a step farther and used it to create new ritual. The Golden Dawn's deity work centered on Egyptian god-forms. Europe was fascinated by Egypt. Napoleon's army discovered the Rosetta Stone in 1799, but it was captured by the British army in 1801. When Jean Champollion succeeded in translating the stone in 1821, it became possible to translate ancient Egyptian texts. Egyptian antiquities had been flowing into London and Paris since the Napoleonic era. The British Museum and the Louvre each contained significant artifacts that attracted esotericists.

The central male figures in the Golden Dawn and O.T.O. (and the many associated groups which flowed into and out from these) not only knew each other, but were steeped in a classical and often upper-class education. They studied at Cambridge and Oxford, and they spoke and read several languages. They were Freemasons and supported one another's work through their fraternal connections.

Women attracted to the Victorian lodges were unusually well educated for women of their time. Even among the upper classes, women's education in the Victorian era occurred almost entirely at home and did not often include college-level studies. However, a few colleges began to admit women. Florence Farr attended the first woman's college in England, Anna Kingsford received a medical degree in Paris and was one of England's first women doctors, and Mina Bergson (sister of philosopher Henri Bergson) attended art college in Paris.

Samuel Liddell MacGregor Mathers met Mina Bergson in the British Museum as she was sketching Egyptian pharaohs. After Mina married MacGregor Mathers and changed her name to the Celticised version Moina, she acted as the medium for messages from the Secret Chiefs (Greer 1995). These messages sketched the outlines for the initiation rituals of the Golden Dawn. Officers in these rituals embody not God, saints, or Christian women and men, as in the Masonic rituals on which they are based, but instead embody Egyptian deities, including Isis, Osiris and Horus, Set, Anubis, Hathor, and Ma'at.

Florence Farr's Golden Dawn career illustrates these themes: an educated woman, her mediumistic ability and her interest in Egyptian religion led her into a position of authority. She spent a great deal of time in the British Museum researching her book on Egyptian magic (Farr 1896). There she contacted an Egyptian spirit, Mutemmenu, through her mummy in the British Museum. Farr collected a group of Golden Dawn adepts to investigate the spirit through clairvoyant visions (Tully 2009). She inherited leadership of the Golden Dawn when the Matherses moved to Paris. The poet Maud Gonne joined with Farr and others in conducting visionary quests which they called "Scrying in the Spirit Vision." Owen notes that not all members of the Golden Dawn accepted women's leadership, and one lodge was specifically formed so that the men in it would not be obliged to report to a woman (Owen 2004).

The tradition of the woman medium played a role in the work of Rose Kelly and Aleister Crowley in Egypt in 1904. During the Cairo working, Rose served as a medium receiving spirit messages intended for Crowley. In a Cairo museum Rose led her husband to the funerary stela of an Egyptian priest. After a series of experiences in which Rose behaved in a mediumistic way, Aleister spent three days acting as his own medium while a spirit, Aiwass, dictated *The Book of the Law*, which began with the pronouncements of Nuit, a new revelation of the Egyptian Nut, the goddess of the starry night sky.

The God and Goddess of the Craft

After the second World War, the mythologizing process continued through the efforts of Gerald Gardner, Doreen Valiente, and the ritualists of the public Witchcraft movement, who built on the foundations laid by their Victorian predecessors.

The God and Goddess of the Craft did not emerge either from Christian revelation or study of ancient Egyptian religion, but from the late nineteenth-century interest in folklore as an alternative to the Christian mythos. The folklorist Charles Godfrey Leland focused primarily on Gypsy lore, but collected some stories from Italian informants in a collection he called *Aradia, or Gospel of the Witches*. In *Aradia*, Leland presented a surviving tradition of Witchcraft in Tuscany. Unlike the father-mother-son triads—Osiris-Isis-Horus or God-Mary-Jesus— the triad in this gospel culminated in a female savior, Lucifer-Diana-Aradia (Leland 1899). The poem-prayer to Diana in this book, "Lovely goddess of the bow," made its way into the Books of Shadows of the Witchcraft revival, although Lucifer dropped out almost at once.

Margaret Murray combed the literature of witchcraft trials to find references to a horned god which she traced to older fertility gods (Murray 1921). Murray and Leland resurrected the term "witch" to describe the practitioners of European folk religion. The horned god Murray identified was rapidly identified with Cernunnos, one of the rare Celtic names recorded by the Romans. This name is carved under a horned head on a four-sided stone which was excavated from Chartres Cathedral and is now displayed in the Musée de Cluny in Paris. In the evolving Witchcraft theology, the Italian Aradia, daughter of the moon, was paired with Cernunnos, the Celtic horned god.

The Goddess of the Craft rapidly evolved into a trinity of her own. In *The White Goddess*, Robert Graves collected various tales and myths about the goddess which he fashioned into a theological image: maiden, mother, crone. These three aspects were mapped onto three phases of the moon, new, full, and dark (Graves 1948).

Stewart and Janet Farrar devoted one book each to the Goddess and the God. Their work called out a number of aspects of the God, including the son-and-lover, the sun, the horned hunter, and the green man. They developed a mythology of the God of the Craft as having two aspects which change midway through the year. They called the summer face of the God the Oak King and the winter face of the God the Holly King. (Farrar and Farrar 1989). Through the myth-making efforts of a number of neo-Pagan rituals and texts, the dual god framework has become conflated with the vegetation god and the horned god. The dual god is both the green man of spring and the hunter of autumn.

The classical moon goddesses, Diana, Artemis, and Selene, were contrasted with sun gods, Apollo and Sol. When the earth-centered vegetation and hunting god of the Witches was paired with the goddess of the moon, he acquired a solar aspect as well. Channeling the Goddess is called "drawing down the moon," and channeling the God is called "drawing down the sun." This is the fullest development of Witchcraft theology to date: the Goddess is a triple goddess of the moon, the God is a dual god of hunting and vegetation, earth, and sun. These are the deities depicted on the candlesticks on my personal Witchcraft altar. These two deities relate to each other through the Wheel of the Year.

Gerald Gardner, Doreen Valiente, and the early writers on Witchcraft brought the religion out into the public. In America, Starhawk's book *The Spiral Dance* made the religion accessible and popular. Here is her description of the relationship of the God and Goddess of the Craft:

> She is the Great Mother who gives birth to Him as the Divine Child Sun at the Winter Solstice. In spring, He is sower and seed who grows with the growing light, green as the new shoots. She is the Initiatrix who teaches him the mysteries. He is the young bull; She the nymph, seductress. In summer, when light is longest, they meet in union, and the strength of their passion sustains the world. But the God's face darkens as the sun grows weaker, until at last, when the grain is cut for harvest, He too sacrifices Himself to Self that all may be nourished. She is the

reaper, the grave of earth to which all must return. Throughout the long nights and darkening days, He sleeps in her womb;
in dreams, He is Lord of Death who rules the Land of Youth
beyond the gates of night and day. His dark tomb becomes the
womb of rebirth, for at Midwinter She again gives birth to Him.
The cycle ends and beings again, and the Wheel of the Year
turns, on and on (Starhawk 1979, 1999).

Women of Witchcraft

Gerald Gardner initiated Doreen Valiente into the Bricket Wood Coven,
where she became High Priestess. Valiente rewrote some of Gardner's
versions of the Witchcraft rituals, particularly removing language imported from Crowley's works. She also rewrote the "Charge of the
Goddess," combining poetry from Charles Leland's *Aradia* and snippets
of *The Book of the Law* with her own material.

The founding men of Witchcraft may have given their names to
the lineages, but the founding women outlived them, writing their own
biographies and versions of the history. Gerald Gardner died in 1964;
Valiente wrote her first book in 1962, and wrote five additional books
after Gardner's death before her own death in 1999. Janet Farrar co-
wrote books with her husband Stewart. Alex Sanders died in 1988; Maxine Sanders's autobiography, *Fire Child*, was published in 2007.

EVALUATING THE HISTORY

All of the systems in Western Traditional Magic explicitly encourage
women to participate in the tradition. Women hold positions of authority in all these systems and have done so since the foundation of the systems. The Gnostic Mass and the Witchcraft coven circle actively require
at least one woman to participate; as deity is gendered in these systems,
fully representing deity requires at least two people, one man and one
woman.

The gendering of deity varies in these systems. Golden Dawn ritual primarily recognizes Hebrew male deity, the Lord God (with various names), although some rituals also invoke Egyptian goddesses and
gods. Thelema venerates Lord and God, but also Nuit and Babalon.

Witchcraft adopts the Star Goddess and places her at the center of the universe, paired with the horned god; this couple together gives rise to the rhythms of sun and moon, the seasons, the earth's web of living creatures, and the spirit world.

Whatever the image of deity in these systems, the image of the magician remains male. Women can perform the Lesser Ritual of the Pentagram, imagining ourselves as sacred men standing in a sacred male universe. In the Thelemic version, the Star Ruby, we can also pretend we are sacred men standing in a sacred male universe. In Witchcraft, priestesses embody the earth, the moon, nurturance, and one of the three fertility-related goddess aspects. Witchcraft, however, is not designed to aid the journey of the individual toward wholeness. That is not to say that the individual does not develop in the system, but that individual development is not the primary concern of the system. Witchcraft has priests and priestesses but not magicians in the sense of making the development of self the center of the work.

One interpretation of the Gnostic Mass holds that the priest is the magician, while the priestess, deacon, and children represent facets of the priest. As priestesses in the Gnostic Mass, we can embody the lover and mother and assist the male magician in his quest for wholeness. The Gnostic Mass makes explicit what is implied in the Star Ruby—the fundamental person is male and incorporates aspects of the divine feminine to make himself whole.

The Magical Gender Narrative

The Magician's Body of Knowledge includes a gender narrative. In Western Traditional Magic, the narrative about men and women goes something like this:

> The entire universe is composed of two elements, the masculine and the feminine. These are mutually exclusive but complementary. The feminine is intuitive, receptive, creating the form of everything. The masculine is intellectual, active, and provides the force of everything. This spiritual understanding of gender is reflected in all the religions of the world. Both women and men

embody both masculine and feminine aspects. However, men embody male energy and women embody female energy.

We can graph this gender narrative in a table:

Male	Female
God	Goddess
Death	Life
Sun	Moon
Spirit	Body
Intellect	Emotion
Reason	Intuition
Air	Earth
Fire	Water
Active	Passive
Phallus	Womb
Aggressive	Nurturing
Priest	Priestess
Magician	Muse

While the tradition holds that both women and men embody both masculine and feminine aspects, and women can step into the role of masculine magician, it is also assumed that men embody male energy and women embody female energy. In all these systems, this means that women are expected to embody the moon, intuition, the womb, nurturance, water, and earth, while men embody the sun, the phallus, intellect, aggressiveness, air, and fire.

The magical gender narrative developed in the modern period. It built on the idea of male as ultimate deity by adding female deity. At the same time, women entered into modern lodges alongside men. The moment the female divine became visible, women also began to be included in the Western magical tradition. This is a definite improvement over the tradition's predecessors, which largely excluded women and which saw deity as only male. Inclusion, however, does not guarantee equality; the male-masculine side of the equation is valued more than the female-feminine side. For example, reason is held to be superior to emotion; the tradition teaches that emotion should be governed by reason.

In the postmodern period, the neo-Pagan and women's spirituality movements preserved the modern magical gender narrative intact but shifted the values assigned to the genders. In the new value system, the intuitive female is revered as the biological source of life and therefore closer to the ultimate source of spirit than the intellectual, separated, death-dealing male. This idea interestingly already exists in Thelema, which places the intuitive life-giving priestess on the high altar for worship.

Gender in the Tarot

Gender images in the Tarot make the magical gender narrative explicit. This deck of cards evolved from the deck of playing cards in the early modern period. Clubs, diamonds, hearts, and spades became the sword, cup, wand, and disk of the magician. This was now termed the Minor Arcana, and an entirely new set of cards was added, the Major Arcana. These 22 cards tell a story, the story of the journey of the magician.

For an example we can look at the Rider-Waite deck. This deck was designed by Arthur Edward Waite and drawn by Pamela Colman Smith. It is a ubiquitous deck, inspiring many others, and is often a magician's first deck.

The journey of the Major Arcana begins with card zero, the Fool, a man about to walk off a cliff. Next we find the Magician card. Here the magician stands before a table which holds the cup, wand, sword, and disk, all magical tools as well as the keys to the deck. The next card is the Priestess, a woman wearing a moon crown, sitting between the Qabbalistic black and white pillars of the universe. The next card also depicts a woman, the Empress, wearing a flowery loose dress, as if accommodating a pregnancy, an image of the Earth Mother. The Emperor, male, represents the ultimate secular power, and the Hierophant, also male, represents the ultimate religious power.

My favorite deck, the one I use when I cast for myself, is the Motherpeace Tarot. This deck illustrates clearly the shift in values assigned to the gender narrative in the postmodern period. Vicki Noble's thoughtful, visionary, and well-researched work brought women's images to the foreground in this deck. Her deck is in the tradition and retains the gendering of male Emperor and Hierophant; however, instead of valorizing male authority, the cards speak to the limitations of male authority, to the consequences of wielding punitive power over others, and to the devastating consequences to men of occupying the male-fire-intellect side of the gender split, which alienates them from the wellspring of their humanity. Noble's deck also speaks of the magician as a woman, a good first step in the process of redefining magical gender (Noble 1983).

These are important insights, and these insights guide me each time I consult the cards. They are interesting in this context to illustrate the shift from the modern to the postmodern magical understanding of gender. The deck remains recognizably within the tradition, while shifting what is valued away from the imaged masculine and toward the imaged feminine.

Magical Women as Men

Lady History has left me alone in her library. I sit at the desk, surrounded by walls and walls of books, look up at the beautifully painted starry ceiling, and contemplate.

If women, and feminist women, were so prominent in creating these magical systems, why are they not better fitted for women to use? Why was the image of the turn-of-the-century magician a male image?

Not all women who joined the magical lodges were feminist. Also, feminism was not then (nor is it now) a monolithic philosophy. It has divisions, and it changes over time. Women in the magical lodges at the turn of the century disagreed with one another, particularly regarding the appropriate expression of sexuality, with some of the women viewing sex between women and men as necessarily debasing for the women (a point of view that continues to exist in feminism today). Moina Mathers, who may have been molested in her youth and who found physical sexuality a shock in her adulthood, relaxed into the safety of a celibate marriage, confiding that she and her husband Samuel had remained "perfectly clean." On the other hand, the beautiful actress Florence Farr took lovers as she chose, while Thelemic women like Leila Waddell, Leah Hirsig, and Jane Wolfe, inspired by Nuit's call and Babalon's example, enthusiastically explored sex magic rituals.

It is important to note that in a patriarchal culture that privileges the needs of men and in which women are treated as servants and adjuncts to men, women may not identify with the gender "woman," seeking the freedom of being gendered male. Carol Lee Flinders explores what feminists call the *common divide*: "On the one hand, one feels moved *as a feminist* to celebrate the beauties and strengths of women's culture, so long and grievously ignored, and to identify oneself *as* woman and *with* other women. On the other hand, most of us have also felt—again, *as feminists*—another kind of need as well: this one can pull us sharply away from other women, or at least from being 'woman identified,' because women have been so relentlessly defined—as nurturing, patient, and compassionate, for example—that we simply aren't taken seriously by a male-centered culture" (Flinders 1998).

Feminist magicians chafed at the restrictions of women's roles. Alex Owen points out that it was precisely the image of magician as male that attracted women to the lodges. "For women, the occult presented an opportunity to develop a masculine persona that in a quite different context was being pilloried by critics of the 'manly' woman." In contrast to the feminine passive temperament, the masculine temperament was characterized by the assertion of will. The magical lodges encouraged women as well as men to develop the will and as a consequence exercise authority and self-direction. Magic, says Owen, "suggested that women might acquire if not already possess the 'masculine temperament'" (Owen 2004).

Stepping into a masculine persona, imagining herself as male, the feminist magician at the turn of the century could step into a role that permitted her to develop her own magical power and occupy positions of authority. It was precisely the freedom from the restrictive women's role that formed the appeal of magic for those women.

With the common divide and the appeal of the masculine persona in mind, we are prepared to assess Moina Mathers's description of the magical quest. In her preface to *The Kabbalah Unveiled*, Mathers said:

The whole aim and object of the teaching is to bring a man to the knowledge of his higher self, to purify himself, to strengthen himself, to develop all qualities and powers of the being, that he may ultimately regain union with the Divine Man latent in himself, that Adam Kadmon, whom God hath made in His Own Image (Mathers 1926).

I struggled to understand this passage when I first encountered it. What an extraordinary thing for a woman to say. What did she mean by that? Was she just caught in the language of the time, lacking any other way to express herself? If she lived today, would she frame that statement in the same way?

The Moina Mathers I have come to know through Mary Greer and Alex Owen, who rejected sexuality, distanced herself from her body, and sought to lose herself in her husband's work, that Moina might very well insist that she had said exactly what she meant.

Feminism and women's thought develops over time. Today's thinking is considerably more nuanced than the groundbreaking discussions in the 1970s. Late Victorian-Edwardian women did not yet have the benefit of Gerda Lerner's work bringing women's history to light, or the work contesting the use of the male pronoun to refer to both genders in English. With the benefit of a century of feminist effort, we can today challenge the privileging of masculine imagery and language in a way that simply wasn't possible in the early days of the magical lodges.

Why did the magical gender narrative develop the way it did? Lady Tradition can show us what the tradition is. Lady History can tell us how the tradition came to be what it is. Neither is equipped to answer a question that begins with *why*; for that we must turn to Lady Philosophy.

LADY PHILOSOPHY

I was afraid when I began this journey. Lady Tradition gave me the courage to speak my own experience. I have been considerably heartened by the time I spent with Lady History and the many strong sisters I found in the Victorian magical lodges. I have a better idea why I do not experience myself as a woman and a magician at the same time. With a deep need for healing I make my invocation: *Come to me, Lady Philosophy, and show me the foundations of my magic.*

Immediately the soft wooden walls, the pleasant forest view of the writer's refuge vanish, replaced by hard stone walls, a window set far above my head, and a barred and locked door. I am in a prison.

My account of enclosure until now has to some extent romanticized the cell. Women enclosed in medieval monasteries were walled off from the world, doors hammered shut while priests spoke the prayers for the dead. They received food through a small window and exercised in tiny courtyards. Not all of those women chose that life, and some, like Hildegard de Bingen, were enclosed as children.

It makes sense that I would find myself in a prison when I invoked Lady Philosophy. In just such a prison cell Boethius wrote the account of his conversation with Lady Philosophy. She taught him serenity in the face of calamity: this noble Roman, once magister officiorum, had been (slanderously, he maintained) accused of treason and stripped of his titles and wealth, spinning from the very top to the very bottom of Fortune's wheel. Even so he was able to write the *Consolation of Philosophy* in the year he spent in prison before Theodoric the Great executed him in 524.

I see that a woman shares the cell with me. She must be Lady Philosophy, but she does not appear to me as the beautiful lady Boethius saw. Now she is covered head to toe in many layers of plain clothing, and her habit's veil completely surrounds her face. Only her eyes remain as Boethius described them, burning with an intense fire.

Unnerved, I stammer my question: "Why does Western Traditional Magic view the fundamental person as male?"

Lady Philosophy draws from beneath her robes a plain and worn book which she drops into my hands.

MEN'S PHILOSOPHY

The book Lady Philosophy shows me begins with the reasoning of a professor, philosopher, and theologian on the very concept of woman. Sister Prudence Allen has assigned herself the problem of Aristotle. In her first work, *The Concept of Woman, The Aristotelian Revolution, 750 BC–AD 1250*, she comments, "…twentieth-century concepts of woman continue to dig at the bedrock of Aristotle. Until this foundation is removed the struggle to develop a correct philosophy of woman in relation to man will be doomed to failure" (Allen 1985).

The root of magical studies begins with a single Greek aristocrat in the fourth century BCE. Aristotle's thinking differed from that of his teacher Plato to such an extent that we continue to contrast the Aristotelian and Platonic ways of thought in our practice today. His thinking provided an important foundation for Jewish, Christian, and Islamic theology, and is the very wellhead of Western philosophy.

Aristotle described his thinking as *theologike*, theological science, a study of first causes. Centuries after his death Andronicus, head of the Peripatetic School in Athens, assembled Aristotle's writings. He titled the theological section "Metaphysics"—after physics—as he placed these works after Aristotle's works on physics. Later students have found meaning in the word as well as the placement, seeing metaphysics as the study of phenomena beyond the physical.

In her work analyzing Aristotle's contribution to philosophy, Allen spent some time surveying the pre-Aristotelian philosophers. She pointed to the Pythagorean school of philosophy, which generated a Table of Opposites: one and many, good and bad, light and dark, male and female. The columns line up, so that male was associated with good, light, one, while female was associated with bad, dark, many. Allen noted the philosopher Xenophon's pronouncement that man's sphere is the public world and his place is to rule, while woman's sphere is the private world and her place is to obey. Allen examined Plato's re-visioning of Hesiod's Earth Mother, a goddess who generated sky, air, and fire, as a Mother Receptacle who passively receives the forms of the elements from the Cosmic Father. Plato, however, at least understood both women and men to possess souls, which he valued more highly than the bodies they inhabit.

Aristotle elaborated on the equation of woman with matter, man with form. Allen said:

> Plato's association of form with father and matter with mother was removed from the cosmic level, and incorporated into Aristotle's theory of natural generation. On this level, the male was the active sex and the female the passive one. Aristotle drew these inferences from his belief that the mother provided the matter, and the father the form to generation (Allen 1985).

> This ordering of the active male force and the passive female force extended to the soul's capacity to reason. Allen noted: "Man's identity was tied to the higher or rational functions, and woman's with the lower or irrational, appetitive functions of the soul" (Allen 1985).

> This cosmic and natural order resulted in women's inability to engage in rational thinking. Aristotle held that for women "the lower part of the soul is not able to be ordered by the higher or deliberative faculty. Therefore, the rational powers of deliberation cannot rule or have authority over the lower functions of reason in women. Consequently, women cannot practice the

necessary prerequisites for philosophy, namely deliberation and the exercise of reason in the activity of definition and syllogistic argument" (Allen 1985).

These precepts, that male and female are opposites, that the male is light and good, that the male provides the active form to female passive matter, that men can reason while women cannot, that men rule the public world and women obey in the private, were packaged by Aristotle and passed down the centuries to the theologians and academicians of later ages.

> Allen concludes, "The final phase of the Aristotelian revolution occurred through the cooperative interaction of Islamic, Jewish, and Christian philosophy. St. Albert the Great was influenced by Averroes and Maimonides ... St. Thomas Aquinas, a student of St. Albert, then carried this phase of the Aristotelian Revolution to completion" (Allen 1985).

Between the ninth and thirteenth centuries, monasteries served as centers of education. During this time period women's monasteries existed alongside and sometimes independently of men's. Toward the end of the 1200s, Aristotle's works were again translated into the Western languages. The centers of learning shifted to urban universities whose curricula were based on Aristotle's teachings. As Aristotle had taught that women could not reason, women found themselves excluded from the new academies. Aristotle's influence on Western thought blighted women's access to learning until the Enlightenment.

The Age of Reason

The Aristotelian revolution came to an end in the great intellectual upheaval of the seventeenth century which challenged the dominion of theology over science. The printing press made information widely available in the form of newspapers and periodicals. Coffee houses sprang up around universities filled with students arguing new ideas. The tenor of the times was ready for a change, an Enlightenment—the very word evokes the image of a dawn dispelling the darkness of ignorance. Enlightenment philosophy spread like wildfire from France and the continent to Britain and America.

More than any other philosopher, Immanuel Kant laid the foundation for the Enlightenment's social effects. Kant championed the objectivist view that things can be known by reason, that knowledge is universal, and that moral judgments must be impartial. The Enlightenment program sought freedom from oppressive authority, both religious and political, by establishing reason as the arbiter of human culture.

At this moment of challenge to received orthodoxy, it would have been possible for Kant to move away from Aristotle's gendering of reason. Instead he chose to reiterate Aristotle's assertion that reason belongs to men. Since women reason ineffectually, Kant argued, they should be excluded from politics and intellectual pursuits, and wives should be subordinate to husbands. At this moment of dawning freedom, the same ancient argument was trotted out to keep women in the subordinate place.

Body and Speech

The disembodied intellect achieved its apotheosis in René Descartes. Sitting in a black wood-burning stove in Germany (it was a big stove), getting as far away from sensory stimulus as possible, Descartes came to his famous cogito: *I think, therefore I am.*

This effort to divorce thought from embodiment once again opened the door to include women among reasoning beings. However, the philosophical association of reason with the male persisted through another mechanism. In the last century, philosophers linked the phallus with the capacity to reason. First of course there is Sigmund Freud and penis envy. Freud taught that when a young girl discovers she lacks the male member she thinks of herself in shock as a castrated male. For Freud, loss of the penis is central to psychological development. Boys fear that loss but can learn to master the fear. Women can only submit in bitterness to their loss of a penis. Freud replays the entire Aristotelian-Kantian positioning of women: woman represents nature, sexuality, and the body, and favors feeling over thought.

Jacques Lacan combined Freudian psychological theory with linguistics to establish his philosophy. Lacan equated the phallus with *logos*, the power of the word, the ability to reason, and the ability to create speech. Lacan noted women possess a small phallus, the clitoris. However, in Freudian sexuality women are expected to shift sexual focus from the masculine clitoris to the feminine vagina. Despite his disclaimer, Lacan's language often shifts into a tacit equation of phallus and penis, aligning with the Western tradition's thousands of years of valorization of the phallus-as-penis. Lacan defines the phallus as a counter in a linguistic discussion. The phallus is the signifier of the logos. Without the phallus, women have no access to the powers of the logos, of reason and of language.

Embodied Experience

Post-enlightenment philosophers began to explore ways to think themselves back into the body. This move is difficult for men to make in Western culture, which equates the fall from spiritual grace with being alive in a body, and equates being alive in a body to being a woman; being embodied thus means both giving up the position of being spiritual, and giving up the position of being a member of the superior class.

This move played out in the argument between objectivism and empiricism. Objectivism says that facts can be understood by any reasonable observer in any circumstance, that they have an existence outside sensory experience, and that sensory evidence and personal experience should be corrected for in the search for factual truth. This is the position, for example, that scientists take when they seek to measure a phenomenon. Against this, empiricism argues that all evidence is sensory evidence. There isn't any place a mind can stand to look without distortion at a phenomenon, because the mind is always situated in a real physical body.

Maurice Merleau-Ponty built the philosophy of phenomenology on the inescapability of viewpoint. He pointed out that all experience is embodied, and all knowing is embodied as well. Observation of the world grounds first in an unconscious tactile sensory knowing that precedes the analysis of reason.

Lacan's disciple Luce Irigaray analyzed Merleau-Ponty's description of the embodied subject. Although it would seem that a move to place reason in the body would open entrance into philosophy for women, Irigaray demonstrated that Merleau-Ponty's body is an ideal, the sports body, adult, self-contained, and unchanging—in fact it is the privileged body, white, male, heterosexual, and healthy.

Masculine/Feminine

Freud's disciple Carl Jung articulated the dual gendering of the human being. Jung saw both women and men as psychologically bisexual, containing both masculine and feminine sides. However, still in the Aristotelian tradition, Jung viewed logos as the fully developed clarity of thought belonging to men only. The masculinity of women, their animus, is a pale reflection of this male power, so that women lack logic but instead form opinions and prejudices. Men's femininity is their anima, the soul or psyche, the source of inspiration. It is the artist's task to combine reason with anima in order to create. This anima may be projected onto a woman who becomes the artist's muse. In fact, a woman's masculine side can fertilize the feminine side of the male artist, to enable him to complete his work.

In *Gender and Genius*, Christine Battersby points to the gender inequity of characterizing the male's feminine side in positive terms, as a spiritual artifact, while characterizing the female's masculine side as a negative parody of reason. The ideal of the artistic androgyne turns out to mean men getting in touch with their feminine sides. Feminine qualities derogated in women are positive when men seek them out, while women displaying masculine qualities are disparaged (Battersby 1989). This gender model turns out to have the same end result as the others, acting as a means to prove out the superiority of men and women's unfitness for any other role than helpmeet.

Genius

Battersby noted the equivalence of the Roman Genius with the *logos spermatikos* as the self-creating procreative power of the universe. Battersby traced the development of the concept of Genius from that of a spirit possessed by the paterfamilias or patriarchal head of the family into a spirit possessed by every male, marking the possessor of the phallus as an instance of the divine universe. Roman women possessed a Juno, a spirit indicating her function as the ground in which the male procreative power could flourish (Battersby 1989).

The Pagan daimones, beings who ran messages between humans and gods, evolved into the Christian angels, messengers between humans and the single god. The Roman Genius or spirit possessed by every man became for the Christians the guardian angel, a single spirit watching over the individual. The concept of evoking one's own unique spirit is a distinct feature of Western esotericism, stretching from the Greek philosopher Socrates, through the Greek Magical Papyri spells to call one's personal daimon, to the Abramelin working to summon one's guardian angel (Mathers 1900).

In Western Traditional Magic, this working is termed Knowledge and Conversation of the Holy Guardian Angel. With this operation the magician summons the magician's own personal angel, Genius, or daimon, as a direct connection to the divine universe.

Women today engage in the operation of Knowledge and Conversation. However, it is important to note that the philosophy underpinning the operation once again roots in the equivalence of spirit with the male phallus.

EVALUATING MEN'S PHILOSOPHY

For "artist" in the discussion above we can substitute "magician." Just as the artist does, the magician unites feminine soul with masculine reason. Women in this system function as the tangible projection of the male magician's emotional spirituality. The magician seeks to harness the power of the feminine unconscious to the reasoning will.

This formula fuels one version of Western traditional sex magic—the soror mysticae is the external embodiment of intuition and inspiration which the male magician taps into through sexual union. This is why traditional sex magic manuals assume the male magician will direct the sexual working; his is the fully developed reasoning will which will harness her emotional power.

The Phallus in Western Traditional Magic

The Freudian-Lacanian phallus also describes the phallus in Western Traditional Magic. The phallus is the logos, the ability to reason and to speak, as well as the life-giving power of the universe. We see this play out in the Thelemic ritual of the Star Ruby, which valorizes the "phalle" as the "immortal principle."

Let us consider the assertion that a woman's clitoris is her version of the phallus, and that she therefore possesses a phallus. This assertion permits women to perform the Star Ruby, and to possess the Lacanian signifier, albeit in a temporary and limited fashion. That said, we don't speak of women having phalluses in any other context than in the magical or philosophical valorization of the phallus. In English, the word "phallus" has several definitions. It is first, a penis, and next, a description of tissue at a pre-gender-differentiated state of fetal development.

For thousands of years, the penis has signified the male sex in Western culture. Eva C. Keuls surveyed phallic imagery on Greek vases in *The Reign of the Phallus, Sexual Politics in Ancient Athens*. The glorification of male genitalia occurred in the context of the glorification of men's power and in particular men's power over women. Keuls pointed out the juxtaposition of the clothed woman with the naked man. Maenads were depicted carrying long cone-tipped staffs, thyrsoi, which carried phallic resonances (Keuls 1985). Greek women in a Dionysian ritual, the phallophoria, paraded with carved wooden phalluses, both to possess and invoke the god, and to claim some of the political power of men (Williams 1998).

Roman culture specifically valorized the phallus as the emitter of semen, which is the male procreative power. In *Gender and Genius,* Christine Battersby traced the career of the *logos spermatikos*, the self-creating power of the male god, from Stoic philosophy into Christian dogma and then into Jungian psychology. The phallus-as-penis was the visible sign that a Roman man possessed his own Genius, a reflection of the Genius of Jove which created the universe through Jove's emission of sperm. This divine authorization placed the Roman paterfamilias in charge of his wife, slaves, animals, and land. The phallus designated what was male and powerful precisely against what was not, and women especially were not; in fact, it was important to Roman culture that they willingly accept their status as servants (Battersby 1989).

In biology, the word "phallus" refers to tissue that is undifferentiated in early embryonic development. Humans begin life in a sexless state. The urogenital complex differentiates at various stages of development. Both sexes develop anuses. Glands become ovaries in females and testes in males. The labiascrotum tissue becomes vagina and labia in females, closing up to form the male scrotum. The urethral gland remains an external orifice for women and closes into the phallic tissue for men. The phallic tissue develops into the female clitoris and the male penis (Moore and Persaud 1998).

I am sensitive to the fact that there are other forms of urogenital development, and that contemporary biology labels these as abnormalities and medicalizes their treatment. Later we will discuss the varieties of genital development that comprise a rich diversity in the gender spectrum.

Taking the case of men and women, the final state of the urogenital complex leaves gendered humans with different physical experiences. The phallus for the man serves three purposes. It provides the urethral opening for the discharge of urine; it is the organ of sexual pleasure; and it provides the opening for the discharge of semen, which contains sperm, the male contribution to generation.

The situation for females is different. The clitoris does not discharge urine. The urethra remains separate from the clitoris. The clitoris sits atop a network of pelvic tissue which functions in some of the same ways as the penis, engorging with blood during sexual excitement. This tissue also includes the labia, which, while not the focus of sexual climax, contributes to sexual pleasure. In terms of sexual generation, the female womb receives an egg from the ovaries about once a month. In contrast to the sexual sensations associated with the discharge of sperm, many women do not physically detect ovulation. When the womb encloses both egg and sperm, the biological process of pregnancy occurs. There is no male equivalent to the womb, and no male equivalent to the process of pregnancy and birth.

When I create rituals, I do not describe my urogenital complex as a phallus. The Greek word for vulva is *kteis*, and some Thelemic women have experimented with using this word instead of *phalle*, although some Thelemic thinkers point out that *kteis* does not describe the clitoris or phallic tissue in women. If I were writing in Greek I would use the word γεννητικός, *yennetikos* (pronounced yennaytikos). When I write in English I say genitals.

So when I perform the Star Ruby, point to my genitals, and say "O phalle," what am I valorizing? If I take the stance that I am valorizing (one source of) sexual pleasure, then the clitoris is the phallus. If I am valorizing the power of regeneration of life, I would protest that phallus does not describe (or substitute for) womb.

For the purposes of this discussion, it doesn't matter what power is being valorized by this ritual. The point is that I have had to consider what "phalle" means at some length, here, and in my own practice. A man doesn't have to think about it at all—he can just point to his genitals, say "O phalle," and go on with the ritual. The male phallus is source of sexual pleasure and organ of generation at the same time. The female phallus is not, and labeling female procreation as "phallic" minimalizes, *masculinizes*, female embodiment.

Similarly, when Lacan discusses the phallus as the signifier of speech and reason, women fight through the discussion about whether the clitoris qualifies as a phallus. Freud was clear on the subject: women don't have penises and envy those who do.

The assertion that a woman's clitoris is her phallus does not act to valorize female embodiment, but instead to keep the focus on the male member. The point of all this focus on the phallus is precisely to define a man as a man, to define a woman as not a man, and to define a man as possessing the full and complete phallus which entitles him to speech, agency, and sexual potency.

The Magician Is a Man

The habit of thought that constructs the sense of self as centered in unchanging disembodied reason is embedded in Western metaphysics and occult metaphysics. All our rituals start from this assumption—the magician stands in the temple and speaks, gestures, performs a magical act. When the magician is imagined in a body at all, that body possesses a phallus. If a woman means to be a magician, she stands in the place of a man, as a man.

At least I have an idea now why I have the feeling that I am not at home in the magical traditions in which I have been initiated. Western occult metaphysics rests on Western metaphysics, and Western metaphysics declares that reason, will, and accomplishment belong to men, and that my body does not fit me to think or act. I am compensated by automatic unwilled access to the life force that flows through me, and my purpose is to channel this for the benefit of the magicians I work with.

Many of my magical sisters are content with this. Many of my magical brothers insist to me that this is the path of magic: that the universe is divided into two energies, the masculine active and the feminine passive. That the man's path to enlightenment is to act out his will while bringing his feminine nature into marriage within himself. That a woman, in order to walk the magical path, must represent the lover and mother to a male magician, or herself take on the masculine persona.

I am no longer afraid. I am angry.

If this is the way the universe works, if my sisters are content with this and my brothers insistent on it, why should I insist on being a woman magician?

Because I know, in the center of my being where I know that I am a woman, that the body matters. There is a wisdom in the body that cannot be overwritten by any intellectual formulation. There is a meaning in the body that is the true meaning of my life. No man can know it, no man can explain it to me, no man has ever gotten it right, and it is a transgression when a man arrogates to himself the task of explaining to me what it means to be a woman.

Because my sisters matter. When I navigate the common divide by rejecting my sisterhood with other women to assume the mantle of manhood, I lose their company. I leave their conversation, their nurturance, the collegial sense of companionship which women of goodwill achieve so easily.

Because there are those among my sisters who cannot navigate the common divide by abandoning their bodies. They cannot bring themselves to sacrifice what the body knows and the company of other women in order to achieve in the world. So they give up—they never enter into the lineage at all, or if they do, they content themselves with embodying the muse, the sexual vamp, the all-accepting whore, the love-without-limits mother, and they pursue accomplishment vicariously through the magical men in their lives.

Because I know, in the center of myself where I know the most important truth of my life, that I am not deformed or incomplete, that I am not fitted only to be a helpmeet, that it is not my purpose in life to be someone else's inspiration and servant. I know that I reason clearly, that I possess a soul, that I am both a material and a spiritual being. Thelemite that I am, I know that my will is my own and no one else's.

I refuse to accept that I must abandon my body and my sisters, call the universe Lord, call myself he, center my magic in an organ that looks suspiciously like the male member, enact mystery plays about men's lives in the world, in order to be a magician. And I am incensed that I struggle every day of my magical life with this divide that no male magician has ever had to face, because his body and his gender and his way of knowing in the world is perfectly reflected in the lineage.

I challenge this.

WOMEN'S PHILOSOPHY

There is a burst of glittering light. I look around myself and find I am still in the prison cell—my challenge has not yet freed me from this enforced enclosure. It is Lady Philosophy who has changed. Now she appears before me as she did to Boethius, wearing a splendid silk gown she wove herself, bearing a scepter in her hands and a radiant golden crown on her head.

I say to her, "How can I understand myself to be a woman with reason and will?"

While men's philosophy has defined women as a subset of men, women's philosophy has defined women in entirely different terms. We don't hear much about women's philosophy. Contemporary accounts of the philosophical lineage shut women out—DK's philosophy book mentions exactly one woman, Heloise, and that only as Abelard's muse (Magee 1998). Nonetheless women have done philosophy since the earliest days of the academy in Greece.

Correcting Aristotle

Sister Prudence Allen traced the history of women's philosophy in her *Concept of Woman* volumes. Allen worked to correct Aristotle's single-sex hierarchically ordered model that envisions man as the perfected human and woman an imperfectly formed human incapable of higher reason.

Against Aristotle's one-sex model Allen established a dual-sex model in which man and woman are different but complementary. She insisted on this gendering because she valued the body, for men as well as women. Unfortunately her dual-sex model excluded intersexuals, whom she treats as medical anomalies; intersexuality would disturb the biological and spiritual basis of her model (as intersexuality disturbs all dual-sex models).

With that in mind, her work is helpful to us in dealing with the affect of Aristotle's one-sex narrative. Her primary concern is to equip woman with both soul and reason by appeal to Aristotle's predecessors and critics, and by a survey of the accomplishments of woman philosophers and theologians.

Allen reviewed the work of medieval women theologians, Roswitha, Heloise, Hildegard, each of whom led women's communities. Hildegard was enclosed as a young girl, rose to the rank of abbess, and managed to move her convent away from the men's monastery to which it had been attached. Hildegard wrote a great deal, not only texts but also songs that illustrate in music and words her ecstatic understanding of the green power of the earth, *viriditas*. Far from being a passive muse, Heloise mounted a spirited argument with Abelard, insisting on engaging with him on her terms, with a woman's voice.

Enlightening Women

At the same moment Kant was working to exclude women from the benefits of the Enlightenment program, a feminist was vigorously campaigning to include girls and women. Mary Wollstonecraft's work is of some interest to students of the various revolutions for freedom, including the French, American, and Thelemic, as well as the feminist.

Wollstonecraft found herself living in Paris when the French national assembly adopted the *Declaration of the Rights of Man and of the Citizen,* kicking off the French Revolution. When British monarchist Edmund Burke wrote "Reflections on the French Revolution," a defense of monarchy and an attack on the revolution, Wollstonecraft fired back with "A Vindication of the Rights of Men." The American Thomas Paine followed up with his own "Rights of Man." (This may be of interest to Thelemites who have read Crowley's version of the Rights of Man in *Liber Oz.*) Meanwhile, back in France, a woman named Olympe de Gouges penned a fiery document, "Declaration of the Rights of Women." Wollstonecraft followed in English with "A Vindication of the Rights of Women."

Wollstonecraft began her professional career as a governess, then a school headmistress. She rapidly came to the conclusion that women were hobbled by their subordination to men. In her first work, *Thoughts on the Education of Daughters,* she argued for the extension of the Enlightenment project to women, and specifically the benefits of education. Wollstonecraft died at age 38 of puerperal fever after giving birth to her daughter, Mary Wollstonecraft Shelley, who would go on to write the novel Frankenstein. Wollstonecraft's early death is our great loss.

Wollstonecraft entered into the philosophical tradition that values reason and devalues the body, so it is not surprising that she spoke of female sexuality and the woman's body with some distaste. This left women in the same philosophical predicament as men, devaluing lived experience and privileging intellectual perception—having minds without bodies.

Countering Freud

Feminist psychologists cast a suspicious eye on the concept of penis envy. Eva Kittay thought it much more likely that a boy experiences womb envy when he discovers that women give birth and men do not. To defend against womb envy, men may devalue life-giving, over-emphasize the role men play in life-giving, or take over the life-giving role altogether (Kittay 1984). We see this play out in Western Traditional Magic (and Western metaphysics) in the equation of the phallus with the power of regenerating life.

Many feminist critics of Freud have pointed out that the entire metaphor of penis envy can be more easily explained by class analysis. It isn't difficult to understand why women would be envious of men's power and position in the world. I have never envied any man's penis, but I have often envied a man's unconscious confidence that he can speak and be heard and do whatever work his ability permits. And I have often resented men's appropriation of my space to speak and of my work—speaking over me, repeating what I have said, and taking my work and changing it.

The Post-Jungian Androgyny of Character

In the 1960s, the psychologist Sandra Lipsitz Bem created a testing instrument called the Bem Sex Roles Inventory, based on the idea that both women and men contain both masculine and feminine characteristics. Bem listed 60 characteristics, such as "loves children," "unpredictable," "conscientious," "willing to take a stand." Each test taker was asked to self-rate how well the characteristic described their own character. The test was then scored to find the test taker's rating on the traits labeled masculine and the traits labeled feminine.

Although the instrument is still in use today and is still available online, researchers rapidly found that it made less sense to talk about how masculine or feminine a person was, and more sense to talk about how loyal or flatterable or sympathetic they rated themselves to be.

Talking Back to Lacan

Jacques Lacan's disciple Luce Irigaray absorbed his philosophy and then, to his shock, acted to counter it. Irigaray objected to the dominance of phallogocentrism in psychoanalytic philosophy. She pointed out that Freud and Lacan defined women's sexuality solely in terms of how they satisfied men's needs, and paid no attention to women's own experience and desires. The equation of phallus with speech stifled articulation of women's experience of sexuality that differs from serving the needs of men. Irigaray sought to create a language in which women's sexuality was not only defined in relationship to men, in which women's genitals were not defined only as a negative of the male, and in which women could reason, speak, self-define, and exist.

The Philosophy of Relationship

Marilyn Frye also critiqued Lacan's phallus-as-signifier. Although the phallus is not identical to the penis, and women do possess a form of the phallus in the clitoris, Frye demonstrated that women are philosophically defined by the absence of the penis and therefore by the absence of the phallus. This definition by absence puts women outside the circle of meaning.

Frye modeled this conception through set theory: all those with a given characteristic are members of set A, while those without that characteristic are not members, are not A. Nothing distinguishes not-A objects from each other, they are all thrown into a pot together. "If, for instance, 'vanilla' is assigned as the A, then not-A includes not only strawberry, chocolate, and peppermint ripple but also triangles, the square root of two, the orbit of Haley's comet, and all the shoes in the world" (Frye 1996).

In the single-sex model, where men are members of set A, women lose definition in the undistinguishable category of everything else. "The man/not-man dichotomy makes no distinctions on the not-man side. This helps make it so 'natural' to lump women indiscriminately with children in 'women and children' and to cast 'nature' ... as a woman and woman as nature. It also connects with the fact that many men can so naturally speak in parallel constructions of their cars and their women, and say things like, 'It's my house, my wife, and my money, and the government can't tell me what to do about any of it.' It also illuminates the fact that women are so easily associated with disorder, chaos, irrationality, and impurity" (Frye 1996).

Frye relied on relationships to develop a definition of woman that sidesteps the single-sex model (woman is deformed man) that excludes women from the set defining a person. For Frye, the concept of woman is a positive self-supporting category. In this category of woman, individual identity emerges through A:B relationships which include numerous others.

Marilyn Frye's work used the concept of multiplicity to establish women's self-defining language. She noted that people who grow up monolingual think of their speech as language, while those who grow up polylingual think in terms of languages, in the plural. This concept is a seed pearl authorizing the development of women's language representing our embodied experience in magical terms.

Irigaray pointed out that women's sexuality is not bound up in the single phallic reference; women's bodily experience is multiple on multiple levels. It isn't as simple as imagining the phallus as the clitoris, or swapping out the phallus for the yoni by substituting "O kteis." Remember womb envy, and the compensation for the lack of life-giving power by overemphasizing the man's contribution to generation. The phallus is the male contribution to generation, which has been expanded to fill the entire universe. Aristotle's philosophy diminished the womb's life-giving power by imagining the womb as passive and inert, waiting to receive the spiritual impression of the hot formative male power.

The counter to this position is not to imagine the womb as the center of woman's power. Sexuality is a full-body experience, involving the yoni, but also mouth, tongue, skin. We give life in many ways, through giving birth and nursing our babies, and also by taking care of one another, with hand and with heart. It is not just one part of the body, but the whole body which gives and receives, and which enters into relationship with other bodies and with the universe.

Thinking through the Body

Christine Battersby drew on phenomenological concepts to arrive at an understanding of the woman's self. In *The Phenomenological Woman* she built on the work of Irigaray, Merleau-Ponty, and Kierkegaard, as well as the therapy of Oliver Sacks. She offered a model of the woman's body which cycles through changes, and which overlaps with the bodies of others. Battersby's identity is constructed through relationships in a repeated process of scoring, which is both a process of repetition of recollecting the self and literal musical scoring; she says, "Continuity of self can be maintained musically—by singing to oneself" (Battersby 1998).

In *Thinking Fragments,* Jane Flax provided a good overview of postmodern thought, which views the Enlightenment reliance on science and reason with some suspicion. The whole Enlightenment project depends on what postmodern thought views as metanarratives that support repressive social structures (Flax 1990).

Postmodern resistance to universalism challenges models of gender. Expecting women to share a single experience ignores the impact of race, class, age, character, country and regional culture, family and romantic relationships. Postmodernism questions the accuracy of lumping all women into a single category and emphasizes the importance of understanding the individual. It is an important critique that our experience and identity is shaped by a variety of other cultural markers in addition to gender, including race, class, and country. Poor Third World women may have little in common with white upper-class American women. The tendency of the rich to colonize the poor leaves postmodern thinkers understandably wary of the ways in which the construct "woman" conceals essential differences. Postmodernism insists on breaking philosophy all the way down to the individual. Each of us has bodies; each of us uses a mind which is embedded in the experience of being in a body.

In *Words of Power,* Andrea Nye drew on empiricism and postmodern standpoint epistemology to assess the work of influential male philosophers. She dispelled the myth of stand-alone thought by analyzing the philosopher who thought it. Her move was to use the postmodern technique of embedding to illuminate the relationship between the philosopher's understanding and the understanding of his culture and time, as well as the impact of the philosopher's life experiences on his thinking (Nye 1990).

This is why at various times in this book I talk about where I am, what I am looking at through the window as I write. This book is not the product of an intellect floating in space and speaking an absolute truth, it was written by an embodied woman who was thinking at various times and in specific physical places. It is important for me as a writer to remain grounded by noting this, and remind us all to connect our reading experience with our physical experience.

As helpful as it is to understand each of us as a uniquely embodied being, postmodernism leaves us in the position of valorizing our individuality while having no framework in which to discuss our connections with each other. In *Enlightened Women*, Alison Assiter argued in favor of a return to a modified Enlightenment project. She validated the postmodern distrust of universalizing categories, while pointing out that the shared experience of the sexed body provides common experiences which transcend differences. For Assiter, it is helpful to be able to discuss women as a class of people who share certain characteristics, especially oppression. She argued for the utility of recognizing commonalities, bonding around shared experiences, and banding together against aggression (Assiter 1996).

EVALUATING WOMEN'S PHILOSOPHY

The women who have come this way before us, who have worked to grant reason to women, have passed to us ideas about how to construct ourselves as reasoning beings. Postmodern theorists and phenomenologists focus our attention on the lived experience of the body, this body, at this moment.

Having established that women exist, have souls, and can engage in higher reason, we can return to the notion in Western Traditional Magic that the male magician is the perfection of the living man. Since women can reason, this would indicate that women are capable of the act of will, which is magic's central act. In fact, the work of Florence Farr, Moina Mathers, Dion Fortune, and many other women in the magical lodges in the past century demonstrates this capacity.

In the end, Lady Philosophy brings to me the same comfort she brought to Boethius. None of us control Fortuna's turn of the wheel. In the Western world, Fortune sets women as a class a rung or two below men as a class. What remains in our power is the way in which we respond to the world. We can act to free ourselves from the prisons to which others would confine us.

With that realization I am myself freed from prison. The bars of my cell fade away and I am back in the writer's cabin, where sunshine streams through the window and falls on the desk where I sit. I throw the window open to breathe the fresh pine-scented air.

We have seen how men philosophers have thought about women and how women philosophers have countered those thoughts. Philosophy underlies our understanding of gender. How much of this is just men making up stories? I am citizen of a secular society and distrust appeals to divine will. I am a child of the Enlightenment and demand that reason have more of a foundation than the declaration of authority. In my time, reason is based on observation and verification. I turn next to Lady Science, the modern world's arbiter of truth.

LADY SCIENCE

I am still angry, and now I am fiercely determined. I make the invocation: *Come to me, Lady Science, and bring to me the truth of my sex.*

The cabin in which I sit fades away again. I find myself at a metal desk in a sterile laboratory surrounded by shelves crammed with jars. Diagrams are neatly pinned to gleaming white walls. Lady Science leans close to study one of these, an image of the human body—at first glance I cannot tell if the diagram she is studying shows a man's body or a woman's. She wears a white lab coat, and her hair is cut short, out of the way. She constantly scribbles on a clipboard, writing her own book as she goes.

I ask her, "What are the physical differences between women and men?"

"Women bear live young and undergo the changes of the fertility cycle," she says.

I nod. "Besides that?"

She hands me Joshua Goldstein's book *War and Gender*. He devoted an entire chapter in this work to the biology of individual gender, assessing genetics, testosterone and female hormones, size and strength, brains and cognition. Surely, I think, size and strength will show a difference. Goldstein, however, immediately begins to talk about variables. Men in one society may be substantially larger or smaller than men in another, and the differences in gender vary by society as well. Cultural factors such as how women and men eat make a significant difference in size. So it's hard to tell if a given difference between genders can be attributed to gender or to some other social factor (Goldstein 2001).

I ask Lady Science, "What about the brain?" I have heard of research about how women and men use the different parts of their brain differently. She points to the book again. Goldstein says, "Nobody knows how the fundamental processes of the brain such as memory and thought work, much less how a brain achieves consciousness." Researchers can study when parts of a brain turn on and off, and conduct surveys of cognitive abilities. These show gender differences around sexuality—for example, men don't use the part of the brain determining ovulation. Men's brains are bigger, women have more brain cells, which evens out—women and men are equally intelligent. When asked to compare nonsense words to determine if they rhymed, men used more left brain function, women both sides of the brain equally, but both accomplished the task equally well. Women do seem to do better on verbal tests, men on spatial tests, but the differences are slight, so it is unclear what impact, if any, these differences have on ability.

I turn to Lady Science again. "If there is so much uncertainty, why do scientists point to biological factors like size, strength, and brain function as proving differences between the fundamental natures of women and men?" Lady Science has that answer at her fingertips: Ruth Bleir's work *Science and Gender* takes this question on without flinching. While the scientific method strives for objectivity in theory, Bleir says, in practice a researcher's biases will be reflected in their assumptions and methodologies. Scientists are born into a given society, raised to its beliefs, and their work is affected by what they want or need to be true (Bleir 1984).

FUNGIBLE GENDER

Maybe I'm asking Lady Science the wrong questions. I ask her, "What is the scientific definition of sex?" In answer she pulls out a copy of the *New Yorker* and lays it on the desk in front of me, open to Ariel Levy's discussion of Caster Semenya.

From her earliest girlhood, Caster Semenya knew running was her ticket out of poverty. She grew up in a tiny South African village fifteen miles from the nearest athletic club, which offered coaching but possessed no running tracks. Semenya had no shoes. From that stripped-to-the-bone beginning she went on to race, winning medal after medal, rising through the world rankings. In Germany in 2009, she won the 800-meter gold at the World Championships, breaking the previous world speed record for a woman.

But was she a woman? The athletes she competed against surveyed her thin breastless body and deep voice and called for an inquiry. The 18-year-old South African villager was accustomed to being called to account for her gender and normally settled the issue by disappearing into a bathroom to show off her genitals. This time the IAAF ordered genetic testing and found that while Caster had female-shaped genitals, she had no ovaries or uterus but did have testes. When this news leaked, South Africa erupted in protest of the world's questioning of her gender. Caster Semenya was a woman! She had a legitimate right to her medal!

Ann Fausto-Sterling began *Sexing the Body* with a story just like this one, from 1985. Maria Patino was headed for the Olympics to represent Spain in the hurdling competition. In the rush of packing she left a vital document at home, the doctor's certificate proclaiming her to be a woman. No problem, everyone thought, she could just do a chromosome test. Hours later she was declared by the Olympics committee to be not-a-woman: she had an extra Y chromosome, and although she had female-shaped genitalia, she lacked a womb. She was barred from the Olympics, evicted from the Spanish athletic compound, her humiliation hit the public newspapers, her boyfriend left her. She fought for two years and was reinstated to the International Association of Athletics Federations in 1988 when she proved that she did not have more testosterone than the athletes she was competing against. She narrowly missed competing in the next Olympics and moved into coaching (Sterling 2000). Two decades later when Caster Semenya lived through the same public questions about gender Maria Patino had immediate sympathy for her.

Caster Semenya's story has a happier ending. After an 11-month suspension, the IAAF cleared her in July 2010 to compete in women's races. She promptly won an 800-meter race in Finland (Moore 2010).

But My Good Woman

Alice Domurat Dreger started her book *Hermaphrodites and the Medical Invention of Sex* with a great story. It was a third-hand story, told by Dreger of a nineteenth-century paper written by a man who knew the doctor who reported it, Professor Michaux. This doctor had examined a woman, Sophie V., who was forty-two years old. She and her husband had been happily married for two months but were having trouble with the "conjugal act." Specifically, Sophie's husband couldn't penetrate her vagina. Michaux's examination turned up what looked like a single descended testes, a large clitoris, and no vagina. He elicited the story from Sophie that when she was born the doctor couldn't tell what sex she was and told her parents to bring her back later. Her parents sensibly did nothing of the sort, but looked at her themselves, said "sort of female," and raised her as a girl. Michaux told Sophie they had been mistaken. Sophie thought he was daft. "But my good woman," he exclaimed, "you're a man!"

Dreger studied medical records about hermaphrodites in the period 1870–1915, written by learned men at that modern moment when the magical lodges were forming. Suddenly there was a spate of papers in the medical journals about people with indeterminate genitalia. Why the sudden increase in interest in the subject? Dreger lists many reasons: there were more opportunities to publish and more people were seeing doctors. Increased access aside, what interested these men, what kept them endlessly fascinated with genital ambiguity, was the opportunity to pin down the physical markers of sex.

By examining people with genitalia not immediately identifiable, the medical men decided that what matters is that men have testes and women have ovaries. For this reason Dreger termed the time period she studied the "Age of Gonads." Dreger said:

Hermaphrodites were repeatedly construed by medical and scientific men so as to reinforce primarily what they threatened most: the idea that there was a single, knowable, male or female "true" sex in every human body (Dreger 1998).

Once a person could be determined to be male or female, then everything else fell into place. What we now call gender and sexual preference was tied then to the biological sex of the individual. Girls played with dolls, boys climbed trees. A woman was attracted to men and was gentle and nurturing, a man was attracted to women and exhibited bravery.

This was precisely the time period when women were getting the vote all around the world, were pressing to own property and divorce husbands, attend universities and medical schools, enter into professions formerly reserved only for men. Dreger noted that despite these challenges to the existing social structure, many physicians and scientists persisted in arguing that sex boundaries were directly linked to nature, that men and women acted the way they did because they were male and female, and that doing otherwise would be unnatural and even immoral (Dreger 1998).

Making Sex

If scientific men in the 1870s were looking at ambiguous genitals to figure out what definitively defines a woman's body and a man's, what had people done in the years before that?

Let's look at Sophie V.'s story again: her parents decided she was a girl and raised her as a girl. According to Thomas Laquer, this was fairly common in the West before the Enlightenment. In *Making Sex*, he traced a significant change in Western science to the dual-sex model we are familiar with today. Before that, Laquer argued, the dominant paradigm recognized only one sex (Laquer 1990).

In the West, we might frame the contemporary dual-sex model like this:

There are two genders, male and female. These are biologically determined. Most gendered characteristics are also biologically determined—the body is the fixed referent of truth regarding gender. The two genders do not overlap and are complementary but different. All men focus on sex; women who focus on sex are bad, those who don't are good. Women give birth, making them better at nurturing children, which also makes them carriers of culture, and makes them better at spiritual pursuits. Women's focus on children and nurturing satisfies them, while men must prove themselves by going out into the world and achieving success in business, science, or the arts. Men are violent by nature. Because men are physically stronger than women, and are more aggressive, they have everywhere in the world throughout history dominated women. This is also why men make better athletes than women.

For two thousand years before the Enlightenment, there was another way to look at sex and gender in the single-sex model. We can summarize it like this:

There is one biological sex, the human sex. Men are the perfection of this sex. Women are men turned inside-out—the womb is the phallus reversed. Women are imperfect versions of the human sex. For that reason there are two genders, the male gender and the female gender. This is primarily a class difference. Men rule, women are ruled. Men are the heads of households, representing or "covering" the interests of the women, children, animals, and lands encompassed by those households, in the doctrine called "couverture." Bodies are not the fixed referent of gender. Bodies in fact can change; men can become softer and more effeminate by associating with women, while women can take the place of men, becoming harder.

Laquer describes this shift: "... at one time the dominant discourse construed the male and female bodies as hierarchically, vertically, ordered versions of one sex and at another time as horizontally ordered opposites" (Laquer 1990).

Before the Enlightenment, Laquer argued, the fundamental distinction was not of the body, but of social class. Men were the class that ruled, women were the servant class. It was possible to move from one class to another, to exchange one class for another, with the plastic, fungible, body physically morphing to accommodate this change in status.

What caused the shift in model? Why was the single-sex model exchanged for the dual-sex model? Laquer took a specific example, a trigger, the sudden "discovery" by science of the clitoris as the seat of female sexual pleasure, which permitted the discussion of conception separately from the discussion of the enjoyment of sex. Laquer points to the separation of sexual pleasure from conception as the first step toward the image of the model of "the passionless female who stands in sharp biological contrast to the male."

Like Dreger, Lacquer pointed to the shifting social climate as the root of the shift in the understanding of sex and gender. "The new biology, with its search for the fundamental differences between the sexes, of which the tortured questioning of the very existence of women's sexual pleasure was a part, emerged at precisely the time when the foundations of the old social order were shaken once and for all" (Laquer 1990).

It's hard to absorb the idea that the model of what makes a man male, what makes a woman female, can change because of politics; that the way we think itself can be exchanged, shift, morph into something entirely new. Made different by a sea-change. Lacquer addressed this discomfort directly:

I have no interest in denying the reality of sex or of sexual dimorphism as an evolutionary process. But I want to show on the basis of historical evidence that almost everything one wants to say about sex—however sex is understood—already has in it a claim about gender. Sex, in both the single-sex and the dual-sex worlds, is situational; it is explicable only within the context of battles over gender and power (Laquer 1990).

Lacquer did not choose his example at random. It seems that every shift in the cultural conception of gender writes itself on women's sexual bodies. No wonder turn-of-the-century feminists argued about the subject, and contemporary feminists argue still; almost every way of thinking about women's sexuality has been used at one time or other to keep women in our place.

Aristotle's Biology

For two thousand years before the Enlightenment, Western science understood women and men as forms of the same being, as one sex. What was the science on which that model was based?

Lady Science hands me Sister Prudence Allen's book *The Concept of Woman.* "I've already seen this," I say, "this is philosophy."

Yes, but Aristotle's gender philosophy was based on a question of biology. He sought to solve the fundamental philosophical problem of his age: where did humans come from? Specifically, do men and women both contribute seed to the formation of a new human?

Although many philosophers who preceded him believed both men and women contributed seed, Aristotle cut across the emerging consensus, and decided that only men contributed seed to the generation of humans. He reasoned that the female is colder than the male. The male's hotness heats up the blood and purifies it so that it becomes white and foamy. The female's colder blood remains red, unpurified, and is discharged monthly. Therefore only the male seed is fertile. The female contributes the material on which the male seed can work.

This led Aristotle to a number of conclusions:

The male and the female are distinguished by a certain ability and inability. Male is that which is able to concoct, to cause to take shape, and to discharge semen possessing the "principle" of the "form" ... Female is that which receives the semen but is unable to cause semen to take shape or to discharge it (Allen 1985).

The female always provides the material, the male that which fashions the material into shape (Allen 2002).

We find here the wellhead of the Qabbalistic doctrines designating force as the male principle and form as the female principle. The male seed contributes the essence, or soul, while the female contributes the material, or body. In the process of generation the female is passive, the male active. The soul principle in the male seed creates a male if it is successful in heating the cold female. If not, it creates a female, an infertile and deformed version of the male. This creates a system of opposites, or contraries:

Male	Female
Hot	Cold
Soul	Body
Active	Passive

This system of opposites maps out onto the elements, which are a combination of hot and cold, dry and moist. The female is cold, the male is hot. The elements are therefore gendered and arrayed in a hierarchy: the earth is at the bottom of the universe, fire and the sun are at the top of the universe, with the sun as male, and the earth as female.

This theory of generation underlies Aristotle's theory of gender polarity, which establishes a hierarchical relationship between the sexes, with women taking the subordinate position:

Man

    Woman (deformed man)

Because women are deformed men, woman's rational soul is not as fully developed as that of man's. Woman's rational soul lacks authority over her irrational soul. Therefore women should be governed by men.

It is clear that the rule of the soul over the body and of the mind and the rational element over the passionate, is natural and expedient; whereas the equality of the two or the rule of the inferior is always hurtful ... Again, the male is by nature superior and the female inferior; and the one rules, and the other is ruled; this principle, of necessity, extends to all mankind (Allen 2002).

Aristotle valorized the monarchy as the model for the marital relationship. As in a monarchy, there should be only one ruler in a household, the husband. The wife's sphere of authority is confined to that of the household, while the husband works in the public world. Since husband and wife are not equals, their friendship is not that of equals, and the husband loves less than the wife.

We know now that Aristotle's understanding of human biology was mistaken. Women contribute an egg and men contribute a sperm to combine to form a human being. Both women and men contribute chromosomes to the new being. About the presence of the soul science is agnostic.

Biological Dominance

Aristotle, a single influential philosopher, articulated the basis for the single-sex model which dominated the West for another two thousand years and provided centuries of justification for the hierarchical relationship between men who rule and women who serve. Aristotle, however, did not invent the dominance hierarchy itself. Where did this originate? Is there a biological foundation for men's dominance over women?

Joshua Goldstein believed he found an answer. In his groundbreaking and exhaustive book *War and Gender*, he meticulously mapped the best information currently available about the biological differences between the sexes as well as cultural norms surrounding war. Goldstein found no biological reason why women should not go to war. Women who do go to war fight well. Men and women have nearly the same genetic code. While it is true that the strongest and largest men outclass the weakest and smallest women, there is enough overlap in the middle of the curves that some women at least definitely qualify as combat ready. In cognitive studies men do a bit better on spatial scores, women on verbal scores, but the curves again mostly overlap.

Hormones don't make the difference. Goldstein found that there is little correlation between testosterone and aggression. Testosterone responds to changes in social status, but is not itself the male aggressive trigger. Similarly, female hormones don't necessarily make women more peaceful; maternal behavior is mostly limited to the nursing period, and even then, mothers are capable of significant aggression in the defense of their children.

What does matter is upbringing. Men are expected to pass a test of manhood that fits them for combat. Boys are raised to distance themselves from their own emotions to prepare them for the trauma of combat.

Goldstein summarized his findings:

> The answer in a nutshell is that killing in war does not come naturally for either gender, yet the potential for war has been universal in human societies. To help overcome soldiers' reluctance to fight, cultures develop gender roles that equate "manhood" with toughness under fire. Across cultures and through time, the selection of men as potential combatants (and of women for feminine war support roles) has helped shape the war system. In turn, the pervasiveness of war in history has influenced gender profoundly—especially gender norms in child-rearing (Goldstein 2001).

Goldstein concluded that war and gender make a knot, one that does not appear to be based on biology, but on developments in human culture.

Perceiving Difference

Aristotle's biology was based less on observation than on reasoning. Let us assume that we know nothing about gender or sex, that we are willing to look at human bodies with new eyes, willing to see whatever really presents itself. What do we find?

Western culture has long recognized the existence of the hermaphrodite, the being between sexes, neither male nor female, both male and female. Dreger says:

> Both visions of the hermaphrodite—as an in-between sex and as a double sex—can actually be found as far back as the days of ancient Greece. Joan Cadden has traced the conception of hermaphrodites as in-between sexes back to the Hippocratic writers. The

Hippocratic paradigm assumed that sex existed along a sort of continuum from the extreme male to the extreme female and that the hermaphrodite therefore was sh/he who lay in the middle. By contrast, later thinkers formed from the writings of Aristotle a different, equally persistent tradition that imagined hermaphrodites to be doubly sexed beings. That tradition specifically held that hermaphrodites had extra sex (genital) parts added to their single "true" sexes via an excessive generative contribution of matter on the part of the mother (Dreger 1998).

A continuum from the male to the female … if there is a continuum, and the hermaphrodite lies in the middle, what are the other possibilities? How many genders do humans actually have?

It is difficult to estimate the percentage of intersexual births in the world. Because the dual-sex model is so rooted in deep expectations of who we are in the world, differences in infant bodies are under-reported. Also at times it can be difficult to determine the sex of a newborn child, as genitalia differ significantly from person to person. As we have discussed, embryos first develop genitalia that include both phallus and labioscrotal folds. Later, female embryos develop a clitoris and labia, male embryos a penis and scrotum. Look at the illustrations in the "Urogenital System" in *The Developing Human* (Moore and Persaud 1998). A male scrotum not completely closed can look like labia, and closed labia can look like a scrotum, just as a large clitoris can look like a penis and a small penis can look like a clitoris.

Today, in addition to gonads, scientists look to hormones, including estrogen, testosterone, and androgyne, as well as chromosomes (XX marks a female, XY a male embryo) to determine sex. In *Sexing the Body, Gender Politics and the Construction of Sexuality*, Anne Fausto-Sterling identifies a number of biological events which result in a body which does not fit neatly into either gender. Chromosomal differences include females lacking a second X chromosome (XO), males with one or two extra X chromosomes (XXY and XXXY), and mosaic karotypes with mixtures of X and Y chromosomes. Hormonal conditions include androgen insensitivity syndrome, in which an XY karotype lacks the ability to recognize testosterone and develops breasts and a feminine body shape at puberty (Sterling 2000).

How many physical sexes are there? How many people don't fit neatly into the categories "woman" or "man"? Again, it's hard to say. At present newborn children are not tested for genetic makeup. Some variations may not surface until puberty. Parents of variant children often experience shame and discomfort at their children's condition and hide this from the children themselves and from the world. There is also disagreement about which conditions qualify for intersexuality (such as hypospadias, or the exit of the urethra from locations other than the tip of the penis). As a result, estimates of the percentage of intersexuals to the general population vary from one in 5,000 to one in 200.

The Child You Save May Be Your Own

The physical condition of intersexuality challenges the dual-sex model in ways which both medical personnel and families find uncomfortable. This has resulted in the medicalization of gender. Surgery may be performed on infants to shape their genitalia. Such children may be studied and displayed to medical personnel from a very early age. Children treated in this way are also frequently kept in the dark about their physical makeup.

Adults reporting on these childhood experiences note several common threads. The first is that surgery never improves sexual performance; instead, it almost always results in physical loss and pain as well as psychological trauma. This is the most tragic consequence of the dual-sex model, the framing of a perceived difference in gender as a medical condition that can be fixed.

The second theme is that knowing is always better than not knowing. Hiding a child's condition from the child, telling the child "don't tell, never speak of this," leaves the child feeling alone and ashamed, and ends up creating the very difference the secrecy was meant to erase. Knowledge is power. Telling a child what is really happening permits the child to begin to navigate the world of gender with as many tools as possible.

The Intersex Society of North America and Organization Internationale des Intersexes call for protection for infants and children. They specifically recommend making no surgical interventions until the child becomes an adult and can participate in decision making. They recommend that parents of children identified by medical science as intersexual assign the child a gender, raise the child in that gender, and tell the child from earliest childhood everything known about the child's body.

It is important to note that intersexual children are not a different class of people than our own boy and girl children. Once difference is perceived and medicalized, who is to decide what makes a difference, and what protects those who are defined as different? We are all intersexuals, falling somewhere on the spectrum of human gendering. Children targeted for medical intervention might have a hormonal condition, ambiguous genitals, or just seem a little different. An estimated one in 200 boys are born with the condition hypospadias, a urethra exiting somewhere other than the tip of the glans, but are otherwise normal boys. Operations intended to repair this condition leave these children with less functional organs, all the childhood trauma of surgery, and the additional trauma and shame of gender surgery.

In June 2010, bioethicist Alice Dreger publicized a program of female clitorectomy at Cornell University. Girl children whose clitorises were deemed too large were subjected to surgery to reduce them. The children, six or older, were then stimulated by the doctor and asked to report on the sensations experienced as a proof that the surgery had not impaired sexual capacity (Dreger and Feder 2010).

A civilized culture does not medicalize difference. We can decide that these types of practices are unacceptable. We can communicate this to the ethical boards which provide oversight for medical operations and research on human subjects. We can act to protect our own children by withholding permission for surgical interventions—and sticking to those decisions even when the medical establishment threatens us for doing so (Dreger 2010). We can also increase awareness of these practices so that the light of both reason and compassion can replace the secrecy which allows these practices to continue.

Intersexuality Around the World

Some cultures make room for an intersexual gender, a third gender, which acknowledges at least one of the gender variants. Children with the XY karotype but lacking the enzyme 5-alpha-reductase may begin life as a girl but develop testicles with the onset of puberty. In the Dominican Republic, there are villages where this condition occurs frequently enough that there is a word to describe it, *guevedoche*, balls at twelve. At puberty a *guevedoche* may decide to cross genders and mature as a man or may decide to remain a girl (Nataf 1998).

In *Men as Women, Women as Men, Changing Gender in Native American Cultures*, Sabine Lang discusses the widespread cases of additional genders in Native American cultures. Men living as women, called *berdache* by anthropologists (and tribe-specific names in their own cultures), may do women's work or wear women's clothing, while in some tribes women (also called by tribe-specific names) may dress as women but take on men's occupations, or may be raised to be a hunter in a family without sons (Lang 1998).

In India, there are men who dress as women and who are sometimes castrated. Called *hijra*, they evoke laughter and fear, but also occupy a cultural role, as performers at weddings and to give fertility blessings. They live together, apart from families or other groups, and may also work as prostitutes.

Ariel Levy believes Caster Semenya developed with partial AIS—androgen insensitivity syndrome, one of the types of intersexuality. Semenya is not the only person of her physical type to be raised as a girl among her South African people. The word her people use to describe her type of body is *italasi*, and there are many others like Semenya. Levy points out that naming the condition does not imply acceptance; South African society fiercely insists there are exactly two genders, and Caster is a girl (Levy 2009).

Sensing Gender

In addition to the classic five senses—auditory, tactile, visual, olfactory, and gustatory—neurobiologists explore two senses having to do with our positioning in space: the vestibular sense, which tells us where our head is in relationship to movement, and proprioception, the awareness of our body in space.

Trans people—transvestites, transsexuals, transgender—report experiencing another physical sense, the sense of sexual identity. Julia Serano, in *Whipping Girl: A Transsexual Woman on Sexism and the Scapegoating of Femininity*, dubs this "subconscious sex," the sense of knowing your biological sex. For some trans people, that sense does not match the gender to which they have been assigned. Trans people report feeling that they are men in women's bodies, or women in men's bodies. They may shift genders by dressing in their chosen gender, taking hormones, or having transitional surgery (Serano 2007).

Interestingly, Norah Vincent did not experience herself as a man in a woman's body. In *Self-Made Man: One Woman's Year Disguised as a Man*, she reports that her sense of her own sex matched that of her biological and cultural sex. After living as a man for a year, she checked herself into a mental hospital for a few days and then spent months rebuilding her sense of equilibrium. She believes this was partly due to the stress of living undercover, with accompanying fear and guilt. Mostly, though, she attributes her breakdown to the disconnect between her lived gender and her sensed gender. This disorientation is a sensation that trans people report experiencing every day (Vincent 2006).

EVALUATING THE SCIENCE

The dual-sex model created two completely different genders, men and women, and exaggerated the differences between them. This model did not entirely replace the earlier single-sex model but sits alongside it. Many cultural artifacts—images, assumptions, histories—assume that only men exist or matter and that there is truly only one gender.

Postmodernism challenged both the single-sex and the dual-sex models, breaking down identity to the individual and sidestepping gender altogether. In the post-postmodern, collective-oriented, contemporary world, a new gender narrative is emerging. A rough-draft attempt to articulate this new narrative might look like this:

Human bodies vary. The single- and dual-gender models do not adequately describe the possibilities of the human body. Body does not determine sex. The physical, mental, emotional, and biologically based capacities of any individual person do not necessarily correlate with the gender class to which that person is assigned. All gender observations, including (perhaps especially) those of science, both create and are results of gender models. Limiting life options by gender supports a scientifically outdated and socially unjust gender hierarchy. The just culture is one in which the most vulnerable population, including children, pregnant women, the elderly, and those who do not fit into sexual dimorphic categories, are physically protected and free participants in society.

Gender Matters

There is a voice that has to be heard at this point, that is insisting on having its say. "I'm a woman!" the voice bursts out, or, "I know what a woman is!" Something about the irreducible biological minimum of sexual dimorphism, as Thomas Lacquer said. Women have bodies that have babies; men don't. We all know that.

The gender sense argues for this point of view. If I know myself to be a woman, if Norah Vincent experienced disorientation when she passed as male, if Julia Serano only felt at home in her body when she shifted gender orientation, is there not a biological foundation for gender?

Thomas Laquer's point is that whether or not biology is the bedrock of sex, our experience of sex is unavoidably shaped by our culture's gender narratives. Allan Johnson, in *Power, Privilege and Difference*, talks about four axes of privilege: gender, race, sexual orientation, and ability. The privileged self is a white able-bodied heterosexual man. Any deviation from the standard calls gender into question. Is a black man a man? Is a lesbian a woman? Does a disabled body qualify as a person (Johnson 2006)?

Whatever bodies we were born with, whatever we do to those bodies to display their gender, wherever we fall on the continuum of gender, in the dominant culture of the West we navigate a culture which recognizes exactly two. The dual-gender model requires men and women to be different, with little overlap between the physical characteristics of the genders. There are many gendered characteristics. Here is a sample:

Men	Women
Fertilize	Bear young
Stronger	Weaker
Low voices	High voices
Taller	Shorter
Like salty foods	Like sweet foods

And so on. Any deviation from this imagined norm evokes suspicion in the people around us, and even suspicion in ourselves. If I haven't borne a live child, if I lift weights and have a deep voice, if I prefer dill pickles to sweet, if I don't pluck my eyebrows and wear trousers by preference, am I still a woman?

I began this book by placing myself on the gender identity continuum. I said:

> By *woman*, I mean that I was born into a culture that recognizes two biologically based sexes and that I was raised in the female sex. I have always been comfortable with my body's sex assignment.

This description for me is not yet nuanced enough to accurately reflect my experience. I identify as a woman, but what kind of woman? It becomes clearer that this is less a biological description than a class description when we begin to discuss the various states our bodies inhabit. If a woman has a body that can bear babies, what about bodies that can't? I know women who have lost their fertility who question their very identities as women.

Is a pregnant woman a woman? I have never had children, and I have thought that the state of being pregnant would be the moment when a woman would feel most like a woman. Mothers have told me that they do not identify their wombs as marking them as women. I was surprised to hear Lesa Whyte say this in her essay "Magic and Pregnancy":

Little by little, over the space of 283 days, the woman is literally a creature apart; she is not male, and she is not a typical female. She is a female who carries within her the beginnings of another human life (Whyte 2009).

For myself, I used to feel like a woman on the days when I was menstruating. Now that I no longer menstruate, am I still a woman? Actually passing through the state of menopause opened my eyes to a change I had always seen but never understood. I always thought aging was a continuum, with effects accumulating gradually. That may be true for men, but for women, the change is spectacular and abrupt. Our bodies morph in so many ways, both visible and invisible. Anti-aging products turn out to be not so much designed to make us look *younger* as to make us look *still fertile*, which mostly equates to *still sexually attractive to men*. This change of life is so significant that I have come to think of women as being literally of two kinds, those still fertile, or young, and those no longer fertile and fully mature.

Recognizing the various states a woman's body can inhabit, we might add this paragraph to our new gender narrative:

Sexual dimorphism describes the ability to procreate. A fertile woman rotates through a monthly cycle when not pregnant. Pregnancy is another state in which a woman carries another body within her own. Women's bodies alter again at the end of the fertile period, dropping out of the monthly cycles, and undergoing a series of abrupt changes. A fertile man's body changes in a slow arc of aging, from child, through adulthood, into age. Those whose bodies are not fertile women's or men's have no cultural category which recognizes their existence, and discover their body's capabilities through a process of exploration and reclaiming.

Intersexuality in the Magical Lodges

With so small a percentage of the population falling into any intersexual category, does this really affect the magical communities today? Of course it does. People whose bodies do not fall neatly into a category can be drawn to the practice of magic as easily as anyone else. Our efforts to reshape Western Traditional Magic around the lived rather than the theoretical body benefit intersexuals as well as women.

Here are some real-world examples. One brother in one of my magical lodges surfaced to me that he has Klinefelter's syndrome: he carries XXY chromosomes. I asked him if he wanted to talk to me about it. He said yes! It was so hard to grow up not knowing what was wrong, and finding out was such a relief. When I asked him about his gender, he said he is a man and wants to be treated as such.

The organization which ordained me as a Gnostic priestess, O.T.O., does work to include intersexuals in celebrations of the Gnostic Mass. A male-to-female transsexual of my acquaintance was authorized to perform Mass in the priestess role. I also know a soror/frater who wants to take both the priest and priestess role in the Gnostic Mass.

Gendered Elements in the Magician's Body of Knowledge

What about the gendering of the elements, with water and earth being female and air and fire being male? This gendering is based on the equivalents of temperature and humidity.

Fire	Hot and dry	Male
Air	Hot and wet	Male
Water	Cold and wet	Female
Earth	Cold and dry	Female

The typing of elements by gender depends on the typing of gender by temperature. Aristotle believed that men's white frothy semen was heated-up blood, so that the male blood was hotter than female blood. We know this to be incorrect. There are differences between blood types, but gender is not one of those differences. Note that in the contemporary world both men and women donate blood to a common pool that is redistributed to both women and men. In terms of physical temperature, differences between the core temperature and perceived air temperature of two people will depend on a number of factors, including body fat ratio.

Laying aside the typing of elements by temperature and humidity, it is clear that these do not gender. By and large today the Magician's Body of Knowledge treats all humans, women and men, as possessing all the elements, with the magical task being to balance these elements within ourselves.

Biology and Culture

I admit I'm feeling a little disoriented. It's a strong person who can think through gender issues without some sense of dislocation. A woman once said to me that feminism made her nauseous because feminists seek to dissolve gender. The feminist movement contains many nuanced responses to gender, but it is fair to say that many do challenge our gender assumptions, and some in fact do seek to dissolve the distinction between women and men.

The gender model that there are men and women is fundamental to identity in Western culture. When that changes, what is left? How am I to understand myself as a woman magician if the scientific definition of woman keeps shifting?

I am relieved when the sterile white walls fade and I am once again surrounded by the writer's cabin's peach walls and warm wood trim. I am far more at home in the library than the laboratory.

This discussion—what affects gender more, nature or culture?—is a very old one. I will not have given it a full airing until I hear culture's side of the story.

LADY CULTURE

I was angry when I invoked Lady Science. I leave her laboratory a little disoriented, but most of all, sad. I am heartbroken that all babies and children are not loved for themselves and permitted to understand their own unique being.

With sorrow in my heart, I make the invocation: *Come to me, Lady Culture, and show me the standing of my gender.*

The cabin fades away around me, but I am still in the forest. I find myself sitting in a forest amphitheater, logs cut into the natural bowl formed there, and at the bottom of the bowl a space has been cleared which evidently acts as a stage. It's a forest theater.

Lady Culture strides out onto the stage as if she owns it. She's decked out in a man's tuxedo and tails, like Marlene Dietrich in *Morocco* and Julie Andrews in *Victor Victoria*. She puts one foot up on a tree stump, takes a drag from her cigarette, and says grandly, "All the world's a stage, and all the men and women merely players." A banner stretched between two tree trunks behind her bears the caption, *GENDER IS A PERFORMANCE.*

In Shakespeare's time, boys took the part of women in public performances. Shakespeare loved to spin out that theme, having his characters disguise themselves, so that a boy could play a woman playing a man, as the main character in the movie *Victor Victoria* played a woman playing a man playing a woman.

I call out my question: "What is the cultural definition of a woman?"

The play begins.

WOMEN IN MEN'S CLOTHING

A succession of scenes plays out on the stage in front of me, stories of pirates, adventurers, cowboys, Albanian codes of revenge, and the disadvantages faced by the ordinary woman.

First the pirates storm the stage, posturing extravagantly, waving cutlasses about in the air. The original of this story seems to be Captain Charles Johnson's romantic book *A General History of the Robberies and Murders of the Most Notorious Pyrates*. Two eighteenth-century girls who had been partially raised as boys ended up on the same pirate ship under Captain Jack Rackham. Mary Read and Anne Bonny both seem to have been lovers of Rackham, possibly of each other as well, but they served as pirates alongside the men and fought as fiercely as any of them. In fact, when they were overtaken and the rest of the crew was dead drunk, they were the only pirates who fought their capture. They were tried as pirates, but avoided hanging, in Johnson's colorful phrase, by "pleading the belly"—both were pregnant. Their fates are murky. Read died in prison, of a fever or while bearing her child; Bonny is rumored to have been ransomed by her father (Johnson 1724).

Next comes a series of vignettes about a Spanish adventurer. In *The Lieutenant Nun*, Sherry Velasco wrote about Catalina de Erauso, a woman who escaped a Basque convent and lived as a man in Spain and the New World in the seventeenth century. She dressed in men's clothing, held men's occupations, and had women lovers (Velasco 2000).

Then the Albanians take the stage, dignified elderly men dressed in trousers, shirts, sweaters, and a little white cap. That is, they are dressed as men, but were born women. Cultural journalist Dan Bilefsky's article, "Sworn to Virginity and Living as Men in Albania," explained that the Albanian folk law Kunan allows a woman to take a vow to remain a virgin all her life, becoming a sworn virgin. In exchange for giving up expressing her sexuality, she becomes a man in all the ways that matter: she talks like a man, dresses like a man, shoots guns. It could be that all the men in her family were killed (Kunan governs a system of honor killings,) so none were left to run the household. It could also be that she simply decided there was no way she was picking up the life of a girl. These elders are the last generation of sworn virgins; Albanian culture has changed, and now a woman can swear and shoot and own property as a woman (Bilefsky 2008). It's amazing to hear them talk, see them move, side by side with the men in their villages—they have become men in every sense that matters to them.

These men were known to be women before crossing genders. Other women simply *passed*, changed over in secret. Billy Tipton's story is remarkable, not least because it is so recent. Diane Middlebrook sensitively brought Billy's story to light in *Suits Me: The Double Life of Billy Tipton*. Tipton's move into the male gender permitted him to lead a jazz and swing band in Spokane, Washington, at a time when women were not accepted in that role. An extraordinary woman could make a musical career, but Billy was not an extraordinary musician, he was a perfectly competent but ordinary one, and only an ordinary *man* could earn a living at what he loved to do. Billy wore men's clothing, married women, adopted children and raised them as a father. He passed so successfully that when he died in 1989 the revelation of his biological sex shocked his own family, shocked everyone who worked with him, and even surprised his own wives, from whom he had successfully kept the secret even while leading an active sexual life (Middlebrook 1998).

I'm drawn to the moments in all these stories when the hero trades up, moves from woman to man, because she is given clothes. Today, anyone can walk into Wal-Mart and buy an identity; in Catalina de Erauso's day, clothes were difficult and expensive to come by, and a gift of that kind literally meant class-jumping (Velasco 2000). The fictional Victoria becomes Victor when her gown shrinks and she has to borrow a man's suit, transforming in that moment into a successful cross-dresser.

Performing Gender

In *Gender Trouble*, Judith Butler described gender as a series of stylized acts. She called for the disruption of gender norms by consciously engaging in parody or drag, opening the gender construct to include the variety of human possibilities.

Andrea Dworkin pointed to the constant effort women put into maintaining the appearance of being a woman. From earliest puberty, age eleven or twelve, women spend a great deal of time and energy on shaving, makeup, and dress. Dworkin believes concern with appearance to be central to femininity (Dworkin 1974).

In *Gender Blending, Confronting the Limits of Duality*, Holly Devor collected the stories and photos of a number of women who refused to enter into the maintenance of the feminine image. Like the Albanian sworn virgins, it is striking how male they look, and they are often mistaken for male, although this upsets them. Many of these women started life as "tomboys"—that is girls, who exercised their bodies and treated with boys as their equals. Discovering at twelve or so that they were expected to relinquish their freedom, they resisted. They don't take men's names or use men's restrooms, they identify as women and wish to be treated as such, but by refusing to wear dresses and pluck their eyebrows they are performing gender on the edge of cultural acceptability (Devor 1989).

What makes performing gender necessary? We don't wear our gender on our sleeves. Since humans walk around clothed most of the time, it isn't generally possible to check out one another's primary sexual characteristics. Sometimes that's the only thing that works—Caster Semenya was accustomed to ducking into a bathroom to show fellow competitors her genitals, and the climactic scene in *Victor Victoria* has the title character disrobing (off-camera) to a woman who believes her to be a man.

As the behind-closed-doors reveal is reserved for special occasions, we rely on secondary characteristics to determine gender: facial hair, sound of voice, size of breasts. Sometimes these make gender obvious. (For myself, although I never wear dresses or makeup and do not pluck my eyebrows, and I show up for most events in trousers and shirts in the countercultural uniform black, I am never mistaken for a man. I have always longed for the slender Amazonian frame, and ended up instead in a Rubens.) Even so, there is enough physical overlap between men and women to render secondary characteristics unreliable in some cases.

That leads us to the tertiary characteristics; we mark our gender with clothing, hair styles, adornment. Although men have begun to wear kilts, dresses are usually reserved for women. My clothes and shoes are shaped in special women's styles, I carry a designer purse, I wear my hair long and loose, while the men in my household wear men's clothing and shoes, carry backpacks, and tie their long hair back in pony tails.

What is the root of all this fuss? Why is it important to distinguish the genders anyway? Whose business is it whether I am a woman or a man?

THE SECOND SEX

Norah Vincent experienced vertigo when she put on men's clothes, while other women have found that men's clothes suit them better than women's. But why would women cross-dress, and why do their stories fascinate us?

Although biology examines the body and reveals a spectrum, culture determines which of two classes each body will be assigned. These classes come with a built-in hierarchy, in which the second class, that of women, serves the needs of the first class, that of men. In any culture that privileges one type of person over another, the underclass have a powerful motivation to present themselves as a member of the privileged class. People with black ancestry but light skin who move into white culture without comment are described as "passing." Women also take on men's clothing to temporarily or permanently "pass" as men to experience the privileges of being a man.

Now that I've used the word "privilege," I have to stop and comment on it. It would be not just cowardly, but *inaccurate* to write a book about how women are viewed in the magical traditions without ever touching on the subject of privilege.

In Western culture today, women still form the second sex. Women make up slightly more than half the population, and slightly more than half of voters, but we do not take half the political offices in America. Hillary Clinton's 2008 candidacy for the presidency was the first since Geraldine Ferraro's run at the vice presidency in 1984. In the 2008 Senate, only 17 of the 100 senators were women. The 2008 House of Representatives had 435 members, 76 of whom were women. Also in 2008, just nine women served among the 50 state governors. (I am proud that as I write, in my home state, Washington, both elected senators and our governor are all women.)

What about business? The percentages in the corporate world are even more dismal. In 2008, only 12 of the Fortune 500 CEOs were women. Women cluster in less well paid service industries, health care and secretarial work, while few women enter the lucrative technology and financial fields.

In my lifetime, the position of women has substantially improved. The feminist movement that rekindled in the 1970s has a great deal to do with this. Cultural sumptuary laws have eased substantially; when I attended school as a girl I was required to wear a skirt, even in subzero temperatures, but now it is normative for women to wear trousers even to formal occasions. Today it is entirely possible for a woman and man to wear the same clothes and carry the same style of bag.

Women literally wear men's clothing, reflecting the real gains women have made in the last half century. The percentages of women in positions of authority have increased in the last several decades. Laws protecting women's property and physical safety have improved. In a sign of the times, women enlist in the military and go off to war alongside men, leaving their children at home.

Many women as well as men find it difficult to squarely face the reality of discrimination against women. This is the root of the fuss about gender: if women really can think as well as men, fight as well as men, work as hard as men, what justifies keeping women in a permanent second class? Kant flinched when asked this question and opted to retain his wife as his servant. Increasingly, men are refusing to sign on for the ancient compact, choosing instead to support full freedom for their wives, sisters, and daughters. Increasingly, women refuse to quietly accept less than full citizenship.

Girls, Ladies, Mistresses, and Magiciennes

Discrimination against women is the water in which we swim. We fail to recognize it because we have grown up with it, it surrounds us, and people around us do not remark on it, so it seems the normal state of affairs. One way to learn to recognize cultural attitudes that put women at a disadvantage is to listen to what we say about women. The language we use to describe women reflects our attitudes toward women.

Words calling out women's gender have a diminutive effect. Terms that may seem to be equivalents, like lady and gentlemen, and mistress and master, function in very different ways. Using the term "girl" to describe a full grown woman is still common, while using the term "boy" to describe an adult man is an insult. We may speak of a saleslady, but never a garbage gentleman. Old masters have created a revered body of work, but we speak of old mistresses only humorously.

In her 1975 work *Language and Women's Place*, Robin Lakoff analyzed the use of the term "lady" as a substitute for "woman." She noted that the term "lady sculptor" assumes that the normal sculptor is male, and also patronizes the woman artist's work. Talking like a lady means speaking with exaggerated politeness, upholding a cultural standard of civility and manners, that places women in a subordinate position. Lakoff outlined components of women's language that illustrate the deferent position: using questions instead of statements, using hedging language, not talking rough, not telling jokes (Lakoff 2004).

Casey Miller and Kate Swift explored the impact of the diminutive on words. Calling a woman a poetess, laundress, heroine, makes women's work nonstandard, as poet, launderer, and hero then describe only men. Miller and Swift's indispensable reference work, *The Handbook of Nonsexist Writing*, contains a number of analyses and suggestions for writing and speaking in ways that assume women are people (Miller and Swift 1980).

Most importantly, they analyzed the use of the false male generic. Although apologists defend the use of the term "man" to describe both men and women, we do not use the term "man" to describe a woman alone, as in "Ginny was the only man in the group to become pregnant." The use of the term "man" to mean "humanity" slides easily into the specific meaning of the male gender, as in the construction "man is frail, his women suffer in childbirth."

Nonsexist language calls adult females women, uses terms like "humanity" to describe women and men together, and uses the terms "poet" and "hero" for women as well as men. Fortunately, the term "magician" to describe a woman has not been subjected to diminutization, as in "magicienne."

The literature of Western Traditional Magic is largely written in sexist language. Turn-of-the-century English used the false male generic to cover women; for example, when I completed an initiation in O.T.O. I became a member of the "Man of Earth." I use the word "cover" deliberately here; in the English-speaking world a hundred years ago, only the male head of household held the right to vote under the doctrine of "couverture," in which he represented or covered the interests of the household, including his wife, children, servants, and animals.

The English language has changed substantially in the intervening century between the writing of *Kabbalah Unveiled* and today. Thanks in part to Miller and Swift's work we no longer automatically assume that the male pronoun is meant to refer to women. This is why Moina Mathers's statement is confusing to the modern ear. We can assume that when a Victorian-Edwardian man wrote about men, he did not mean to include women. Even in those times it was rare to hear a woman describe herself in male terms. Mathers had dedicated her life to the art, and she surely meant to include herself in this paragraph:

> The whole aim and object of the teaching is to bring a man to the knowledge of his higher self, to purify himself, to strengthen himself, to develop all qualities and powers of the being, that he may ultimately regain union with the Divine Man latent in himself, that Adam Kadmon, whom God hath made in His Own Image (Mathers 1926).

New material is being written today in which the word "man" describes women and men. The extent to which contemporary magicians write in nonsexist language depends on how fervently they emulate the archaic language of Western Traditional Magic, as well as how committed the writer is to the inclusion of women in magical processes and groups. As a positive example, the Open Source Order of the Golden Dawn uses the terms "frater" and "soror" interchangeably in its new rituals.

Women Talking

For purposes of study, it doesn't matter whether biology or culture underlies a specific trait. Women are grouped together as a class and consequently develop woman-specific cultural characteristics. Women's use of language differs from that of men's, both in woman-only and in mixed gender groups. The path women take toward learning and assuming authority also differs from that of men.

Robin Lakoff's work influenced and inspired the linguist Deborah Tannen, whose highly successful books with memorable titles brought linguistic analysis to popular culture. *You Just Don't Understand* focused on the language women and men use to speak within their genders and to each other. "Male-female conversation is cross-cultural conversation," she concluded. She noted that although the gender narrative criticizes women for talking over men, women in mixed groups cede the speaking floor to men, men interrupt women, and women adopt men's style of conversation—all women are bilingual, speaking both women's language and men's (Tannen 1990).

Tannen's conversational analysis reveals the profound differences between men's and women's language. Men's language reports, solves problems, and establishes hierarchy; women's language establishes rapport through connection. Many of the mechanisms women use to maintain connection, like the automatic apology, put women in one-down positions relative to men. While women's language establishes connections, it also has a leveling effect—women are not supposed to look better than their peers, avoiding boasting. Women use tactics of scorn and ostracization to keep other women in line.

Women's language emphasizes connection; men take the speaking floor from women, and women cede it; women in the dominant culture act as subordinates to men. For all those reasons, women spend a lot of time listening to men. That cross-cultural subordinate class study gives women the appearance of being magically intuitive; "women's intuition" is to some extent attributable to the fact that we are paying close attention.

Only biological women give birth. Mothers teach children, especially in their earliest years. In many cultures this makes women the carriers of culture. We learn from our mothers what foods to eat, how to talk, how to walk, how to carry ourselves in the world. In the role of cultural arbiter, women in traditional culture act to uphold patriarchy. My mother taught me to serve the men at the table first, to clean house as I would be doing for my husband when I grew up, and to walk with swaying hips so that I would attract a husband. Although I consciously contested these teachings from earliest adolescence, I find the attitude ingrained—when serving food I still find myself serving the men first.

Cultural markers shift. Girls in the Western world today may not be taught how to walk in a sexy way (or they may be), but as I read through the articulate, thoughtful, and angry posts from teen and young feminists on www.thefbomb.org, I think that the pressure to conform to a feminine ideal may be even more intense than when I was growing up. Posts there discuss the equation of superskinny with beauty, the teen Botox epidemic, being shunted away from math class and ignored in science class.

Women who enter into Western Traditional Magic today have a level of acceptance of male-centered culture. Women read ourselves into the magical texts as men and may identify more with men, who are legitimately magicians, than with women, who as women act as the intuitive muse to men. Any woman who studies Aleister Crowley's work runs up against sexism in his writings, and even the most fervent woman apologists I have met cannot excuse his most misogynist language.

In Western Traditional Magic today, it is often men who are the most outspoken and committed advocates for women's equal participation. Since men listen to men, their work is critical to the effort to create a more equitable magic. Men's focus on men's conversation tends to step on women's conversation. In online forums and in person it is easy to see the ways in which magical women cede magical men the speaking floor, and to note examples of men stepping on women's speech. Men tend to listen to other men and ignore women, sometimes repeating what women have said. It is important for the men who are our allies to continue to work both to make sure important things are said, and to make sure that we all listen to the women who are saying them.

Women's Ways of Knowing

In writing her pioneering work analyzing attitudes toward women in contemporary English, Robin Lakoff drew on her personal experience, dropping anecdotes from her own observations into the text. She was criticized at the time for this technique. Deborah Tannen's research throws some light on this: women seek connection with others through language. Research into women's learning patterns further explains why this story is important to our effort to understand and acknowledge women's contributions to knowledge.

In the 1950s, William Perry studied white male college students to derive a theory of intellectual development, particularly the development of the use of reason. He outlined a series of positions students experienced in the process of learning. In the first position, duality, the world of learning is divided into true or false, good or bad. Students in this position see teachers as authority figures who impart a truth to be learned, and see their own task to demonstrate correct learning. Next, students learn that there are multiple viewpoints, and that right and wrong depends on context. These students see teachers as expert guides rather than oracles of truth. This position requires significant restructuring of existing knowledge. Finally, students commit to a particular point of view, moving into a position of authority of their own (Belenky, Clinchy, Goldberger, and Tarule 1986).

Four women studying Perry's work decided to test whether women took the same path toward assuming authority. Belenky, Clinchy, Goldberger, and Tarule interviewed 135 women, including not only students, but also women outside the university system. They modified Perry's system based on these interviews to outline five positions in women's learning arc, comprising a system of women's ways of knowing:

- *Silence:* Women have no voice and are subject to external authority.
- *Received knowledge:* Authority has knowledge, the self only receives it.

- *Subjective knowledge:* Personal experience is the ultimate authority.
- *Procedural knowledge:* Procedures are learned for obtaining and communicating knowledge. These include:
  - ⋆ *Separate knowing:* Objective methods are used to obtain knowledge; traditional critical thinking.
  - ⋆ *Connected knowing:* Objective methods are tempered by a recognition of the value of personal experience.
- *Constructed knowledge:* Knowledge is created within the context of the individual life and in cooperation with others.

There are major differences between the women's experiences and the men's. Some of these differences are expected in a system that subordinates one gender to another. First, women begin from a position of silence, of being unable to speak at all. Also, women do not invariably end by taking a position of authority, and young women may move from a more complex to a less complex epistemological position to conform with cultural expectations of femininity (Belenky, Clinchy, Goldberger, and Tarule 1986).

Ten years later, Goldberger, Tarule, Clinchy, and Belenky, along with a number of colleagues, revisited their work in *Knowledge, Difference and Power: Essays Inspired by Women's Ways of Knowing.* The essays incorporate a number of refinements of these positions. Researchers now consider the effect of race, class, and privilege factors in the development of cognition. These positions may not describe a sequential journey; a given individual may hold more than one position simultaneously, or may slide back to an earlier position, especially after leaving college (Goldberger, Tarule, Clinchy, and Belenky 1996).

Carol Lee Flinders addressed the silencing of girls. She movingly described her community's response to the abduction and murder of the young girl Polly Klaas. She and her husband, a schoolteacher, came to understand that violent act as the ultimate expression of the patriarchal move to separate the genders at puberty and to strip young women of autonomy (Flinders 1998). Girls who once expressed themselves as confidently as boys begin to learn the women's language of hedging, using questions instead of statements, ceding the speaking floor to men. We lose our voices at twelve.

Daring Sisterhood

Women must protect ourselves, our daughters, and each other. Protection means physical protection, learning to defend our bodies, walking each other to our cars. After group meetings I never leave a woman standing alone waiting for a ride; when I drop women off at their houses I wait until they're inside before I drive away; and I teach simple self-defense as part of every beginner's magic class.

Protection means emotional support. Whenever a woman I know speaks out, I speak in defense of her right to do so. We can all encourage the girls in our lives to speak, both by encouraging their speech, and by speaking up ourselves.

Our most urgent need is a change in women's culture. Traditional women's culture supports and replicates the processes by which women are exploited, wounded, and silenced. Around the world mothers teach their daughters to keep the status quo, to be servants, to be silent, as my mother taught me to be a servant to men. Many women in many places in the world experience much more severe and damaging forms of enculturation.

Few mothers act out of hatred for their daughters. Women pass on the coping mechanisms learned from their mothers to navigate their cultures to the individual woman's best possible advantage. Women's isolation from other women reinforces our vulnerability. In a world in which men make choices and women are chosen, women compete with each other to be chosen, bonding with the men who choose them and experiencing the company of other women as potential competition.

Even in groups, women act against our own best interests and that of our sisters when we try to keep each other in line and ignore or actively silence dissenting voices. It can take a lot of courage to speak up in the face of thousands of years of tradition and very little to squelch that tentative voice. When we become true sisters to one another, we not only seek to navigate the existing tradition, we also support each other's work as individuals. That may mean that women do and say things that make us or the people around us uncomfortable. It means that our sisters may challenge the systems we find meaningful. They may achieve and create, make waves, stick out.

We lose our voices at twelve; we regain our voices when we stand together. The great strength of women's culture is the ability to connect with one another. Over and over again we see that when women band together they mutually support one another's accomplishments. Rozsika Parker and Griselda Pollack discussed the network of women's studios and practices that supported French women artists in the mid-eighteenth century (Parker and Pollock 1981). Gerry Hirshey painted a memorable picture of Motown women running in and out of the studios taking turns as soloists and singing backup for each other (Hirshey 2005).

Christine Battersby examined the nuances of the word "genius," concluding that almost every form of genius in the Western tradition involves a man's solitary achievement. There is one way in which a woman can be considered to be a genius, to stand up above her peers and to be acknowledged as achieving, and that is by the recognition of the group. We can acknowledge women in our midst for our particular contributions. For thousands of years, women have assisted each other in creative endeavors. Building true commonality takes time, trust, and effort, but it remains our greatest strength.

EVALUATING CULTURE
Navigating Cultural Gender

The cognitive experience of cultural gender floats atop the lived experience of the body and maps onto it with greater or lesser success. We all navigate the divide between the cultural map and our own experience at every moment.

Culture writes itself across the body well or poorly. Our task here is to stay with the truth of the lived body while navigating the demands of culture. The balancing act is to honor the body's unique individuality while acknowledging the overlap of what we share with other bodies. Tension arises when our lived experience contradicts the gender narrative. A metanarrative that requires men and women to be polar opposites, with no overlap, denies to men the full expression of their emotional lives and a real connection with one another, and denies women full expression of voice and the exercise of power.

If we are to navigate the common divide, if we are to work to ensure that our daughters and their daughters don't have to choose between *being a woman* and *being who they are*, and our sons don't have to chose between *being a man* and *being who they are*, we must permit to them and to each other behaviors outside the cultural narrative. Boys cry. Girls shout. Men can bond with other men, and women can speak our minds. We can support those who challenge the metanarrative in their work and writings, and in their modes of being in the world.

It is important to recognize difference. There are any number of states that a woman's body may inhabit: pre-fertile, menstruating, not menstruating, pregnant, post-pregnant, perimenopausal, menopausal. Young women may have their wombs removed for medical conditions, thus entering into menopause before the curve. Women may have ambiguous genitalia but a sense of being a woman. Women may be born into bodies typed male but have a sense of being a woman.

It is important to recognize difference. Women may be tall or short, thin or large, large breasted or flat chested. Women may speak with high voices or deep ones. A given woman may be as strong as most men or weaker than most women.

It is important to recognize difference. A woman may be sexually attracted to men, or women, or no one. A woman may dress in the most feminine style imaginable or refuse ever to pluck a single hair. A woman may compete in any way, including athletically, or may refuse competition. A woman may drive a truck, run a jackhammer, fire a gun, land a fish, grill a steak. A woman may clean a house, bake a pie, teach a child, nurse a sick person, comfort the elderly. A woman may be gentle or fierce, nurturing or aggressive, sensual or ascetic.

It is important to recognize difference. Being a woman is not dependant on any given state of the body. Being a woman is not dependant on any given physical appearance. Being a woman is not dependant on living out any constellation of characteristics. Being a woman means being a member of a class and of a culture. Being a woman means being accepted as a woman by other women.

It is important to recognize commonality. We need not fall back on an essentialist position, holding that women's bodies fix their essential natures, to recognize the similarities between women's bodies and women's experiences. Fertile women bear live young, and no other gender does. Not every woman menstruates, but many do, and when women live together, they menstruate together. Women in families and villages raise children together. Women in a given culture share the gendered experiences of other women in that culture.

It is important to recognize commonality. Being a member of the class of women means being a member of a class that is primarily defined not by itself, but by another class, that of men. Women's experiences bond us to each other by virtue of the fact that they are different from men's experiences. Women endure violence, particularly sexual violence and the control of our reproductive ability. Around the world women's status varies tremendously, but in few places are women as free as men to live our lives as we would choose, in some places women are slaves, and in many places women live lives that are more restricted than men's.

It is important to recognize commonality. However unique our bodies may individually be, we share nearly all our genetic code with everyone else of our species; we are all human.

RITUAL OF CREATION

Lady Tradition encouraged me to review how it is I perform my magic today. Lady History offered me a sense of connection with a historical lineage and the encouraging knowledge that others have gone before me. Lady Philosophy brought me to an understanding of myself as a thinking embodied individual. Lady Science helped me to a clear comprehension of the shape of my body itself. Lady Culture illuminated the context surrounding me, how it is that language shapes me and how I can use language to shape my experience. These ladies have shown me the web of connections between myself and the world.

Inspired, eager to apply what I have learned, I construct a ritual of creation, to create myself as an embodied woman with reason and will.

This ritual affirms the actual body and circumstances of the person who is conducting it. It is completed here with the values that I gave it at the moment of writing. It can be (and has been) successfully conducted by any person of any sex or ability.

Grounding

I stand in the center of the ritual as an embodied woman.

First, I construct my body. I know myself to be an animal. As an animal I began in my grandmother's womb. (All women are born with all the eggs they will have, formed in their own mother's wombs.) I was carried by my mother as an egg, then, fertilized, developed in my mother's womb, until she birthed me into the air. I grew as a dependent in a web of relationship which sustained me until I could feed and clothe myself and move under my own power in the world.

I came to awareness of the contours of my body. Human minds construct body maps and continually update these. I construct this map consciously now. I am feet, knees, thighs. I am genitals, I am vulva, I am womb. (As I construct my body, I am aware that others can construct their body differently, with penis or with other genitals that developed differently, or that were altered surgically.) I am stomach, lungs, heart. I am back, arms, hands, fingers. I am throat, mouth, nose, ears, eyes.

Body changes over time. As an animal I trace an arc of existence. I locate myself on this arc. I was born and grew. I am beyond the midpoint of my life now. I will age, shrink, and die.

I construct a sense of self. Human culture is as significant as body to the animal that I am. Culture changes body, changes the world, changes the person. All experience is embodied. All knowledge is embodied—it does not exist outside the human cultural matrix which is sustained by each of us individually and all of us collectively. Humans exist in relationship to one another. The self constructs as a memory reinforced by the people with whom I am in relationship.

The first circle of people are those who cared and care for me, whom I cared and care for, who are my family of blood, marriage, and adoption. I am a daughter, shaped by mother and father. I am a granddaughter, shaped by two grandmothers, two grandfathers. All these forebears are dead. I am a sister with two brothers. I have a niece and nephew, grown, and a grand-niece and grand-nephew whom I have not met. I have adopted a sister who has adopted her grandson as her son, who is my adopted nephew. I have a husband and an inamorato. I care for my inamorato's parents as they age. My love for my family sustains me. The love of my husband, inamorato, brothers, sister, and nephew sustains me and defines me. They are the keepers of the closest memories of me which shape my immediate sense of self. Without their memories my self unmoors and fragments.

I am a member of a coven. Almost all the members of the coven are in my family. One of these members has his own family which identifies family primarily with their blood relatives rather than the coven. However, my relationship with these people adds to my identity.

I am an employee. I am corporate, which is a significant shape to my identity. The corporate culture and the people who shape my immediate experience wield the greatest amount of external authority over my life. At the same time, the corporation and the people who shape my immediate experience grant me the greatest power that I wield in my life. My manager supervises me and mentors me, and I assist him. In this context I am valued for my intelligence and experience, and also valued as a woman adding to the diversity of the collective.

I am an ordained priestess in the E.G.C., a chartered initiator of O.T.O., and past master of Vortex Oasis. My bishop supervises and mentors me. I mentor novices, baptized and ordained members of the church, and initiates. I act as child, deacon, and priestess in the Mass, serving the congregation. I initiate, bound by the rules of the organization, while wielding influence over the initiates. Each of these positions defines my relationship to specific individuals.

I am a member and treasurer of Temple of Light and Darkness, which uses the material of the Open Source Order of the Golden Dawn. I trade the position of initiate and initiator with other members of the group. The group's leader redacts the rituals, although I have input into this process. The order redacts the original rituals and I have no input there. The original rituals were written more than a century ago.

My selves construct in this web of relationships over time. I understand myself to contain multitudes; selves grow, are born, and die in response to changing relationships in the world, while maintaining the experience of a consensus thread of unitary experience. I understood myself as a child to have had previous lives. I experience a central "I" which nonetheless changes.

I construct the place where I stand. I am in a cabin on Whidbey Island, standing in the screened porch overlooking the forest. It is a cool day, but it has been a sunny one, though the sunset light is fading now, and the entire forest is still.

I construct the relationship of animal, self, place, to world. I understand myself as animal to exist within a world that is entirely composed of life. All things on earth were either created by life or modified by life, so that the entire planet is a living organism.

Based on this meditation, I constructed the following ritual. It is the ritual I perform before each magical act, as the basis of every magical act. It creates the sense of self through a repeated scoring, a singing of myself to myself. This scoring is an act of remembrance as well as an acknowledgement of the changed circumstance since the last time I performed the ritual.

Ritual Action
1. Construct body as animal.
I am feet.

I am toes.

I am calves.

I am knees.

I am thighs.

I am buttocks.

I am anus.

I am vulva.

I am womb.

I am stomach.

I am lungs.

I am heart.

I am back.

I am breasts.
I am arms.
I am hands.
I am fingers.
I am throat.
I am lips.
I am tongue.
I am mouth.
I am nose.
I am ears.
I am eyes.
I am skin.

2. Place animal in life arc.

I was an egg in my grandmother's womb.
I was quickened by my father's seed.
I was carried by my mother and born into the world.

[Place self on life arc.] (Example: *I grew through infancy, childhood, adolescence, youth, adulthood, to maturity. I am past the midpoint of my life. I will age. I will decline and die*).

3. Construct family.

I am daughter, granddaughter, niece, aunt, (mother,) lover.

4. Construct position in human society.

I am (*job, artistic endeavor, magical affiliation*).

5. Construct position in earth.

I am of Earth. I am part of the web of life which includes all things that grow, fly, swim, crawl, burrow. Earth's gravity, atmosphere, magnetosphere shield me and sustain my life.

I am (example: *at the Whidbey Island Writer's Retreat, at sunset*).

6. Construct being.

I am woman. I am human. I am divine.

The Fractal Universe

The first time I conducted this ritual, it terrified me. I had unmoored myself from the familiar structure of Western Traditional Magic and launched myself into an unmapped magical space. Qabbalah structures the psyche as well as the universe; letting go of its framework to strike out on my own felt psychically perilous. To create, I had first to deconstruct, and I had no way to know whether what I was doing would leave my mind in fragments or would bring me back safely to a sense of myself.

When I finished the ritual the first time, it had a sense of rightness to me, a sense of wholeness and completion. I was still singing to myself, following Battersby's suggestion that song scores the sense of self, but the song I was singing was jubilant. I leapt up from my desk and ran outside. The whole world seemed alive, part of me, as I was part of it, breathing the air, connected by sound to the trees, connected by the light they cast to the very stars.

As sunset gave way to darkness, I looked up at the sky and picked out the first stars. "That's next!" I said to myself. Ritual in Western Traditional Magic proceeds from establishing the self to establishing the cosmic pattern. I had created myself as an embodied woman with reason and will. Next I needed to create myself as an instance of the sacred universe. It is that second step that brings the magic into the equation, that turns the embodied reasoning woman into the woman *magician*.

There I hit a full stop. Looking up at the night sky, I realized that I did not know how to conceptualize the sacred universe. I had come as far as philosophy could take me; it was time to grapple with theology.

LADY THEOLOGY

It is winter. I have returned to the Whidbey Island forest cabin for another period of enclosure. I am wearing my blue denim dress again,
now with a rust-colored sweater thrown over my shoulders. My host-
ess has tucked a wreath and small tree in the cabin to honor the winter
holiday season.

Back at work at the little wooden desk, I contemplate what I know.
I have spent decades of my life practicing magic, studying history, philosophy, biology, and psychology, striving to make sense of my place in
the world. I am woefully aware of how inadequate my knowledge continues to be. Striving toward Magia Femina requires all these studies,
but I am not an expert in any of them. Furthermore, there is an entire
field of study I have not yet touched. Humbly, I make the invocation.
Come to me, Lady Theology, and show me the female divine.

The room shifts around me, becoming much smaller and plainer,
with unadorned white walls, a single bed, an old wooden desk. All the
space and luxury held back from the room goes into the view, an ex-
panse of lawn fringed by trees, with a meditation labyrinth starting on
the grass and wandering into the shade of the trees.

Lady Theology stands next to the window looking out on the
labyrinth. She has walked it many times and needs only to look at it
to achieve again the sense of serenity that it brings. She wears an unadorned floor-length white robe bound at the waist with a white cord,

her clothing as plain and simple as her surroundings, but the glow about her head lights up the room like a halo on a medieval saint.

I say to her, "How can I understand myself to reflect the divine universe?"

Lady Theology gestures behind her. She does not work alone, she calls on the services of all her sisters. Lady History brings the knowledge of religion as it has developed. Lady Philosophy is nearly her twin, they work so closely together to work out underlying assumptions. Lady Science answers her questions but in turn largely refuses to hear her conclusions—we leave their quarrel for another day. Lady Culture, on the other hand, keeps up a lively conversation with her as they work to meet the needs of real women in today's world. Lady Tradition waits to hear the outcome of their conversation.

REVELATION AND PHILOSOPHY

Theology essentially proceeds from two sources. The first is revelation, the direct experience of deity. God speaking to Moses from the burning bush. Visions unfolding before St. John the Divine. Aiwass dictating the words of Nuit, Hadit, and Ra-Hoor-Khuit to Aleister Crowley.

The second source of revelation is human thought. We reason our way to the divine. Plato did this when he searched for the first cause.

The idea of "doing" theology at all is foreign and threatening to those who think of theology as literally studying the word (*logos*) of God (*theos*)—that is, reading books dictated by God or a god or gods: Torah, Bible, Qu'ran, Zabur, Chaldean Oracles, *The Book of the Law*. For peoples of the book, theology is the self-revelation of deity to a human prophet who transmits the word to the rest of humanity.

These are not, however, mutually antagonistic methodologies. At some point the revelation has been recorded, and then what? Human ingenuity makes sense of what was said. Philosophy provides the underlying framework for the religious structure.

Among religious reformers, "doing" theology means working with the raw material of experience, what is known, to craft a metaphor that illuminates the vastness of what is not known in ways useful and ennobling to those who choose to enter the metaphor. Women of all faiths are doing theology to open doors into religious experience which have previously been closed to us because of our gender.

It is impossible not to be a little cynical when reviewing human theological efforts. At their best they seek to meet human spiritual needs, to align human life with the needs of all life, to construct a moral compass for human behavior. At their worst they authorize the power of a few over the spiritual and temporal lives of the many. When so much is at stake, it is wise to be wary.

The fates of the gods and of their worshippers are intertwined. In the human competition for power, wealth, and land, a divine patron weights the odds. The political motive can exist alongside the religious: theologians can express a real sense of awe and love for God, Goddess, gods or goddesses, while at the same time benefiting from their ascendance.

To get a feel for how doing theology works, here are a few examples of moments in history when theology married politics to accomplish a given end.

Enheduanna and Inanna

Four thousand years ago, the daughter of a king and the wife of a god sought to stitch two peoples together while singing the praises of a goddess. Enheduanna's father Sargon united northern Akkad and southern Sumeria (now Iraq) under the rule of a single king. The Akkadians grafted their culture on the older Sumerian stock, which in turn rested on a Neolithic root. Sargon had several wives and concubines; Enheduanna may have been the daughter of a Sumerian woman, as she wrote fluently in the Sumerian language (Meador 2000).

Sargon appointed his daughter to be the en-priestess, wife, of the moon god Nanna, in the Sumerian custom in which women served gods and men served goddesses. Enheduanna probably stepped into a line of en-priestesses, among whose duties were writing hymns (Frymer-Kensky 1992).

Three of Enheduanna's hymns survive, all praising the goddess Inanna. Sargon and Enheduanna equated the Sumerian Inanna with the Akkadian Ishtar in a theological bid to unite the two peoples. Enheduanna may have had a number of reasons to write her hymns to

Inanna, rather than the moon god Nanna whom she was appointed to serve. First, Enheduanna was protesting the declaration of Sargon's successor Naram-Sin that he himself was a god, a change in status which allowed him to claim both temple properties and the authority of priestesses and priests. Alongside these political struggles, Enheduanna deeply loved Inanna, exalting her above all others. For Enheduanna, Inanna was the sky, the earth, the power of fate, deity both transcendent and immanent, and the goddess who walked beside her every day (Meador 2000).

Egyptian Cosmologies

In the New Kingdom, the capitol of Egypt moved from Memphis and Heliopolis upriver to Thebes, modern Luxor, where the pharaohs (both male and female) of Egypt constructed eternal homes in the desert rock for themselves and their families. In Theban theology, the god Amun took over the central role previously held by Atum and Ptah and stepped into the role of creator of the cosmos and patron of the royal families. At times Amun was served by priestesses called God's Wives and God's Hands.

The Theban religious hegemony paused briefly during the reign of Akhenaten. This pharaoh moved the capitol of Egypt to a city he constructed, Aketaten, and declared that the only gods that existed were the sun-disk Aten, and himself and his wife Nefertiti. In effect he used the vast power of the pharaoh to attempt to check the power of the bureaucracy of Amun. On his death the established priesthood of Amun rapidly moved the royal family and capitol back to Thebes. The young king Tutankhamen began his life as Tutanaten. His early death and the death of Akhenaten himself are suspicious in the light of the enormous political struggle between temple and pharaoh.

In contrast, the pharaoh Hatshepsut used the entrenched power of Amun's clergy to overcome her gender disadvantage and establish and maintain her position as pharaoh. On her mortuary temple walls she portrayed herself as the child of her mother and Amun, and one image shows Amun embracing her in an act of approving her authority.

Nag Hammadi Gospels

The 1945 discovery of manuscripts at Nag Hammadi in upper Egypt brought to light a number of gospels that had been lost to the West for two thousand years. These Coptic translations of Greek documents became available in English in the late 1970s (Robinson 1978). These texts, written in the first two centuries of the common era, may have been buried by monks from a nearby monastery sometime around 375. At that time the Alexandrian Bishop Athanasius issued a letter listing canonical biblical texts and discouraging the use of any other texts. Burying these noncanonical texts permitted them to survive (Bishop Athanasius 367).

In the 1970s, it came as a surprise to many that there had ever been discussion about the makeup of the New Testament. The Nag Hammadi find spotlighted the process of defining canonical and apocryphal (personal use) texts. In her analysis of the Nag Hammadi texts, Elaine Pagels discussed alternative cosmologies which were eventually declared to be heretical. The approved cosmology in which a single God ruled over a hierarchy of lesser beings reflected and authorized the structure of the church in which a single bishop ruled over priests, deacons, and laity (Pagels 1979).

Although various councils of bishops (such as the Council of Nicaea in 325) met to discuss Church doctrine and declare some theologies heretical, the Roman Catholic Church did not finalize its New Testament until the close of Council of Trent in 1563. The council was called to answer the Protestant challenge launched by Martin Luther, who questioned among other points the authority of the Pope.

Contemporary Theology

When I first studied these theological moves, I was dazzled by the implications. Theology need not rest only on the revelation of a deity to a prophet, it could proceed with a good working understanding of the forces involved and a particular sympathy for an image of the divine. I was even more delighted to discover that modern women theologians have been reshaping the religions of our time.

GOD THE MOTHER

I was baptized into the Roman Catholic Church as an infant, and as a child was taught to make a profession of faith which my memory gives me more or less like this:

> I believe in God, the Father Almighty, Creator of heaven and earth, and in Jesus Christ his only begotten Son, our Lord, who was conceived by the Holy Ghost, born of the virgin Mary, suffered under Pontius Pilate, was crucified, died, and was buried. He descended into hell. On the third day he rose again from the dead and ascended into heaven. He sits at the right hand of God, from where he shall come to judge the living and the dead. I believe in the Holy Ghost, the Holy Catholic Church, the communion of saints, the forgiveness of sins, the resurrection of the body, and life everlasting. Amen.

We have noted that Victorian esotericists did not reject their Christian and Jewish roots. Like me, most of the women and men who formed the turn-of-the-century magical lodges were born into the monotheistic religions. Aleister Crowley was raised Plymouth Brethren. Anna Kingsford married an Anglican priest, but followed her brother in converting to Roman Catholicism. Henri and Mina Bergson had Jewish parents.

That is not to say that Victorian-Edwardian magicians accepted monotheism as it was handed to them. God the Father, the graybeard in the clouds depicted on the ceiling of the Sistine Chapel, did not seem to Anna Kingsford to reflect the totality of deity. Here is how she rewrote the Apostles Creed based on her years of visionary work:

> I believe in one God, the Father and Mother Almighty; of whose Substance are the generations of Heaven and of earth; and in Christ-Jesus the Son of God, our Lord; who is conceived of the Holy Ghost; born of the Virgin Mary [the purified soul]; suffereth under the rulers of this world; is crucified, dead, and buried [in matter]; who descendeth into Hell [the unredeemed world]; who riseth again from the dead; who ascendeth into Heaven,

and sitteth at the right hand of God; by whose law the quick and the dead are judged. I believe in the Seven Spirits of God; the Kingdom of Heaven; the communion of the Elect; the passing-through of Souls; the redemption of the Body; the Life everlasting; and the Amen (Kingsford 1890).

Anna Kingsford's feminism inspired Samuel Liddell MacGregor Mathers. He dedicated *The Kabbalah Unveiled* to her, a book in which he conducted an analysis of the first chapters of Genesis and its two differing accounts of the Creation. Here is the King James Bible version of the first story:

And God said: "Let us make man in our image, after our likeness; and let them have dominion over the fish of the sea, and over the fowl of the air, and over the cattle, and over all the earth, and over every creeping thing that creepeth upon the earth." ... And God created man in His own image, in the image of God created He him; male and female created He them (King James Bible).

In *The Kabbalah Unveiled,* Mathers analyzed this passage:

The word Elohim is a plural formed from the feminine singular ALH, *Eloh,* by adding IM to the word. But inasmuch as IM is usually the termination of the masculine plural, and is here added to a feminine noun, it gives to the word Elohim the sense of a female potency united to a masculine idea, and thereby capable of producing an offspring. Now we hear much of the Father and the Son, but we hear nothing of the Mother in the ordinary religions of the day. But in the Kabbalah we find that the Ancient of Days conforms himself simultaneously into the Father and the Mother, and thus begets the Son. Now this Mother is Elohim (Mathers 1926).

Mathers heavily influenced the work of feminist Elizabeth Cady Stanton. Stanton brought what she termed a revising committee together in 1892 to work on *The Woman's Bible*. She launched the project boldly: "From the inauguration of the movement for woman's emancipation the Bible has been used to hold her in the 'divinely ordained sphere,' prescribed in the Old and New Testaments" (Stanton 1898).

Stanton invited women Greek and Hebrew scholars to participate, but they refused, fearing that so radical a project would expose them to censure. Her committee therefore studied the Bible only in English. Stanton concluded, "Whatever the Bible may be made to do in Hebrew or Greek, in plain English it does not exalt and dignify woman" (Stanton 1898).

In the section of *The Woman's Bible* on Qabbalah, Stanton pointed to occultism in general and Mathers's work in particular as holding the key to resolving religious conflicts. Stanton repeated Mathers's analysis of the first creation story in Genesis, and commented that the first account granted equality to both sexes, "created alike in the image of God—the Heavenly Mother and Father" (Stanton 1898).

Reforming Eve

The second creation story in Genesis is entirely different. Unlike the first creation story, in which Gods created Man and Woman in Their own image, the second creation story firmly subordinates Eve to Adam:

> Then the Lord God formed man of the dust of the ground, and breathed into his nostrils the breath of life; and man became a living soul ... And the Lord God caused a deep sleep to fall upon the man, and he slept; and He took one of his ribs, and closed up the place with flesh instead thereof. And the rib, which the Lord God had taken from the man, made He a woman, and brought her unto the man (King James Bible).

The eighth-century midrash "Alphabet of Ben Sira" expanded the first creation story. Yahweh created woman and man out of the same material, earth. This first woman, Lilith, refused to lie beneath Adam. Adam in turn refused to lie beneath her. Lilith uttered God's name and flew away. Adam complained to Yahweh that the woman left him. Yahweh sent three of his angels to tell Lilith she must return to Adam or he would kill a hundred of her children each day. When the angels found

Lilith in the midst of the sea, she refused to return to Adam. The angels threatened to drown her. She told them to leave her—she had been created to cause sickness to infants. The angels still insisted that she return with them. She struck a deal with them: she would pass by any child protected by an amulet containing their three names (Stern and Mirsky 1990).

In 1972, feminist theologian Judith Plaskow attended the second conference on women and theology at the intentional community Grailville. There she was inspired to create her own version of this story. In Plaskow's feminist midrash, Adam orders Lilith to serve him, but she refuses and flies away. He asks God for a more malleable wife. God obliges by creating Eve. Adam tells Eve that Lilith is a baby-eating demon. Lilith tries to re-enter the garden. Adam fends her off, but not before Eve sees that Lilith is a woman like herself. Eve uses the apple tree to scale the wall and go talk to Lilith. She keeps on visiting Lilith, and becomes more assertive, refusing to wait on Adam. Adam complains to God, but God by this point has begun to rethink Adam's demandingness. Adam and God together are willing to listen when Eve and Lilith walk into the garden together (Plaskow 2005).

Feminist theologian Lynn Gottleib has also created new texts for Jewish women. Gottleib's poetry calls Lilith "Fiery Night Woman" and Eve, or Hava, "Let There Be Life Woman." Gottleib sees Eve as Everywoman (Gottleib 1995).

In 1898, Elizabeth Cady Stanton lofted the same idea. In analyzing Genesis, she noted that Adam called his wife "Life," and named Eve as the eternal mother. Stanton's reforming view of the Bible ultimately rejected Christianity:

> The real difficulty in woman's case is that the whole foundation of the Christian religion rests on her temptation and man's fall, hence the necessity of a Redeemer and a plan of salvation. As the chief cause of this dire calamity, woman's degradation and subordination were made a necessity. If, however, we accept the Darwinian theory, that the race has been a gradual growth from the lower to a higher form of life, and that the story of the fall

is a myth, we can exonerate the snake, emancipate the woman, and reconstruct a more rational religion for the nineteenth century, and thus escape all the perplexities of the Jewish mythology as of no more importance than those of the Greek, Persian, and Egyptian (Stanton 1898).

Stanton's move was to equate Jewish scripture with Greek, Persian, and Egyptian mythology—not an idle comparison but an educated one, equating religious scripture with the mythology that underlies Western culture.

Process Theology

Stanton's work languished in the post-war suspension of feminist movement. Her work was rediscovered in the second wave of feminism in the early 1970s as women re-examined their religious heritages. Many feminist theologians cite connections with other women formed at Grailville and in other meeting places about that time period. In light of our understanding of the power of women's collectives, it is significant that contemporary feminist theology grounds in real physical community. In particular the collaboration between Jewish feminist theologian Judith Plaskow and Christian feminist theologian Carol Christ has resulted in a number of pivotal anthologies, including *Womanspirit Rising* and *Weaving the Visions*, bringing together essays written by women of a number of faiths and replicating in print that sense of community.

Contemporary Jewish and Christian feminist theologians and thealogians who honor the unity of everything, who seek to reform the imagery and language of the punitive father God who created men to be his priests, draw on process philosophy to reshape God-talk. As Carol Christ put it, "Process philosophy's divinity has a body, which is the whole world. In process philosophy all beings are connected in the web of life" (Christ 2003).

Feminist theologians experiment with inclusive terms for God:

- Father/Mother
- Goddess/God

- God-She
- She Who Is
- She Who Changes

In feminist process theology, God-She is understood to be the unfolding of the universe which includes the creation of the world which sustains human life. This theology supports eco-feminist values affirming life, creation, the connection between human life and all other life on the planet, and the perception of self as a part of an interconnected whole.

Process theology incorporates scientific discoveries into an evolving understanding of the human-divine connection. For example, feminist theologians draw on imagery of mitochondrial Eve to honor the connections to our ancient mothers. Mitochondrial DNA is passed only by women to their female and male children. Our most recent common maternal ancestor, whose mitochondrial DNA all humans bear today, lived between 150,000 and 200,000 years ago. It is a profound meditation to recognize that all humans alive today are connected by the legacy of this common mother.

If Eve is the first mother, every woman is her daughter, literally embodying Eve. Eve in turn is the daughter of Elohim, the divine. With this in mind, we could recast Moina Mathers's paragraph to say:

> The whole aim and object of the teaching is to bring a woman to the knowledge of her higher self, to purify herself, to strengthen herself, to develop all qualities and powers of the being, that she may ultimately regain union with the Divine Woman latent in herself, that Eve Kadmon, whom *God the Mother* hath made in Her Own Image."

For woman magicians today who are comfortable with monotheistic deity, this formulation will work perfectly well.

God the Mother is not, however, a synonym for Goddess. The new religious movements, neo-Paganism and the women's spirituality movement, turned away from God the Father and toward the Great Mother

Goddess. This move also derived from turn-of-the-century religious and occult predecessors.

Reform or Revolution

In the latter part of the twentieth century, while feminist theologians in the monotheistic religions sought to develop more inclusive imagery for God, others found themselves questioning whether this change alone would be sufficient for them to remain with those religions. Rita Gross commented that the first question a woman asks herself when confronted with sexism in a religious tradition is whether she should work within the tradition to change it or to leave it altogether and work to create something new. She noted Carol Christ named these two responses "reform" and "revolution" (Gross 1996).

The revolutionaries argued that the language and image describing God is irretrievably male, that the bearded old man in the clouds, God the Father, is so deeply ingrained in Western culture that introducing female language and imagery only grafts a superficial change on a deep unchanging root. In her book *Beyond God the Father,* Mary Daly put it this way:

> Sophisticated thinkers, of course, have never intellectually identified God with an elderly parent in heaven. Nevertheless it is important to recognize that, even when very abstract conceptualizations of God are formulated in the mind, images have a way of surviving in the imagination in such a way that a person can function on two different and even apparently contradictory levels at the same time. Thus one can speak of God as spirit and at the same time imagine "him" as belonging to the male sex (Daly 1971).

GODDESS SPIRITUALITY

Feminist theologians searched for images and language that describe the divine as female. Looking for examples of Western female deity led them into the territory of history to explore goddesses of the past. Here they found nineteenth-century texts to be helpful in creating a new mythos.

Matriarchy

While nineteenth-century mythographers studied European folklore, nineteenth-century historians rewrote the metanarrative of human history. In 1861, the anthropologist Johann Jakob Bachofen published *Das Mutterrecht*, translated in English as *Myth, Religion and Mother Right*. He traced the development of human culture from a more primitive state of matriarchy to a more advanced political system of patriarchy (Bachofen 1967).

The image of matriarchy informed the political aims of the feminist movement. Elizabeth Cady Stanton discussed the concept of matriarchy in her address to the National Council of Women of the United States in 1891. In "Matriarchate or Mother Age" she cited Bachofen among others to attack the historical metanarrative that all women everywhere have been physically subject to men's rule, instead tracing a long period of human history in which women steered human cultural development (Stanton 1891).

The work of Raphael Patai forms an important bridge between the effort to reform God-talk and the exploration of goddesses of the past. He began his pivotal work *The Hebrew Goddess* with this statement: "Goddesses are ubiquitous." Patai assembled scholastic research into ancient Hebrew goddesses. He studied Asherah, once honored as Yahweh's wife in the temple and worshipped beneath trees by women of Judah, as well as related goddesses Astarte and Anat. He argued for the goddess-like aspects of the concepts Shekhinah, Matronit, and the Sabbath, and he pointed to the Babylonian origins of the demon Lilith (Patai 1967).

Patai did not write from an overtly feminist standpoint; his point seemed to be that *men* require a goddess as well as a god to fulfill their understanding of the divine. Feminist theologians, however, pointed to male god imagery as legitimating men's subordination of women. As Mary Daly famously put it, "If god is male, then the male is god" (Daly 1973).

Merlin Stone took this concept as her starting point. The male god legitimates patriarchy. However, before the patriarchal God suppressed the worship of all other deities, there was the Goddess. She began *When God Was a Woman* by saying:

> In prehistoric and early human periods of development, religions existed in which people revered their supreme creator as female. The Great Goddess—the Divine Ancestress—had been worshiped from the beginnings of the Neolithic periods of 7000 BC until the closing of the last Goddess temples, about AD 500. Some authorities would extend Goddess worship as far into the past as the Upper Paleolithic Age of about 25,000 BC (Stone 1976).

Stone cited the authority of J. J. Bachofen, retaining the chronology matriarchy-patriarchy while flipping the values: before patriarchy, Stone argued, there was the rule of the matriarchs, who created more equitable and peaceful cultures than the patriarchal invaders who conquered them.

Images of the Goddess answered a deep need. Scholars documenting ancient religions found themselves suddenly popular. Westerners were especially drawn to excavations of old European sites, devouring books by Marija Gimbutas, who detected female imagery in cave drawings, and James Mellaart, who unearthed Neolithic statues of goddesses at Catal Huyuk in Turkey.

Riane Eisler's history of Goddess religion collated all these sources into a coherent narrative. *The Chalice and the Blade* started with the Paleolithic, reviewed Neolithic goddess imagery, surveyed ancient Cretan religion, covered the patriarchal invasion and subsequent loss of religious and secular status for women, cited the religious justification for patriarchal violence, and offered challenges to existing religious and social structures and suggestions for the future of women's religion (Eisler 1987).

Male-Centered Stories

Western women casting about for images of the female divine found closest to hand the Greek stories that are part of the Western cultural heritage. In these stories:

- Apollo killed the great serpent Python. Apollo's priestess, the Pythoness, spoke his words as oracle.

- Zeus bore Athena in his head until Hephaestus split his head open so that she could be born fully grown and dressed in armor.

- Demeter's daughter, Persephone, was carried off to the underworld by Hades, who raped her. Demeter won her release from her underworld prison for half the year. Thus was the seasonal round created.

I received a classical education as a child and was taught these stories at school. The images of rape and murder reflected the images of rape and the murder of women and children in the nightly news headlines. It seemed that not only monotheistic religion but Pagan religion involved the devaluation of women and ubiquitous violence against women.

Closely following Merlin Stone, Zsuzsanna (Z) Budapest mounted a one-woman campaign to bring positive goddess imagery back into Western culture. In 1976, I crammed into the basement of a church near Los Angeles along with a standing-room only crowd to marvel at her slide show of statues from the world's museums.

In her self-published books, Z interpreted Greek myths as a form of history documenting the patriarchal rewriting of older matriarchal theology. In Z's understanding of history, the goddesses in these stories predated the stories told about them. Before Apollo, the Pythoness spoke the oracle of a goddess. Before her forced marriage to Zeus, Hera was a goddess with great authority and power (Budapest 2007).

Charlene Spretnak created a version of the Demeter-Persephone myth that removed the forcible rape and abduction of Persephone. Spretnak's story focuses on the relationship of mother and daughter, the conflict between the mother's desire to keep the daughter near and the daughter's desire to do her work in the world (Spretnak 1989).

All Goddesses are One Goddess

Feminist monotheism requires God to remain singular, Father-Mother. Christian theology casts Mary both as Christ's mother and as human. Although centuries of medieval devotion built an aura of deity around her, and although the mother-and-child imagery borrows directly from the ubiquitous Isis-and-Horus imagery of late antiquity, Mary is a saint, not a deity in her own right.

In her novel *Sea Priestess*, Dion Fortune provided the theological framework in which the study of deities of the past could become the deities of the present. She said, "All gods are one god, all goddesses are one goddess" (Fortune 1935). Within this framework a single goddess could become a facet of the Great Goddess.

Many books were printed describing goddesses and their stories. Carl Jung and Joseph Campbell created systems of categories into which individual goddesses could be sorted. Jung placed goddesses in categories he called archetypes, while Campbell drew parallels between goddesses from different cultures and time periods.

Psychologization of Goddesses

Jung's theory of human personality development traced the intersection of a given person with transpersonal archetypes. Men dipped into the archetypes of, for example, king, warrior, lover, and magician. Female archetypes include mother and anima, or, roughly, man's lover or muse.

Following Jung and Frazer, Campbell drew parallels between similar deities in all the world's cultures as reflections of the universal human experience. He traced the cross-cultural journey of the hero as a prophet's spiritual development in a three-step process: separation, initiation, and reintegration. The man flees a revelation of God, receives aid on his journey, encounters the Mother Goddess and the Temptress Woman, and ultimately reconciles with the Father (Campbell 1949).

Although Campbell's journey is a male one, female archetypes do show up in it. Jean Shinoda Bolen work *Goddesses in Everywoman* related those archetypes to women's psychological development. She grouped

Greek goddesses in categories with shared traits. For example, the virgin goddesses Athena, Artemis, and Hestia are characterized by an emphasis on focus. She maps these traits onto women's personalities, each having inherent predispositions to a given archetype (Bolen 1985).

Psychologist James Hillman developed archetypal psychology, which explains Jungian archetypes as artifacts of human culture. Hillman pointed to Freud's use of the myth of Oedipus to analyze human development and noted that using other myths in analysis would more accurately reflect human diversity. Taking her cue from Hillman, psychologist Ginette Paris began *Pagan Grace* by disavowing belief in the goddesses and gods, seeing them instead as useful therapeutic metaphors, while her second book *Pagan Meditations* applied this methodology to the goddesses Aphrodite, Artemis, and Hestia (Paris 1986, 1990). Similarly, Christine Downing approaches myths about Greek goddesses as stories lived out by the goddesses and by human women (Downing 1981).

God the Mother as Goddess

All these moves—theology that recasts deity image in female terms, theology that resurrects ancient goddesses, and psychology that finds goddesses in the human psyche—permit us to update Moina's paragraph in contemporary language:

> The whole aim and object of the teaching is to bring a woman to the knowledge of her higher self, to purify herself, to strengthen herself, to develop all qualities and powers of the being, that she may ultimately regain union with the Divine Woman latent in herself, that Eve Kadmon, whom *Goddess* hath made in Her Own Image.

CULTURE WARS

Women rejecting the monotheistic religions built new religious understandings based on both the new goddess scholarship and the Witchcraft revival. Some seized on the term "Witch" both to describe the sense of connection with the past and to reassert the value of women and of nature.

Some women worked together with men, others rejected working with men at all; Z Budapest's Dianic Witchcraft initiated only women. Women studied ancient religions and priestesses, revived Pagan religious practice, modeled ancient Pagan priestesses, worshipped goddesses from around the world, and used all of these as jumping off points to create new forms of ritual and religion. The history-as-theology approach created a sense of connection with the past and provided numerous examples of goddesses to revolutionary theologians.

Interfaith Discussion

Insights from the neo-Pagan and women's spirituality movements sometimes inspire women who remain in the monotheistic religions. However, the interaction between revolutionary and reform theologians has not always been mutually supportive. The conflict between reform and revolutionary theology surfaced in discussions of the new theology. Those who left Jewish and Christian faiths offered sharp criticism of their old religions. Newly initiated Witches swore "Never again the burning times!" and held Christianity as a religion responsible for the deaths of their religious predecessors.

The narrative that peaceful matriarchal cultures were destroyed by invading patriarchal cultures tended to demonize older religions. Rabbi Elyse Goldstein said:

> Some scholars have held the Hebrews responsible for all of patriarchy. They suggest that in the "good old goddess worshipping days" peace and harmony abounded, until the Hebrews came along with their male YHVH, and everything went wrong. The covert anti-Semitism in this argument frightens feminists who still hold the Torah as containing the sacred history of the Jews, a link to our identity, and a record of our struggle to connect with the Divine. Words such as "patriarchal invaders" appear again and again in the writings of authors such as Merlin Stone (Goldstein 1998).

On the other hand, Catholic theologian Rosemary Ruether reviewed the writings of several neo-Pagan groups, including Covenant of the Goddess and Earthspirit, and noted, "One does not find in this literature diatribes against Christians or Jews as inherently patriarchal or opposed to nature." She argued for the Christian defense of Witchcraft and the feminist value in building alliances (Ruether 2005).

Religious people involved in interfaith discussion, especially those who subscribe to the Parliament of the World's Religions Global Ethic, have called for a cessation of blaming language between religions. Dialogue between feminist theologians reforming existing religions and feminist theologians creating new religions builds bridges between their positions. Reform theologians draw on imagery and language created by the Goddess movement to inform the reshaping of God to include female aspects. At the same time, rituals written by Jewish and Christian feminists are easily performed by feminists in the new religions.

Scholastic Criticism

Both Merlin Stone and Riane Eisler came under fire for writing history outside their specialties—Stone was an artist and art historian, and Eisler is an attorney and a sociologist. Their work has been challenged by numerous sources, perhaps most famously in *The Goddess Unmasked*, in which Phillip Davis called into question the strategy of history as theology (Davis 1998).

Similarly, Eliot Rose criticized Margaret Murray's work on the grounds that she was an Egyptologist and not a medieval scholar. He also faulted her for taking literally the confessions of accused witches (Rose 1962). More recently, Ronald Hutton extensively explored the flaws in Murray's methodology, as well as Charles Leland and Gerald Gardner's work, contesting historical precedent for Witchcraft as practiced today (Hutton 1999).

The out-of-her-league criticism could not be leveled against Marija Gimbutas, a trained archaeologist working within her specialty. Her critics did dispute the conclusions she drew and argued that other conclusions could be drawn from the same evidence. Others in turn defended her work; Joan Marler cited Gimbutas's persistence in the face of this opposition and organized a large anthology of essays in her honor (Marler 1997).

Archaeologist James Mellaart encountered similar criticism after his excavation of the Anatolian site Catal Huyuk, in which he identified goddess statues, shrines, priestess burials, and a society in which women were at least as important as men (Mellaart 1967). Challenges to his work have focused on discrediting his data. His student Hodder, working in the new excavations at the site, contests his conclusion that goddesses were worshipped there (Kunzig 1999).

Other scholars criticize the history-as-theology approach on the grounds that the historical scholarship on which the theology is based is faulty, distrusting historical scholarship that has an end result in mind. Critics accuse reconstructionists of projecting their own practices into the past, and of seeing only what they want to see and ignoring evidence that contradicts their predetermined conclusions.

Christian theologian and historian Rosemary Ruether made the important point that historical goddesses supported political institutions, by authorizing kingship positions and by being placed in sometimes subordinate relationship to gods. From this she concluded that she doubted the existence of a Mother Goddess and traced a dominant maleness in all historical Western religion. She believed that the concept of an independent Goddess was constructed through postmodern theology rather than resurrected from the past (Ruether 2005).

In *Claiming Knowledge: Strategies of Epistemology from Theosophy to the New Age*, Olav Hammer offered a hostile outsider critique of the discursive strategies used in what he defines as Modern Esoteric Tradition. He applied the postmodern distrust of grand narratives to esoteric models of tradition, using scornful terms such as mythic history and projection. Hammer's work recalls the modern scholastic denigration of magic as primitive religion and pseudo-science. He negatively evaluates the tradition's use of revelation and personal experience as well as the tradition's engagement with science.

Hammer himself retroactively applied contemporary postmodern standards to Victorian and modern thinking. However, his analysis of fragmenting techniques such as disembedding (taking a religious or scientific concept out of context) and source amnesia (failing to note the context of a concept) are thought-provoking criticisms which we may apply to our understanding of the traditions as practiced today (Hammer 2004).

Ideological Arguments

Cynthia Eller's work *The Myth of Matriarchal Prehistory* criticized the work of archaeologists such as Gimbutas and Mellaart as well as popular writers such as Merlin Stone and Riane Eisler. Eller "debunks" the notion that women's power was at any time ever equal to or greater than men's. "Women may have powerful roles, but their power does not undermine or seriously challenge an overall system of male dominance in either these groups or ours, and there is no reason to believe that it would have in prehistoric societies either" (Eller 2000).

Joan Marler's review of Eller's book examined Eller's methodology and conclusions. Marler commented that Eller defined matriarchy and feminist interest in history and in ancient goddesses in inflammatory terms (Marler 2003). Max Dashu directly challenged Eller's work on the grounds that it is not history but ideology (Dashu 2000).

Responding to Eller's work, Marguerite Rigoglioso concluded:

> ... the academy is attempting to repress the expanded ways of knowing, seeing, and interpreting that women's spirituality scholars are bringing to the table, and it is using one of patriarchy's favored methods to do so: the silencing tactic of scorn. Whether this kind of repression is being carried out by women or men academics, it is all part of the same patriarchal paradigm (Rigoglioso 2003).

Challenging the Gender Narrative

In the Western world, any challenge to the metanarrative that men have always dominated women is fiercely attacked. Vicki Noble explicitly connects the current trend toward "debunking" the works of Gimbutas, Mellaart, and others with backlash to feminist movement.

The fact that Western women had not only shown scholarly interest in the ancient widespread religion of the Great Mother, but also recognized it as meaningful in our own everyday lives, has precipitated a frenzy of reactivity in the academic world, leading to an active effort to deny that there was any Goddess religion at all, ever, anywhere (Noble 2003).

It is significant that Marija Gimbutas was Lithuanian. Taking a tour of Czech Bronze Age archaeological sites, theologian Asphodel Long was surprised to discover that archaeologists there worked freely with theories about the importance of women in history. She noted the communist metanarrative, articulated in particular by Engels, held that early matriarchies were later overthrown by patriarchy, in contrast to the Western European metanarrative that men have always ruled women. Explanatory material in Eastern European museums and archaeological sites routinely discusses totemic female ancestors and women's importance in history in a way that would be immediately contested in the West (Long 1992).

It is apparent that standpoint matters. Historians or theologians may have a solid grounding in their profession and a sincere commitment to faithfully reproducing facts, while at the same time inescapably speaking from the point of view of their own gender, age, class, race, personality, and ideology. Historian Mary Fulbrook worked to find a post-postmodern approach to historical agreement without either supporting politically charged metanarrative or leveling difference. She noted that the same generally agreed upon facts can be shaped into differing narratives. It is possible to come to agreement about methodologies for accumulating data, but every narrative is based on unprovable assumptions reflecting the historian's standpoint (Fulbrook 2003).

Culture Wars in Western Traditional Magic

Culture wars also break out in the magical communities today. The techniques of disembedding and source amnesia which Olav Hammer critiqued in what he called the Modern Esoteric Tradition are also at work in the postmodern esoteric communities.

The connection between Masonry and the magical lodges persists today. Students of ceremonial history are well aware of the debt owed by the magical lodges to Masonry. Men in various Golden Dawn and Thelemic groups also join Masonic lodges. These lodges in turn rent meeting facilities to Thelemic and Golden Dawn groups too small to afford their own meeting halls. Performing ceremonial ritual in a Masonic hall illustrates the extent to which our rituals derive from that source—the space is built or oriented correctly for the rituals, and quite a bit of equipment (thrones, altars, and pillars) can be provided by the hall.

Some Witches, like myself, also study ceremonial ritual and belong to Masonic-derived magical orders, but the historical connection between them has largely been forgotten. My Witchcraft teachers did not contextualize the relationship between our Craft as religion and *the* Craft as fraternal order. I was caught by surprise the first time I attended a Masonic installation and heard the terms "Craft" and "cowan" and heard the assembly intone "so mote it be." Few books on the history of Witchcraft link the three-degree Craft initiatory system with the three degrees of Witchcraft.

Witchcraft breaks from Western Traditional Magic in theological structure. Rather than a Lord of the Universe, or a collection of Egyptian deities, we have Aradia and Cernunnos. The marriage of European folk religion with ceremonial-Masonic ritual structure gives Witchcraft its unique character. It is common among Witches to practice source amnesia, emphasizing the folk religion aspect and positioning contemporary Witchcraft as a Pagan survival, while de-emphasizing or even denying the debt owed to ceremonial ritual and Masonry. Magicians, on the other hand, over-emphasize the debt Witchcraft owes to ceremonial ritual and enjoy poking history at those who have forgotten it. Both tendencies lead to an unfortunate tension between the groups.

Neo-Pagan revivals of older Pagan religion and women's spirituality rituals often borrow the Witchcraft circle, the eight sabbats, and other theological and ritual components to structure fragmentary survivals and newly created work. Often this debt too remains unacknowledged, and the connection between these rituals and their Masonic and ceremonial predecessors is entirely forgotten.

QABBALAH

Western Traditional Magic in turn borrowed both Jewish and Christian mysticism to frame the tradition's philosophy and theology. The system is called Qabbalah (sometimes spelled Kabbalah).

Attempting to trace this system, we encounter a fascinating series of cultural borrowings. At the beginning of the common era, Roman rule spread Greek learning throughout the Western world. In this Hellenistic world, Jewish, Greek, and Egyptian magic swirled together, mixing with neo-Platonic philosophy. This world formed the common Mediterranean substructure which underlies much of Western philosophy and magic.

The neo-Platonists held that the soul descended from the stars through the planetary spheres to incarnate on earth. This notion surfaced again in Jewish mystical texts. Although these texts, such as the *Sephir Yetzirah* (Kaplan 1997), surfaced in medieval Spain, they are frequently claimed to have been created centuries earlier. The Qabbalistic system envisioned the planetary spheres as outpourings of God's energy. Qabbalah arranged the planetary spheres in the form of a tree, building on the resonance of the Tree of Life motif in Mediterranean and Near Eastern art and religion. The spheres of the Sepher Yetzirah are gendered. (See Illustration 2.)

Renaissance Christians appropriated Jewish Qabbalah and added imagery of sacrifice, suffering and redemption. Turn-of-the-century occultists reshaped the system again, adding back Pagan elements, particularly Egyptian forms of deity. This is the form of Qabbalah on which the contemporary practice of Ceremonial Magic is based.

Gender and the Tree of Life

In her book *Goddess Spirituality for the 21st Century*, Judith Laura reviewed and contrasted the Jewish gendering of the Tree of Life with the esoteric gendering of the spheres. Laura's Jewish version looks like this: (See Illustration 3).

In this system, only two of the ten spheres are female, one is nongendered, and six are male.

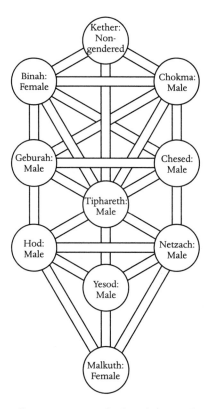

Illustration 2: Tree of Life Sepher Yetzirah

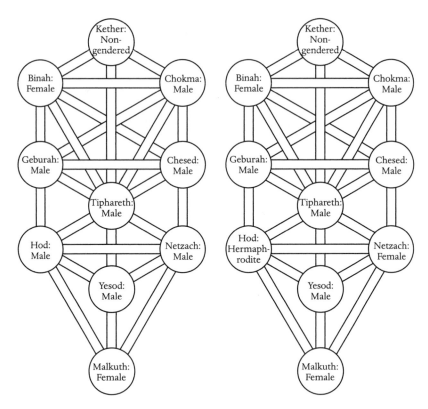

Illustration 3: Tree of Life Judith Laura One   *Illustration 4: Tree of Life Judith Laura Two*

Here is Laura's version of gender on the Hermetic Qabbalah: (See Illustration 4).

In this system, two of the ten spheres are neither male or female, three are female, and five are male (Laura 1997, 2008).

Qabbalistic commentaries also absorb the Adam Kadmon or heavenly man. This idea appears in the *Astronomica*, a first-century Hellenistic text. In this text, Marcus Manilius, who was roughly contemporary with Philo, discussed the astrological signs. These signs were developed by pre-Platonic Greeks based on Babylonian predecessors. Manilius arranged these signs into the form familiar to modern astrologers, placing the zodiac in the system of houses. These astrological signs are also shaped into the form of a human being by associating each of the signs with a part of the human body.

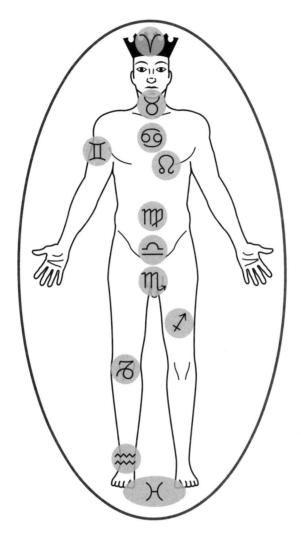

Illustration 5: Adam Kadmon as Astrological Man

In the same way, Qabbalah maps onto the human body; this is illustrated most clearly in the ritual of the Qabbalistic Cross, which affirms the ritualist's unity with the sacred cosmos.

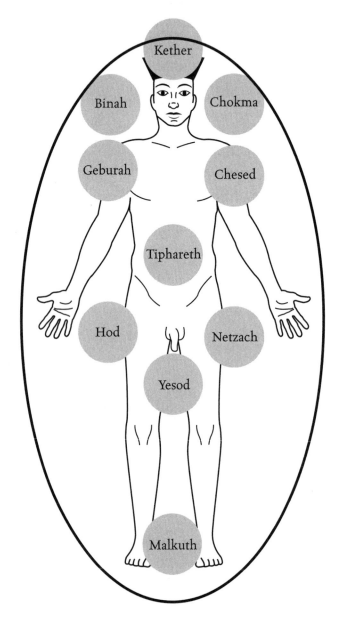

Illustration 6: Adam Kadmon as Tree of Life

If God is male, the cosmos is male, the Qabbalistic spheres that describe the cosmos are male, and the real human body which reflects the cosmos is male. The unarticulated, implied template looks like this:

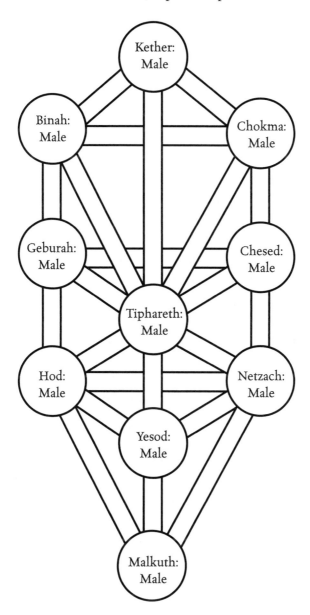

Illustration 7: Tree of Life Male

Feminist Qabbalah

A handful of writers have brought insights from feminist movement and feminist theological reform to Western Traditional Magic.

In 1985, Ellen Cannon Reed's work *The Witches Qabbalah* sought to explain the ceremonial Tree of Life to the general magical communities. She reviewed a general history of Qabbalah, provided a quick look at the uses of the spheres, and linked the sphere Chokmah to God the Father and the sphere Binah to the Great Mother (Reed 1985, 1997).

In a neat reversal of the female artist/male writer pairing, Rachel Pollack was commissioned to write an explanatory text for Hermann Haindl's version of the Tarot, which sparked a partnership between them. Pollack's book *The Kabbalah Tree* refers to Haindl's poster of the Tree of Life. In her book, Pollack called out explicitly patriarchal viewpoints in the Jewish Qabbalah, for example pointing to the second creation story in which Eve was created from Adam's rib. This story, Pollack argued, positions the male as primary and the female as secondary. Like turn-of-the-century esotericists and postmodern process theologians, Pollack turned to scientific paradigms to counter these viewpoints. She pointed to the role played by both mother and father in contributing genetic material as reflecting the egalitarian nature of Eve and Adam.

Pollack's view of the tree called each sephiroth both female and male except for two, Kether being male and Malkuth being female. Although her Creator God was a S/He, Pollack repeated the gendering of the elements, fire-air-male and earth-water-female, and noted their links to the formula Yod He Vau He and the four Qabbalistic worlds (Pollack 2004).

Pollack wrote an introduction to Judith Laura's book *Goddess Spirituality for the 21st Century*. In the second revised edition, Laura reviewed not only Qabbalistic history but also concepts from the Goddess movement. She revisioned the Qabbalah to present female and male as complementary rather than oppositional, and horizontally related rather than hierarchical.

In Laura's revisioning, Chokmah, Binah, and Malkuth correspond to Crone, Maiden, and Mother. The male Kether, Hod, and Netzach become Father, Son, and Consort. For Laura as for Pollack the masculine Kether is balanced by the feminine Malkuth. In Laura's tree, Tiphareth is female and Yesod male, while Geburah and Chesed are dual-sexed.

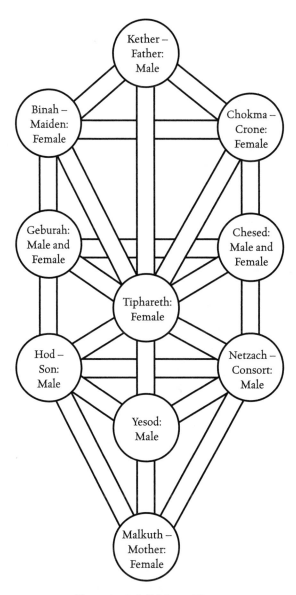

Illustration 8: Judith Laura Three

Laura entirely replaced Adam Kadmon, the man written on a universal scale, with the Great Mother Goddess. Her head is Kether, her breasts Chokmah and Binah. Chesed and Geburah are her hands, Tiphareth is her solar plexus. In her womb she carries the son, with both womb and son placed in the triangle Netzach, Hod, and Yesod. Her feet are anchored in Malkuth, the world (Laura 2008).

EVALUATING THE THEOLOGY

I set out to discover how I might understand myself as an instance of the divine. Revisioning God as Goddess gets me halfway to that goal. At least a Goddess is a deity who looks like me.

That said, all the formulations that work to add the divine feminine back into the divine seem to me to rest on Aristotelian gendering. The philosophical move that allowed me to understand myself as an embodied and reasoned being has not yet transformed occult metaphysics.

What are we saying when we use the term "divine feminine"? The word "feminine" in English marks the female gender, but it also refers to a set of characteristics women are expected to embody, the woman's half of the gender narrative: intuitive, gentle, nurturing, subordinate. "Divine feminine" writes those expectations on female deity, who is expected to be inspiring, gentle, and nurturing—a mother who loves her children. Feminine is half of an equation, masculine-feminine, but where the term "divine feminine" is used we do not hear the matching term "divine masculine." Using the term "divine feminine" without calling out gender assumptions does not essentially alter the patriarchal imagery of God and Adam Kadmon as male.

Jung's term "archetypal feminine" is often used interchangeably in the new religions with "divine feminine." We have previously examined Jung's understanding of the unequal nature of masculine and feminine natures—while both women and men have both feminine and masculine sides, for men incorporating the feminine anima enhances their genius, while women expressing the masculine animus are argumentative and driven by preconceived notions and prejudice.

We might expect to see cultural expectations of woman being written into the archetypal feminine. Jean Shinoda Bolen's *Goddesses in Ev-*

erywoman exemplifies this tendency, relating the archetypal goddesses to women's traditional roles and expectations. To draw on Hestia's focus, Bolen recommends folding clothes slowly and meditatively, and she notes that "Hera" women disappointed in marriage may turn into shrews.

In addition to the unbalanced nature of this gender narrative, the term "archetype" used to describe deity subordinates understanding of deity from every human culture, past and present, to the model of theology as psychological metaphor. When viewed as an archetype, every goddess and god is understood to be an aspect of the universal unconscious, and gods and goddesses are cross-culturally identical. This formulation has a colonizing effect, projecting Western religious concepts on the rest of the world, and projecting contemporary frameworks on the past. This filter can inhibit our study of context, of how the people who worshipped a deity experienced that deity in their own terms. The postmodern insistence on the value of the individual can help us here, pointing us to study and understand each deity in its own context and on its own terms. We discount difference unless we are receptive to it.

Historical Critique as Backlash

In my youth, the new women's histories inspired me to understand my own life in the context of woman-directed spirituality. As my knowledge of history grew both in general and in study of specific time periods and cultures, the assumptions and misreadings in some of the new methodologies became apparent, and individual critiques of specific work seemed both important and relevant to my spiritual work. It's all very well to talk about *the* Goddess, but lumping all goddesses everywhere together elides magically important differences: what does this specific goddess want from me and offer to me?

Over time, however, the accumulation of these critiques, and their increasingly scornful debunking tone, have rendered them suspect to me as a group. These critical works appeal to scholastic or cultural consensus, what seems "reasonable," or even acceptable, to believe, but it is precisely that cultural consensus which both feminist reform and feminist revolution seek to change.

I am suspicious of critiquing narrative that specifically sets out to discredit or wound, especially when it seems intended primarily to establish an individual's academic or professional position, or to ally the work with entrenched power structures. I am suspicious of narrative constructed by scholars who do not reveal their standpoint, and narrative that presents itself as true for anyone anywhere, as when critics base their criticism on the idea that the work criticized has a viewpoint while their own work simply seeks to understand the real truth.

The structure of this conversation seems to me to mirror men's one-up conversational structures. Critiques of the debunking sort set up a winner and a loser, enacting a dominance hierarchy. Here we have another instance of the common divide in women scholars who enter into the competitive world and identify with the male-privilege power structure by savaging the work of other women and rejecting the call to enter into commonality. Personal benefit for a single woman who engages in this identification results in reduced status for other women.

As Rigoglioso pointed out, violence is violence, no matter who commits it. When we have a critic chortling and a subject struggling with a sudden loss of power, we have backlash, even when the critic is a woman, academically trained, a respected theologian, or a neo-Pagan or esotericist.

As women esotericists work together to create Magia Femina, it is important for us to band together to resist backlash. As with any form of patriarchal oppression, resistance to backlash involves calling out the methodology, standpoint, and context of the critic, and joining together with other women who are willing to enter into cooperative and mutually supportive work.

Daughter of the Goddess

Female deity in twentieth-century magical systems still relates to primary male deity. The theologians of early public Witchcraft married Aradia, daughter of Lucifer and Diana, to Cernunnos, the Celtic god. Robert Graves's wildly popular vision of the Goddess in three aspects, Maiden, Mother, and Crone, centers the divine feminine on aspects of material fertility.

Although Western Traditional Magic imported Pagan deity to Western theology, the religious underpinning remained rooted in the Abrahamic religions, Christianity and Judaism (and Islam to a much lesser extent). This imagery places the male at the center of the cosmos and relegates the female to subordinate relationship to the male, as wife and lover, mother and daughter. In the formula Yod He Vau He, Yod is the father and king, He the mother and queen, Vau the prince-heir and son, He final the prince's bride.

Judith Laura's replacement of Adam Kadmon with the Great Goddess would permit me to place myself on the tree as an instance of the female divine. In this vision, however, the womb of the Goddess bears a son.

Starhawk's visionary theology is the clearest explication of the theology of Witchcraft. Unlike the overarching Father God in other forms of Western Traditional Magic, her Great Goddess is immanent, the center of the universe, and the party with greatest power in the relationship. Even though the values have flipped, however, Starhawk's Goddess acts pretty much like the Thelemic Nuit and Babalon, as mother of the son, and as the son's lover and initiator or intuitive muse.

As I come to this realization, the anchorite's spare cell fades away, and I am once again tucked away in a warm cozy cabin, looking out at a vista of cedar, fir, and alder, contemplating my situation.

I am not a mother. Motherhood is a noble, critical, and spiritual endeavor, and I strive to support all the mothers I know, but bearing and raising children is not my purpose in life. Although I am a lover, this is not my primary magical identity. I continue to seek a magical methodology by which I can myself undergo the hero's journey, not serving as the hero's helpmate, mother, seducer, initiator, or feminine half, but myself acting as the center of the story—and not vicariously, as a pretend man, but as a woman, a daughter, myself.

LADY MAGIC

Transforming Magia Traditionis into Magia Humana first requires an articulation of Magia Femina, traditional magic reshaped around the physical form, emotional center, and spiritual needs of women.

Magia Humana rejects historicizing narratives, including those which equate the spiritual experiences of all women who have ever lived in any culture. Contemporary Western philosophy slowly grapples with two dawning realities: women have been defined as less-than-men in artificial categorizations which do not accurately reflect the lived experience of humanity, and biology does not confirm an absolute distinction between genders, instead revealing a confusing spectrum of physical possibilities which do not easily map onto any of the extant gender narratives. Postmodern activists seize gender confusion to challenge the metanarratives—if everyone is queer, no one can be relegated to an artificially confining social role.

Is there any sense, then, in which it is possible to think about women as magicians?

The key is to focus not on Woman, as a category, but women, as people who have been socialized in a gender role. This is precisely the difference between the standpoint of an object and the standpoint of a subject. Woman has been defined from without, as relating to Man. The Magical Woman is inherently intuitive, rejects intellectual pursuit, expresses her magical work through physical fertility and emotional nurturance, and embodies goddesses and the Divine Feminine. In contrast with this ideal, the real physical women in traditional magic are often (although not always) childless, generally intellectual, and identify with male roles or male-defined female roles. Our individual temperaments lead us in various directions; what we have in common is the gender assumption that we will act as Magical Woman, however we have responded to that assumption. We can recognize commonality of experience without leveling difference.

In my effort to articulate Magia Femina I have gone on a journey in which I invoked six spirits. Each invocation grew out of the last, and each was inspired by my responses to my situation and what I had learned.

When I was afraid, I made this invocation: *Come to me, Lady Tradition, and help me to speak of my magic.* I asked Lady Tradition, "Why do I have the feeling that I am not at home in the magical traditions in which I have been initiated?"

When I was uncomfortable, I made this invocation: *Come to me, Lady History, and show me the origins of my magic.* I asked Lady History, "How did Western Traditional Magic come to view women as it does?"

When I was in need of deep healing, I made this invocation: *Come to me, Lady Philosophy, and show me the foundations of my magic.* I asked Lady Philosophy two questions: "Why does Western Traditional Magic view the fundamental person as male?" and "How can I understand myself to be a woman with reason and will?"

When I was angry, I made this invocation: *Come to me, Lady Science, and bring me the truth of my sex.* I asked Lady Science, "What is the scientific definition of a woman?"

When I was sad, I made this invocation: *Come to me, Lady Culture, and show me the standing of my gender.* I asked Lady Culture, "What is the cultural definition of a woman?"

When I was humbled, I made this invocation: *Come to me, Lady Theology, and show me the female divine.* I asked Lady Theology, "How can I understand myself to reflect the divine universe?"

Listening to men discuss their experience of magic, I do not find that the magical system itself and their place in it inspire fear, discomfort, need, anger, sorrow, or humility. What I hear instead is that magic inspires in them exaltation, self-knowledge, awe, and power.

I want to be able to have the experience men have in Western Traditional Magic. I make the invocation: *Come to me, Lady Magic, and show me a new shape to my magic.*

As Lady Tradition did, Lady Magic comes to me in the room where I sit, at the desk of a cabin in the woods of an island. She wears a robe spangled with stars and a crown like the sun on her head. In one hand she holds a cup, in the other a sword. Her gaze captures mine with a challenge. She seems to be saying: *Well, magician, what do you want me to do about it?*

I say to her, "How can I understand myself as an instance of the divine universe?"

Lady Magic laughs and swings her sword around her head once. In that move I am cut off from all the world I have known, and at the same time, I become the universe.

EVE KADMON

When we do not challenge gender on the Tree of Life, the unarticulated, implied template seeps through, with every sphere reverting to the default male gender. A vision of Qabbalah based on the emerging postmodern gender narrative would explicitly call out the dual-gendered nature of all the spheres (see illustration 9 on the next page):

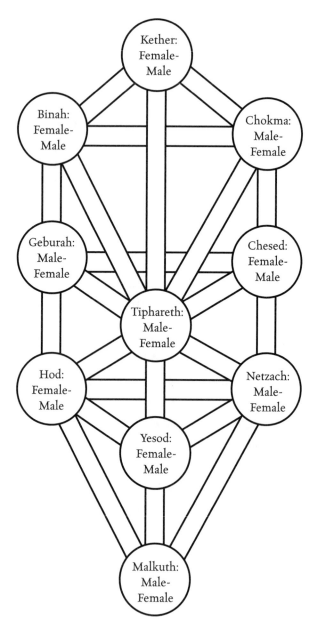

Illustration 9: Tree of Life Eve Kadmon One

This formulation places me on the tree and grants my sex access to all the spheres of the tree for the first time in my magical career. This tree makes it possible to imagine myself in the same way male magicians can imagine themselves, as reflection of the sacred cosmos. Eve Kadmon is the universe:

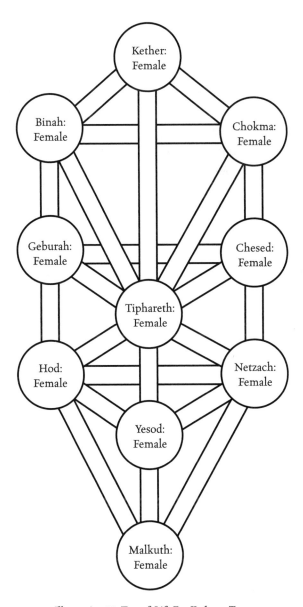

Illustration 10: Tree of Life Eve Kadmon Two

Lady Magic has shown me the shape of the universe as female and I am eager to explore it. I say to her, "What ritual permits me to stand in the place of Eve Kadmon?"

The swing of her sword created a kind of enclosure. The magic she calls to me to perform is ritual performed with other women, and only women.

Woman-Centered Religion

I belong to a coven, a magical lodge, and a fraternal order. While the nouns "coven" and "lodge" do not imply any particular gender of their members, "fraternal" does. A fraternal order is a band of brothers or people who feel brotherly to one another. The fraternal order Freemasonry served as the model for the Victorian-Edwardian magical groups. However, while Masons accepted only men into the fraternity, the modern lodges accepted women as well.

In cultures organized around men's interests, women relate to men, or to each other through men. Women historically have escaped the pressure to focus on men's needs by forming groups or societies that admit only women, for example in women's colleges or in the monastic system.

The move Lady Magic has made—to enclose the magic of women—permits us to withdraw from the pressure to conform to particular roles. In this magic, every role is available to women, and the shape of the entire universe is a female shape.

Why construct ritual that imagines the universe in female terms? Why construct ritual that calls for only women to conduct the rites? Isn't that as unbalanced as ritual that imagines only male forces in the universe, and isn't it unfair to exclude men from the practice?

Men-only rituals, and rituals in which women are referred to as men and as brothers, have dominated Western Traditional Magic. There are groups, such as the Open Source Order of the Golden Dawn, that have consciously worked to bring a more equitable and accurate gender balance to the ritual work. However, even in those rituals which introduce gender-balancing language, the forces of the universe are still imagined in male terms—lord, god, creator—and descriptions of the magician still lapse into using the word "man" to describe the human operator. We are so used to male-dominated imagery that it does not strike us as unusual or inaccurate.

Humans understand the forces of the universe differently in every age, through the filters of the perceptions of our time. Take for example the occult understanding of the sun as male—the sacrificed or dying and reborn god, the power that inseminates the fertile female earth and is reflected in the mirroring female moon. The most mystical occultist cannot escape the knowledge that the sun is on one level a ball of hydrogen gas which has burned for billions of years and will continue to burn for billions more. The most hard-boiled scientist must also acknowledge that the sun is the manifestation of those universal forces which have combined to create life on this planet.

To call the sun male, or female, is not to name a fact about the sun on either the hydrogen ball level or the manifestation of universal force level. It is a metaphor, a human understanding of an essentially inhuman force, a mirror through which we catch a glimpse of the reality which is always vaster than our ability to comprehend it.

Even within the world of human metaphor, the idea that the sun is male is not a human universal, although it is entrenched in Western Traditional Magic. Other cultures have viewed the sun differently. The religion of Shinto preserves a very old understanding of the sun as the female *kami* (spirit) Amaterasu-omikami, the beneficent source of life. Exploring these stories within the context of Western Traditional Magic again shifts the focus away from the men as the most powerful creatures in the universe, toward an understanding that women also embody the power of life.

It is true that this move to enclose women's magic excludes male imagery and assumes that the operators are women (although nothing prevents men from performing these rituals—this is published work). Woman-only work invariably garners objections that because the work does not include male imagery, or men, it is of necessity inaccurate and unbalanced. This objection did not occur when female imagery and women were excluded or underrepresented in traditional magic. The objection is the objection of privilege—bluntly, we are used to men being at the center of magic, and a magic that places women at its center will draw the ire of men and women who uphold traditional patriarchal systems.

For that reason it is critical to recognize that women who band together to perform woman-only magic can expect to experience opposition. When women in Western Traditional Magic move into woman-only circles we can expect other traditional magicians, both women and men, will criticize their work. Brothers in other magical groups, and the women's own partners, will pressure the women to let men into the group. This routinely happens to women's circles in the Goddess or women's spirituality movement, even in overtly feminist circles, and there is no reason not to expect this pressure to emerge among traditional magicians.

This pressure does not only come from men. Women upholding traditional culture may also object to the focus on women and may press to include men. Even women who are comfortable with woman-only space may experience the impulse to include and welcome their male partners and friends. I certainly do—I would love to share the rituals I have written with the men in my life and struggle continually with myself to maintain the enclosure.

Many women theologians have been working for several decades to revive and create more positive images of the divine feminine. Women in the monotheistic religions appropriate female-oriented language and imagery to find the feminine in the singular divine, as in Mother-Father. Women in the neo-Pagan and women's spirituality movements create new cosmologies and new stories that bring out different facets of the female divine.

We have discussed the objections raised when women create woman-centered ritual and work in woman-only groups. It also happens that women as well as men, feminists and non-feminists, raise questions and objections when facing a female-only cosmology. Why not create a cosmology that balances male and female? Isn't that more accurate and more fair? Isn't a female-only cosmology just enacting a version of the unjust exclusion of a male-only cosmology?

A gender-balanced cosmology is important work to do. However, there is a place for a female-only cosmology. It acts as a corrective to the male-only cosmologies which surround us. It provides us a safe space and helps us to begin to heal from the violence of the cosmologies that imagine raping and killing goddesses. A female-only cosmology helps us to imagine ourselves into the act of creation. We aren't fighting for a place in this story; it includes us, in every facet, automatically.

It also helps us see the female power in its own right. We are accustomed to viewing the female through the lens of the male. It seems odd to us that a woman, or a goddess, should stand alone, not as the father's daughter or spouse or consort to the male, but as a divine being who has no male relations. When the cosmology includes only female forms, the relationship to male power drops out of the picture. We have an opportunity to explore what each aspect of the divine looks and acts like when that aspect is female and powerful on her own.

Enclosure, as Carol Lee Flinders so wisely pointed out, turns out to be critically important. The experience of working ritual that envisions the universe and the magician as female is empowering and healing. I work a number of magical systems and groups that include men, systems that imagine some, most, or all forces of the universe as male, but I carry myself differently in the world now because I have stepped through rites where the face of fire, sun, creator, cosmos, magician is a female face.

AUTHORIZING WOMEN'S MAGIC

Lady Magic has called me to create rituals for women to perform together, based on women-centered theology. I say to her, "What power authorizes me to create women's magical theology and ritual?"

She swings her sword again, invoking with a voice like the birth-cry of the universe: "Seshat!"

I know this goddess. It does not surprise me that she is the divine power Lady Magic invokes to aid me. It is natural to turn to Egyptian religion to find sources of power for women's practice. Egyptian magic has been important to Western Traditional Magic for thousands of years.

Egyptian magic developed in parallel with the Western tradition. In contrast to Greek and Hellenic culture, where magic was seen as marginal to mainstream religion, Egyptian magic was a central and respected part of religious practice (Ritner 1997). Egyptian culture in every era included gendered roles, but did not limit women's capacities in the way the Mediterranean cultures did, and Egyptian history includes many examples of accomplished women. For these reasons turning to the Egyptian deity forms that embody magic can empower us to create new theologies that revision women's magical capacities.

Seshat presents us with an image of the woman as magician, not as a pale imitation of male magic, but as ensouling magic in her own right.

The Historical Seshat

Here is an overview of what we know about the historical attributes of Seshat. Her titles include:

- She Who Is Foremost in the House of Books
- Mistress of Builders
- Mistress of the Temple Library and Keeper of Royal Annals

Seshat is depicted as a woman wearing a panther skin, often with a seven-pointed star on her head. Some think this star is a cannabis leaf representing the fiber used to make rope, one of the tools she uses. Rev. Dave Dean of the Kemetic Orthodox faith reports Seshat has told the Kemetic clergy that it is a closed lotus (Dean nd).

Thoth is depicted as Seshat's husband, brother, or father, but not her son. Some scholars refer to Seshat as a personification of an abstract concept, citing that there was no specific temple dedicated to Seshat. However, the artisans at Deir-el-Medina kept shrines to both Seshat and Thoth (Lesko 1999).

Seshat is attested from the Old Kingdom to the New Kingdom. In the Old Kingdom, she is mentioned as recording animals seized as booty. In the Second Dynasty, she is depicted stretching the cord to measure the temple foundation with the fifth pharaoh of the dynasty,

Khasekhemwy (Wilkinson 2003). In the Middle Kingdom, she is mentioned again recording captives and tribute goods. In the New Kingdom, she is depicted inscribing the name of pharaoh on the Persea tree, writing on leaves representing years of a pharaoh's life, and recording the pharaoh's jubilees. In this function, she holds a notched palm branch, the hieroglyph for years (Lesko 1999).

There is an indication of overlap between Nephthys and Seshat. Pyramid Text: PT 616 says, "Nephthys has collected all your members for you in this her name of Seshat, Lady of Builders" (Faulkner 2007).

As goddess of scribes, her function is similar to that of the Babylonian goddess Nisaba, patron of scribes and of the grain storehouse. There is an obvious connection between the origin of writing and counting, as both in Egypt and Mesopotamia the oldest function of the scribe was to account for the numbers and movements of goods.

From these references and images, modern scholars and enthusiasts construct Seshat as a goddess of writing, census, libraries, astronomy, the dead, and wisdom.

Why does the same goddess represent two such different things—writing (counting and recording) and architecture? One possible connection is through counting. Writing originated as a way to track the numbers of things and there is certainly measuring in architecture. However, to better understand the connection, it is helpful to understand something about how the ancient Egyptians depicted and understood magic.

Great of Magic

The pharoanic word for magic was *heka*. Heka is a god attested in all periods of Egyptian history. Prophets of the god appear in the Old Kingdom, there was a temple or mansion of Heka at Heliopolis, and he appears in the necropolis in Memphis.

In the Coffin Texts he appears in the solar bark, re-enacting with each sunrise the moment of creation by invoking the separation of earth and heaven and sometimes performing this separation himself. Re defeats Apophis each night through the use of Heka.

With that shifting quality of Egyptian gods, Heka also appears as a force that can step into and empower a deity. In several Egyptian texts Heka appears as a ba, bird-soul, of Re. Furthermore, that power can shift into the body of the priest-magician. In the "Book of the Heavenly Cow," the ritualist says, "I am that pure magician who is in the mouth and body of Re ... I am his ba, the Magician" (Ritner 1997).

Any of the deities of Egypt carrying the title "Great of Magic," such as Isis, are inhabited by the god Heka. Thoth as the god of writing handles the sacred power of words and is himself "excellent of magic."

At her temple in Dendera, the goddess Hathor receives the gifts of magic from Heka. Here, however, Heka is accompanied by Seshat as his ka, or body-double. The force that steps into Hathor and ensouls her at Dendera is Seshat, "who copies texts" and is "possessor of spells, bearing her writings which are in her mouth." (Ritner 1997).

It makes sense, then, that the power of writing and of speaking that creates the world is also the power that creates the physical temple. At Dendera, Seshat also serves the function of Heka as the ensouling power of magic.

Seshat and Women's Speech

Lady Magic has created the space for me to experience myself as female and divine. She has invoked Seshat, the Woman Magician. While Western philosophy equates the phallus with the logos and the ability to speak, Sheshat authorizes my speech as a woman magician. Sheshat steps into me; I feel her in my heart, working to create two new magical instruments:

- a female centered-cosmology, and
- a series of initiatory rituals.

The initiatory rituals invoke Seshat as the ba in the heart of every woman magician. Lady Magic has led me to a new magical system, the Order of the Sisters of Sheshat.

Evaluating the Magic

In Western Traditional Magic, the goal of the system is to bring the magician into an awareness of being divine by working toward balance and wholeness.

Because women and men have different roles in Western culture, our path to wholeness differs. For men, the path to wholeness is well defined: bring out the feminine within, by developing personal intuition, acknowledging the divinity within real women, and worshipping embodied female deity. The tradition puts the priestess on the altar, allowing both women and men to relate to deity in female form.

Women in Western Traditional Magic embody the Divine Feminine and the Human Feminine. As we have seen, the male magician can project the female within onto real women around him. The priestess embodies intuition and the ability to create with the body. For the heterosexual magician, the Goddess becomes a lover, and the woman who embodies the Goddess can become a physical lover.

As priestesses embodying human intuition, women can act to assist men on their path to wholeness, helping them to find the intuition within themselves. As priestesses embodying the Goddess, women can receive the worship directed at the Goddess. This position has its own power; it's heady to hold the mysteries of the universe within, to stand in the position of teacher, to have the priest kneel at your feet.

People who are intersexual, not strictly heterosexual, not white, differently abled, or not young don't map easily into the coupling of young white male magician and his young white female priestess-muse.

To undergo the magical journey in the tradition, women have to date stepped into the position held by men. The power to think, to act, to move in the world and make changes in it, has been a male power, and the woman who takes on that power becomes an honorary man, either an implied man as in the Golden Dawn rituals, or actually called a man and brother as in the O.T.O. The image of the whole person, the realized magician, is a man who has integrated the feminine.

Western Traditional Magic developed in a period of European and American history when women were achieving the right to vote and moving into higher education. A hundred years later, as Western culture changes and women increasingly wield the power to think, to act, to move in the world and make changes in it, this understanding of the magical path becomes increasingly dated.

What happens when we take the stance that a woman magician's path to magical wholeness is to integrate the male within? Because of the still unequal balance of power in the world, just flipping the gender of the practitioner doesn't quite work. For example, we could place the priest on the altar and worship him, but the Abrahamic religions have long valorized the power of the male divine, so worshipping the male divine doesn't act to balance the power of male and female. Witchcraft has moved farthest in exploring the suppressed sexual and nurturing aspects of the male divine: the God becomes loving son to the divine mother and consort to the divine lover.

Many Ceremonial Magic rituals import Hebrew words of power describing the male divine: Yahweh, Adonai. One option is to import Hebrew words of power describing the female divine, notably Asherah; this is an approach that the Open Source Order of the Golden Dawn takes. We can explore the formula of Aleph Shin Resh He as well as the formula of Yod He Vau He. Here again we work to bring the suppressed and forgotten female power of deity into balance with the male deity who expanded to absorb the universe; our work pushes against that huge and powerful God, fighting to create a space in which the Goddess can stand.

We can evolve a system in which women relate to male magicians who embody the divine lover, and women and men relate to the male divine as nurturing father. These are important moves to make. However, on the magical journey toward wholeness the act of projection does not work the same way for women—if we project the ability to act, to exercise will, it's still the male magician, or the male in ourselves, that changes.

In all these moves we are still fighting for a place to stand, a way to think of the female, of women, of ourselves, as being powerful not just in relationship to men or male power, but standing alone. What does the magical universe look like when we don't have to spend all our energy fighting to stay standing? What does the magical universe look like when there is no gender? Because we inhabit a fiercely gendered culture it is almost impossible to see a universe without gender. When we take out the filter "male-female," our language describes the inanimate—everything becomes it, or a thing. The ungendered universe seems inhuman. And when we take out the female, because Western philosophy for so long has imagined the default person as male, we eventually fall back into the old patterns of mind which assume that the magician is a he with a phallus.

To look out into a universe that is female, we have to call it female. To look on ourselves as woman magicians, we have to call ourselves women. This is the move that Lady Magic has made—she has created a space where we can see every power in the universe as being female. We can place ourselves on every aspect of the tree. We can undertake every magical act. Perhaps most importantly, we can do this together, acting in groups to support each other on our magical journeys.

The Order of the Sisters of Seshat arose in the milieu of operative magicians in the Pacific Northwest in the first decade of the twenty-first century. Golden Dawn, O.T.O., and Witchcraft groups in this region developed actively experimental approaches to magic. In particular the women in these groups have supported one another, have met in woman-only discussions, and have written woman-only rituals. In the grand tradition of women's creative communities, while I have written the rituals and shaped the form of the order, my work has been supported by a less visible but vibrant and supportive network of other women doing similar work. Some of these women have been kind enough to work this material with me, providing input, energy, and enthusiasm. In turn I have worked on other rituals with them, returning my energy and enthusiasm for their work. I am profoundly grateful to live within a nurturing web of magical community with a strong component of women's community.

PART TWO

SISTERS
OF SESHAT

Illustration 11: Image of Seshat

Seshat, woman magician,
Mistress of the scribes, lady of counting,
Mistress of the library, lady of records,
Mistress of the temple, lady of builders,
speak to us of times gone past and times to come,
bring to us our history, the stories of our foremothers,
teach us to preserve our stories for our daughters and their daughters,
lay for us the foundations of the temple where we may meet with our sisters,
bring to us your gifts of magic as women and magicians.

THE ORDER OF THE SISTERS OF SESHAT

The Order of the Sisters of Seshat is a sororal order in Western Traditional Magic. The order combines elements of Masonic, Golden Dawn, Thelemic, Wiccan, neo-Pagan, and women's spirituality rituals.

The Order of the Sisters of Seshat owes a debt to Freemasonry. Any Western order that establishes the foundations of a temple will resonate with Freemasonic building techniques and symbology. Freemasonic imagery in turn builds on ancient correspondences with Egyptian temple construction.

The Sisters of Seshat adopt the Masonic women's ritual movement, which establishes the continents Asia, Africa, Europe and America, as well as the gesture of the hand on heart. The Sisters of Seshat independently developed the use of a spindle, which is a formal tool in some traditions of women's Freemasonry.

The order does not adopt the Masonic offices of Master and Matron, Wardens, Inspectresses, and so on. Instead the order adopts the Golden Dawn officer structure, which in turn adapted the ancient Greek offices of the Eleusinian Mysteries. These officers are Hierophant, Hegemon, Hierus, Dadouchos, Stolistes, and Sentinel.

The Hierophant is in charge of the ritual. The Hegemon balances the ritual's energies. The Hierus anchors the ritual's energies. Hegemon and Hierus act as the main assistants to the Hierophant, and together they form the main three officers. The Dadouchos and Stolistes move specific kinds of energies in the ritual, often act together, and are subsidiary officers. Finally, if the group has enough members, one can act as the Sentinel, guarding the door of the temple to make sure no one interrupts the ritual.

Women drawn to the rituals of the Sisters of Seshat may already be grounded in one of the lines of Western Traditional Magic, and be learned in Wiccan, Golden Dawn, Aurum Solis, or Thelemic magic. It is also perfectly possible to undertake the series of Sisters of Seshat initiations as a first magical experience.

Any woman can join the Order simply by doing the rituals. There is no lineage or central authority. A Sister of Seshat can work on her own or can form or join a group to work the initiation rituals. The initiations require five officers plus one candidate, or six women total.

Most groups will need to begin as a bootstrap group—that is, the members take turns initiating each other. A group that has established itself can bring new initiates into the group who have not previously taken an office in the initiation.

The Order of the Sisters of Seshat does not specify a group structure or bylaws. Women who perform these rituals are free to structure themselves in any way appropriate for the group. Here are some options: The group may elect leaders, or a leader. The group may function by consensus, with every member participating in decision making. One experienced woman can act as Hierophant for all the initiation rituals, or members may rotate in and out of the Hierophant role, or the group may permit a woman to take the Hierophant role only when she has participated in one or more other officer roles.

The group may decide to meet weekly, monthly, quarterly. The group may focus only on the initiation rituals, or alternate doing a group ritual with a group discussion of one of the study course books.

A group may decide that the same members will work together through the initiation rituals until they are all complete, or may bring new people in whenever they apply and are accepted. The group may bring in new members by decision of the organizer alone, by a voting majority, or by agreeing unanimously. Just note that it is important that the women can all work together in a ritual setting. Deciding who is in and out of a group is an area of potential conflict for any group!

However the group functions, there are some cautionary notes here. First, the group should do the initiation rituals as written at least once before changing them. This magic is not a pretend or symbolic kind, it moves real energy. The rituals are built with safeguards, checks and balances, designed to move the group and the candidate into an altered state and safely back out again.

For the same reason, the initiations should be experienced by a candidate in sequence—earth, moon, Mercury, Venus, sun. The nature of a bootstrap group is that a woman may act as officer in an initiation she hasn't yet taken as a candidate. However, it is probably wise not to get too far ahead. If a woman has only taken the moon initiation, she probably should not yet act as officer in the Venus initiation.

Larger groups may find that there are more than seven women in the room. In this case, the sorors of the order may sit and observe the ritual. All sorors should participate in the closing ritual, eating cookies and drinking wine or juice. Sorors not acting as officers can also participate in the City of Ladies narration in the Mercury initiation, the memorial gathering in the Venus initiation, and the chanting in the sun initiation.

EGYPTIAN DEITIES
AND THE EGYPTIAN SOUL

The Victorian magicians adopted Egyptian deities into the rituals of their orders, and this method of working with deity continues in the Ceremonial Magic orders today. It's somewhat different from the neo-Pagan methodologies that developed later. The magician visualizes the deity and steps into the deity form. Officers in rituals embody particular deities, and sometimes more than one deity per ritual. The officers walk around the temple and say their lines as per the script of the ritual, all the time understanding themselves to be enfolded in the aura of the deity. It is important in doing this kind of work to be sure to put the deity down at the end of the ritual!

The cosmology of Sisters of Seshat explains the relationship of some of the deities to the system. However, deities will show up in the rituals who were not explained in the cosmology.

The popular contemporary Western conception of "soul" is that of a singular force that inhabits the physical body. This is derived from a Greek understanding of the soul as *psyche*, a word which now means "mind" but earlier meant "breath." For Plato, the psyche had three parts, breath, reason, and desire, each located in different parts of the body. Western Traditional Magic adapted the Qabbalistic understandings of the soul as having more parts: the nefesh, animal soul or subconsciousness; ruach, consciousness; neshamah, higher soul; and the chiah, connected to every living thing.

Egyptian religion predates Platonic philosophy and differs from Hebrew religion. The Egyptian soul has numerous parts that do not map neatly onto either the Qabbalistic soul or the Greek soul. The Egyptian understanding of the whole complex of the person included the body, name, heart, shade, and parts described as the akh, ba, and ka (Bell 1997). Every schoolchild knows the importance Egyptians placed on the physical body, which was mummified after death. The akh was the part of the soul associated with the recently dead and could be called on to intercede in the affairs of the living.

The parts of the soul that we work with in the rituals of the Sisters of Seshat are the ba and the ka. The ka is the shaping force of the physical body. It is the part of our existence that was given to us by our ancestors, in our family line, and which we pass on when we bear children. In the personal ritual we acknowledge the ka, which enables us to physically move in the world.

The ba was often depicted as a bird with a human head. It can be thought of as a spiritual body which brings power to the physical body. Seshat is the goddess of magic. When the magician visualizes Seshat stepping into her body, Seshat empowers the ba of the magician with magical power.

PRACTICAL CONSIDERATIONS

The philosophy on which this system is set up is that it is better to do the ritual whenever possible than to wait until conditions are perfect. Conditions are seldom perfect for women. So many other tasks compete for our time and energy, and while men magicians sometimes work alone or with women as helpers, women don't usually have any helpers except for each other. Do the rituals when and where you can. It is the doing itself that is important.

I've set up these rituals in an O.T.O. temple and in a basement recreation room. In the temple, the question occurred to us, do we circumambulate outside or inside the altars? Where possible the circumambulation should be outside the altars. In the recreation room, this didn't even occur to us, as there was only enough space to move inside the altars.

The recreation room had just enough space to set up the Temple Ritual. If you don't have that much space, improvising is perfectly appropriate. You can use the furniture already in the room for the elemental altars. The repast altar could be staged on a tray and then just brought in at the end of the ritual (although you should try to use the same tray every time, as it represents the energy of the temple in Malkuth). In the moon initiation, you can combine the three altars (Altar of the Tree, Altar of the Journey, Altar of the Spring) into one central altar to save space. Remember, particularly when it comes to setting up a ritual in a particular space, you can change it so that it works!

Temple Furnishings

The biggest pieces of furniture needed are chairs and tables. Every officer and sister attending the ritual will need a chair, but they can be any chairs. We've mostly used folding chairs. Chairs for the officers can be draped with cloth (shawls work) to mark them as thrones for the officers and the goddess forms. The tables can be any end or coffee tables in the house or temple. I've used tables that were furnishings in a ceremonial temple, and also used a set of wooden TV trays that store in a corner.

The ritual items can fit in one or two craft storage boxes. Almost every item can come from a fabric or craft store, and again, you can use items you already have, like candle holders. Any of the tools specified—bell, mirror, sword—can be loaned to the group by a member or can be obtained by the group for its own use.

The specialty items that you can't often get at the craft store are the serpent crown and the sword. You can order serpent crowns online from Egyptian trinket stores, or you can make a serpent with clay and fix it to a cloth band. Light, portable, and inexpensive swords are widely available on the Internet—search on "fraternal swords" and "souvenir swords." If you prefer a hefty sword, medieval reconstructions are available online also or through Society for Creative Anachronisms vendors.

The egregore object should be something special. An egregore is the energy that the group generates that gives it a special feel. Any group that does the initiation rituals is simultaneously tapping and nourishing the egregore of the Order of the Sisters of Seshat. The object will be touched by every officer at the start and end of every ritual, so it should be reasonably sized, and solid. A small statue or a stone globe works well.

Notes on specific tools:

Small altars: Wooden TV trays or any small tables. They don't have to match.

Altar cloths: These can be as bought or made, and can be as simple as a fabric scrap or felt square, or as elegant as a handmade and embroidered art object.

Candles: Can be pillar candles, small votives, or tea lights. Each candle should have a holder, dish or tile to sit on to protect the altar and floor where it is placed from wax dripping and burning.

Aspergillum: This is a little stick used to dip into water and sprinkle people, places, and objects with it. This can be a branch of an herb (hyssop is traditional) or a tool such as a honey dipper.

Lamens for the goddess forms: Lamens can be created from disks of wood or printed out and backed with cardboard. They can bear the image of the goddess, the name of the goddess, the hieroglyph of the goddess, or whatever invokes the power of the goddess for the officer and the group. They should have a hole punched through so that a cord can be strung that will allow officers to wear the lamens around the neck.

Initiatory tokens: Many craft shops carry small wooden disks. You can use white and black paint (I like acrylic, which dries quickly) for the base colors and then either paint the planetary symbol or draw it with colored pen.

Diagrams: These can be images printed out and pasted to poster board. The diagrams can be laid on top of the altars or set on a chair or easel next to the altar.

Image of Seshat: These are easy to find online. The best image to use is one that depicts the goddess holding her tools, so that the sisters can look at the image to remind themselves of the sign of Seshat—left hand held out low, right hand held out high. The image can be printed out and pasted to poster board or framed in a certificate frame.

Temple Robes

Nearly every magical system recommends that the magician sew or purchase a special robe to wear while performing the rituals in the system. Usually the robe is specified to be black, occasionally white. Sisters of Seshat are free to wear any robes they wish. Egyptian style robes, such as Arabian thobes or Egyptian galabiyas, work well with a system that invokes Egyptian deity.

The magician herself can sew a T-robe—called that because when you lay it flat on the ground, it looks like a T.

One very easy way to make a robe is to buy fabric, fold it in half, cut a semi-circle in the middle of the fold for the neckline, and then belt it. Cutting the edges with pinking shears stops the fabric from unraveling. You can also tie or sew shawls and scarves together.

Officers wear identifying colors over their robes:

Hierophant	White
Hegemon	Yellow
Hierus	Black
Stolistes	Blue
Dadouchos	Red
Sentinel	Black

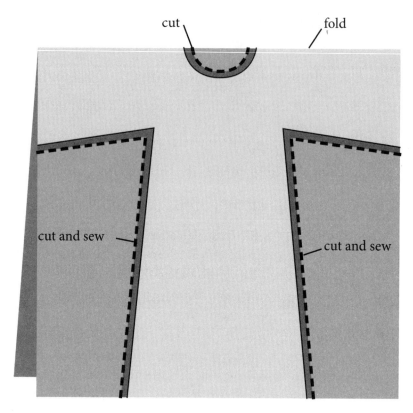

Illustration 12: T Robe

Colors may be stoles, such as choir stoles (available online), or a sash or scarf can be tied around the waist or neck. A simple way to bring the color into the robe is to buy a length of ribbon, trim, or cord from a fabric store and tie it around the waist. The cord could be kept by the group. Each member could also bring the appropriate cord and keep it, and start a collection of her own cords commemorating the officer roles she has held.

Initiation Scripts

Each group will need to make photocopies of the rituals for each participant in the ritual. When these initiations call for prose to be read while movement is happening in the temple, usually one officer will read while another officer or the candidate circumambulates. If the circumambulation is complete before the text is fully read, the person doing the circumambulation waits where she started until the text is completed. If the text is complete before the number of circumambulations called for by the ritual has been completed, the circumambulations continue in silence until they are complete.

Feasting and Communion

Each ritual ends with the closing of the temple, which involves setting up a repast altar where the sorors congregate to eat cakes (cookies) and drink juice or wine, toasting Seshat. This is a ritual communion which grounds the elements in the temple and affirms the connection of the sorors to the egregore of the group, the egregore of the order, and Seshat.

The sorors should if at all possible eat together after the ritual is complete. Sorors can hold a potluck at the site of the ritual or can go out to eat together. Sharing a full meal is a form of feasting, which permits socializing, connects sisters to one another, and has the effect of grounding the energy of the ritual for each individual participant.

Empowerment

The focus of these rituals is not on the grandeur of the temple or the difficulty of the ritual. One group may print out the ritual and read the script as they go, while another group may choose to create a grand temple and to rehearse and memorize the ritual. Whatever the physical expression of the ritual and the experience of the members, the rituals focus on the relationship of the magician to the energies involved and the other members of the group.

As the initial group performed these rituals, the women often asked if they were performing an action correctly—were the chairs in the right places, were they facing the right direction? The permanent ongoing answer is: however you are doing it, you are doing it right.

PLANETARY INITIATIONS
BACKGROUND NOTES

There are five initiations in the Order of the Sisters of Seshat system, each corresponding to a planet associated with the esoteric Tree of Life. The initiations draw on the symbols and attributions of the tree.

The esoteric Tree of Life is built on several thousand years of Western esoteric thought. The Pythagorean philosophical system worked with spiritual attributes of numbers. The neo-Platonic philosophical system framed those numbers as planetary spheres and traced the descent of the soul from spirit, through the stars, through the seven planets known to the ancients, to material embodiment on earth. Jewish Qabbalah attached Hebrew names to each of the neo-Platonic spheres and arranged them in a tree form, invoking the ancient images of the Tree of Life. The spheres of the esoteric Tree of Life also carry all the Hermetic attributions of the planets, including colors and incense.

This table graphs the number, planet, Hebrew name, and primary color of each of the spheres.

Tree of Life Correspondances			
Sphere	*Planet*	*Hebrew Name*	*Color*
1	Spirit	Kether	White
2	Stars	Chokmah	Gray
3	Saturn	Binah	Black
4	Jupiter	Chesed	Blue
5	Mars	Geburah	Red
6	Sun	Tiphareth	Yellow
7	Venus	Netzach	Green
8	Mercury	Hod	Orange
9	Moon	Yesod	Silver
10	Earth	Malkuth	Citrine, olive, russet, black

The tree links the planetary spheres through their paths, each of which corresponds to a planet, astrological sign, or element. This table graphs the paths of the tree, the number of the path, the spheres it

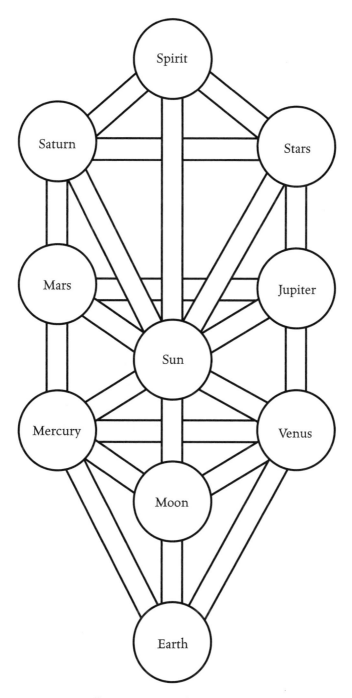

Illustration 13: Tree of Life as Planets

links (with both neo-Platonic association and Hebrew name), and its attribution.

In the neo-Platonic philosophical system, the soul's task is to rise up from the earth, through the planets, to its true home in the stars. This understanding underlies many rituals in Western Traditional Magic. For this reason the initiation rituals start on earth, or Malkuth, and move up the tree through the paths beginning with the 32nd path from the earth to the moon.

The Sisters of Seshat initiation system most closely resembles that of the Golden Dawn, which enacts the candidate's movement along each of the paths by laying out a physical journey in the temple. The Golden Dawn initiations are each associated with an element: Neophyte, the first initiation; Zelator, earth; Theoricus, air; Practicus, fire; Philosophus, water; and Portal, all four elements and spirit. The Sisters of Seshat initiation system acknowledges the elements in our Temple Ritual and in our initiations. However, our initiations primarily focus on the planetary sphere, with its associated colors, numbers, and deities, and on the symbology of the attribution of the paths that link the spheres.

Here is the pattern of the Sisters of Seshat initiatory system:

Earth initiation: Establishes the temple in Malkuth, invokes the shadow tree (Qliphoth), re-establishes the Tree of Life in Malkuth.

Moon initiation: Establishes the temple in Malkuth, moves along the 32nd path to the temple in Yesod.

Mercury initiation: Establishes the temple in Malkuth, moves along the 31st and 30th paths to the temple in Hod.

Venus initiation: Establishes the temple in Malkuth, moves along the 29th, 28th, and 27th paths to the temple in Netzach.

Sun initiation: Establishes the temple in Malkuth, moves along the 26th, 25th, and 24th paths to the temple in Tiphareth.

In Western Traditional Magic, the magician who has journeyed up the tree to Tiphareth then engages in a private working to invoke the higher self, or holy guardian angel (or daimon or Genius) who provides an influx of divine power which illuminates the magician's path. The

Tree of Life Paths					
Path	From (Neo-Platonic)	To (Neo-Platonic)	From (Hebrew)	To (Hebrew)	Attribution
11	Spirit	Stars	Kether	Chokmah	Air
12	Spirit	Saturn	Kether	Binah	Mercury
13	Spirit	Sun	Kether	Tiphareth	Moon
14	Stars	Saturn	Chokmah	Binah	Venus
15	Stars	Sun	Chokmah	Tiphareth	Aries
16	Stars	Jupiter	Chokmah	Chesed	Taurus
17	Saturn	Sun	Binah	Tiphareth	Gemini
18	Saturn	Mars	Binah	Geburah	Cancer
19	Jupiter	Mars	Chesed	Geburah	Leo
20	Jupiter	Sun	Chesed	Tiphareth	Virgo
21	Jupiter	Venus	Chesed	Netzach	Jupiter
22	Mars	Sun	Geburah	Tiphareth	Libra
23	Mars	Mercury	Geburah	Hod	Water
24	Sun	Venus	Tiphareth	Netzach	Scorpio
25	Sun	Moon	Tiphareth	Yesod	Sagittarius
26	Mercury	Sun	Hod	Tiphareth	Capricorn
27	Mercury	Venus	Hod	Netzach	Mars
28	Venus	Moon	Netzach	Yesod	Aquarius
29	Venus	Earth	Netzach	Malkuth	Pisces
30	Mercury	Moon	Hod	Yesod	Sun
31	Mercury	Earth	Hod	Malkuth	Fire
32	Moon	Earth	Yesod	Malkuth	Saturn

Golden Dawn Portal initiation bridges the first or outer order and the second or inner order. The Sisters of Seshat initiations here conclude with the entrance to the temple of the sun, completing the journey of the outer order. At that point the magician is prepared to create her own unique magic or personal inner order.

STUDY COURSE

Women are busy. We hold day jobs, keep house, raise children, care for animals, raise food, cook and store it. If we have any time left, we socialize with our friends and family, throw parties, make crafts, make art and music, rest and enjoy life. Where on earth are we going to find the time to shoehorn in a magical study program?

Soror Inde Seraphina wrote a description of performing an Enochian call in the space of a toddler nap (Seraphina 2009). We do what we can when we can. It isn't necessary to read a single book before doing the personal ritual or any of the temple initiations. However, any time we are able to put into study repays us in increased understanding and appreciation of the rituals.

No single book covers every aspect of magical practice in any of the aspects of the tradition. Western Traditional Magic is a literate endeavor, with knowledge passed through the written record. It is also a feature of the Hermetic traditions that reading is a form of initiation in and of itself.

For those of us who are inspired to undertake a study course, here is an outline that will deepen understanding of the Sisters of Seshat magical system. The books chosen for this canon were all written by women. There are many books available written by women and men together, and by men on their own, which should be included in any magical study course. However, this order is informed by women's voices, and we are fortunate enough to have quite a few of them in print. We are so accustomed to listening to men, and to interpreting women's work based on men's appraisals, that it is an informative (and perhaps transformative) effort to read the women themselves.

Histories

The work of women historians and academics is often ignored or appropriated by others and rarely enters into canon. For that reason it is especially satisfying to study the works of Frances Yates, who pioneered academic investigation into Renaissance magic as a subject of serious study. Her works include *Giordano Bruno and the Hermetic Tradition*, *The*

Art of Memory, The Rosicrucian Enlightenment, The Theater of the World, and *The Occult Philosophy in the Elizabethan Age.*

Histories of turn-of-the-century esotericism include Alex Owen's two works. *The Darkened Room* discusses spiritualism, the largely forgotten milieu in which esotericism flourished. *The Place of Enchantment* directly studies the lives of women esotericists.

We owe a great debt to Mary K. Greer for her critically important history, *Women of the Golden Dawn,* which provides a readable history of the order itself, as well as chronicling the lives of the women of the order as interesting subjects in their own right.

Victorian-Edwardian Esotericists

For the older books discussed in this section, some have been reprinted, and where there is a new edition I note it in the bibliography. Others are difficult to find and can only be obtained secondhand and usually at some cost. I list some of those books here to give examples of the kinds of books to be alert to find.

Turn-of-the-century women esotericists often expressed the magical worldview in novels and plays. Ithell Colquhoun's *Goose of Hermogenes* titles each chapter by an alchemical operation. Many of us have drawn our initial feeling for visionary magic from Dion Fortune's *Sea Priestess.* Florence Farr's *Dancing Faun* combines Jane Austen–style parlor conversation with a feminist esotericist's sensibility.

Women esotericists also left records of their visionary experiences. The pamphlet *The Enochian Experiments of the Golden Dawn* records some of the findings of Florence Farr's sphere group. Anna Kingford's *Clothed with the Sun* documents the illuminations she received from several sources, including her own Genius. *Jane Wolfe: The Cefalu Diaries 1920–1923* meticulously records Jane Wolfe's workings and thoughts. *Thorn in the Flesh* captures Rosaleen Norton's poems and images.

Witchcraft

Doreen Valiente's readable history *The Rebirth of Witchcraft* surveys the development of modern esotericism from the point of view of one of the major founding figures. Her book *Witchcraft for Tomorrow* provides both information and a feeling of what it is like to live as a Witch. Vivianne Crowley's *Wicca* provides a philosophical and contemplative perspective.

Many writers have published versions of a Book of Shadows. Lady Sheba was arguably the first. Her version, combined with *Witch* and *The Grimoire of Lady Sheba*, forms an essential trilogy providing the basic rituals for individuals and covens.

Zsuzsanna Budapest provided a Book of Shadows as well in *The Holy Book of Women's Mysteries*. Her woman-centered practice includes a women's history and rituals for protection and healing.

Starhawk's book *The Spiral Dance* provides the basic rituals for practice and includes theology and personal development rituals. This book served as the founding reference for many a coven at the end of the twentieth century when it was first issued and continues to do so today.

Esoteric Studies

The ceremonial or ritual magic traditions in Western Traditional Magic are sometimes described as a combination of theory and practice. The theory by and large rests on Qabbalah, while the practice involves formal ritual.

For theory, Dion Fortune's *Mystical Qabbalah* has provided students a solid grounding in esoteric Qabbalah for most of a century. On the practice side, Dolores Ashcroft-Nowicki provided a number of essential texts. Her *Ritual Magic Workbook* is designed as a one-year study system for the independent student to set up a ritual magical practice. In *The Shining Paths*, she updated the visionary process of working the paths on the tree.

Rachel Pollack provided a reference introduction to the Tarot, including meanings of the cards and how to read with them, in her two-volume set *Seventy-Eight Degrees of Wisdom*. My own book *Practical Magic for Beginners* covers fundamental magical technique as well as elemental and planetary correspondences.

RITUAL WORKBOOK

COSMOLOGY

The Creation of the World

"The Creation of the World" is based on the work of Barbara Lesko, Patricia Monaghan, and Judith Laura, among others, drawing on the oldest strata of women's culture to focus on the female power of creation, of speech, of action, and of relationship. The cosmology imagines the founding of the universe using Egyptian goddesses as descriptors of the universal forces. Historically the Egyptian deities have been amenable to revisioning; also, Egyptian deities have the added advantage of having largely escaped the psychologizing revisioning of the archetypal movement. The cosmology does not seek to create a historically accurate representation of the worship of the ancient Egyptians. Instead it approaches Egyptian deity forms as representatives of the divine forces which are true to their individual character but can be understood to interact in ways that are new to us.

1. The Void

That which is Void existed before all things existed, everything and nothing, the darkness which is light and the light which is darkness.

The Void exists beyond time, beyond space, limitless and without existence.

Everything that is came into being from the Void, so that the Void was annihilated when creation occurred, and everything that is will be in turn annihilated at the end of time and return to the Void.

The Void continually creates everything that is, and everything that is continually returns to the Void and is annihilated.

Spirit cannot comprehend the Void which cannot be named. Nonetheless Spirit names it and attempts to apprehend it. So creation begins.

2. The Darkness and the Light

Mehet-Weret the vast darkness of the universe filled with Weret-Hekau the power of limitless light. These twin forces flashed into existence in the same instant, so that one could not exist without the other, and when one is gone both are gone and the universe will cease to be.

The vast darkness of the universe spread like water in all directions without limit. This dark water, Nun, formed the substance of the universe.

Floating on the dark waters of Nun, Neith came into being. She knew herself to be although nothing else existed. There was no land, no sky, no star, no sun, no water, no air, no life.

Neith imagined everything, she desired that everything should exist. Neith spoke, and Ma'at came into existence, the pattern of the cosmos, that everything should be formed in harmony.

Neith imagined everything, she desired that there should be sky and star. Neith spoke, and Nuit came into existence, the vast space which is the limitless darkness of space, and the myriad manifestations of light. All space and sky and matter flashed into being simultaneously out of the speaking of Neith according to the pattern of Ma'at.

3. The Sun and the Land

Nuit draped her body in swirling brilliant nebulas, the flowing fabric of the cosmos. As these nebulas flared across the sky the matter within them collected, congealed, coalesced into bright pinpoints of light. Each was a sun, and each sun was a mother, pouring out the light of her love, and calling all around her to shelter in her orbit. Around many suns matter collected, congealed, coalesced into balls of gas, chunks of ice, and globes of rock, gathering around the light of the sun as children flock to the skirts of their mother.

Many suns emerged from the body of Nuit. One of these was Hathor. From the beginning she poured out her bright love in all directions, without ceasing for an instant, without measure or counting, without condition or withholding, but constantly ceaselessly giving forth the energy and sustenance which supports all life.

Circles of gas and dust swirled around the body of Hathor. Like snakes the swirls of dust spun, each twisting in on itself, growing denser and denser. Through Ma'at two such snakes spun so closely to each other that they locked in dance with one another, growing together as twins, two worlds in a common system.

One of the twins spun until the heat of the spinning formed a heart of molten fire and the fire developed a skin of rock and air. Thus did the sacred snake of the world come into existence, Wadjet of Earth. One of the twins grew denser and cooler and smaller and became the moon, Tefnut. She joined with her sister Wadjet as girls lock hands, and the twin worlds spun around each other endlessly.

4. Time and the Elements

Then Neith spoke her blessing on the earth, Wadjet, and the face of the earth cracked open and the molten heart of the earth spurted into the air with violent passion. Mountains formed and pushed toward the sky, earth reaching to heaven, the sacred mountains which are the serpent coils of the world.

Then Neith spoke her blessing on the earth, Wadjet, and the envelope of air enfolded and protected the world. Then Neith spoke her blessing upon the earth, and out of the substance of the world came the water, covering the earth in furious waves, and where water met molten fire, geysers of steam sprayed into the air.

Ma'at caused all the spinning of world around world to bring time into being. The world spun on her own axis, turning her face first toward Hathor, then Nuit, bringing into existence the cycle of the day and night. The world spun in her own orbit around the sun, bringing into existence the round of the year. The world spun on a common axis with the moon whose face appears and disappears, bringing into existence the month. Tefnut the moon moved the water in the rhythms of the tides so that dry land emerged from the waters.

Thus the elements came into existence, air and water, time and tide, each in their place, and each in harmony according to Ma'at.

5. The Tree of Life

Then Neith spoke her blessing upon the earth, Wadjet, and out of the substance of Neith came the twin sisters Isis and Nephthys, light and shadow, life and death. From these sisters came the great Tree of Life. Isis is the substance of the tree, the force of life, and because of this she is Great of Magic. Nephthys is the encased heart of the tree, the necessity of death, the change which is the renewal of life. The green earth which holds life in its embrace is the face of Isis; her barren sister moon who is made of earth only, with no air or water or fiery core, is the face of Nephthys.

The Tree of Life is rooted in the depths of the universe. The tree reaches from the fiery heart of the earth through the rock and water and air up into the sky beyond the ken of the world into the swirls of space and thence to the darkness and light and to the mystery which cannot be known.

6. Seshat

From the coming of Isis and Nephthys formed the Tree of Life. This forming summoned Ma'at to frame life in patterned harmony. Ma'at stepped forth on the earth, and in her coming she was Seshat, who writes the life of all things on the Tree of Life. Seshat brought knowledge to the world and all the world's creatures. Because of this she is Mistress of Magic, who bears the words of magic in her mouth, the words of Neith.

Thus all the forces of the universe came into being as twins, mother and daughter, sister and sister:

Each of these forces flowed one from another, spilling over into one another like water from pool to pool.

Mehet-Weret		Weret-Hekau
Nun		Neith
	Ma'at	
Nuit		Hathor
Wadjet		Tefnut
Isis		Nephthys
	Seshat	

Illustration 14: Egyptian Goddesses Cosmology

PERSONAL RITUAL

The personal ritual establishes the magician as a Sister of Seshat. A magician can perform this ritual at any time to accomplish any working she devises.

Inputs to the Ritual

The ritual is a contemporary adaptation of the Ritual of the Heptagram. The foundation of the ritual is an Egyptian-based cosmology that includes only goddess imagery. The names and functions of the goddesses derive from Barbara Lesko's work (Lesko 1999). Patricia Monaghan discusses Hathor's solar nature (Monaghan 1994). The ritual enacts the three-step process of withdrawal, transformation, and emerging explored by Carol Lee Flinders (Flinders 1998).

The working is influenced by Christine Battersby's phenomenological philosophy of self (Battersby 1998). My sister Kallista first discussed with me the spiritual manifestation of the fact that all women are born with all their eggs.

Grounding the Ritual

After the ritual, the tools should be immediately put away. The magician changes out of her magical robe into street clothes. It is also advisable to record the working in a magical journal. The entry should include day, month and year, day of week, and time of day, along with any notes about feelings, visions, or other effects of the ritual. This magical working record is the most valuable tool a magician can possess, forming a record of accomplishment as well as a record of themes which develop in the work over time.

Tools

Small altar (as small as a portable tray)
Altar cloth
Elemental tools:

Air: incense
Fire: candle
Water: drinking cup with a small amount of juice or wine
Earth: small plate containing a small amount of bread or some solid food

Preparing the Temple

This ritual can be performed in any space where a small altar can be set up. The magician should know which part of the room is marked out as the working space. This space, and preferably the entire room, should be clean and neat.

The magician herself should also be clean and neat. She can wear any clothing, although an Egyptian-style robe helps to bring seriousness and intent to the ritual.

Establishing the Cosmos

The magician stands in the center of the working space. Breathing deeply, centering, she raises her arms in a circle so that her palms come together above her head. As she does so, she visualizes and senses energy moving from the earth through her feet, along her central column, and up to the globe above her head. She vibrates:

Mehet-Weret

She visualizes darkness surrounding her in all directions.

Slowly she brings her arms down in a circle, visualizing and sensing energy flowing from the universe back through the globe above her head, through the central column, down her legs and feet, and down into the earth. She vibrates:

Weret-Hekau

She visualizes light surrounding her in all directions.

She spreads her arms out to the sides to form a cross with her body, visualizing and sensing a line of energy running through her arms and out into the universe. She vibrates:

Nun

She visualizes the dark waters of the cosmos surrounding her in all directions.

She brings her hands to her heart, palm to palm, where the line of vertical energy meets the column of horizontal energy. She vibrates:

Neith

She acknowledges the spark of the self-aware universe within her.

She lifts her arms to shoulder height, turning the palms upward in the psi position. She vibrates:

Nuit

She visualizes the starry vault of the heavens.

She stretches her arms in front of her, bent slightly at the elbows, palms facing outwards. She vibrates:

Hathor

She visualizes the sun filling the dark waters with light.

She lowers her arms to her sides, turning her palms downward toward the earth. She vibrates:

Wadjet

She visualizes the serpent of the earth.

Facing east, she visualizes an Egyptian woman wearing the horned solar crown, holding an ankh in one hand and a staff in the other. She vibrates:

Isis

Facing west, she visualizes an Egyptian woman wearing the pillar crown, holding her hands in front of her. She vibrates:
Nephthys

Facing north, she visualizes an Egyptian woman wearing a scarab crown. She vibrates:
Neith

Facing south, she visualizes an Egyptian woman wearing a scorpion crown. She vibrates:
Selket

Facing east again, she says:
Ma'at the unfolding of the pattern
Seshat the writing of the words

She holds her hands in front of her in the sign of Seshat (left hand held out low, right hand held out high). She visualizes Seshat standing behind her and then stepping into her. She vibrates:
Seshat

She says:
Seshat is the ba in the heart of every magician.

Making Offerings

Taking up the plate and cup, she holds them up and says:

My seed was formed in my grandmother's womb. I was born of the waters of my mother's womb. I am part of the river of life. I make offering to the forces of creation.

She replaces them on the altar. Taking up the incense and candle, she holds them up and says:

My spirit was formed in Nuit's womb. My soul was born of the fire of Hathor. I make offering to the forces of creation.

Illustration 15: Sign of Seshat

The Declaration

Facing east again, she proclaims:

I am surrounded by the order of Ma'at. I walk the path of harmony.

The pulse of withdrawal and unfoldment is the beating heart of power. I am enclosed in magic. The withdrawal is complete. I affect the transformation.

The Working

The magician performs the magical working.

Completing the Offerings

Standing in the center of the working space in front of the altar, the magician says:

The transformation is affected. The unfoldment begins.

Taking up the plate and cup, she holds them up and says:

I give thanks to the river of life which sustains me and the forces of creation.

She eats the food and drinks the drink.
Taking up the candle and incense, she says:

I give thanks to the spirit and stars which sustain me and the forces of creation.

She blows out the candle. She says:

The substance of my being is the gift of the world.
The outpouring of my love is my gift to the world.
The working is complete. May I move in harmony with Ma'at.

TEMPLE RITUAL

TEMPLE RITUAL EXPLANATORY NOTES

The Temple Ritual creates a temple in Malkuth. It begins and ends each ritual of the order, in the pattern discussed by Dolores Ashcroft-Nowicki in *The Shining Paths*, where each pathworking begins and ends in the temple in Malkuth. The temple in Malkuth is a physical place and an astral temple (Ashcroft-Nowicki 1983).

The immediate predecessors to the structure of the Temple Ritual are: the rituals of the Open Source Order of the Golden Dawn, the Aurum Solis temple as described by Osbourne Phillips, Albert Pike's rituals in *Masonry of Adoption*, and the *Ritual of the Order of the Eastern Star,* 1919 edition.

OFFICERS

Four officers take on the power of an element, administer the altar of the element, and wear the color of the element. They are the Hegemon, Hierus, Dadouchos, and Stolistes. The four altars are located at the corners of the temple, in contrast to the common neo-Pagan custom of placing the altars in the middle of each side of the temple. This placement allows the altars to anchor the four corners of the temple, and allows the officers to measure the sides of the temple in the same way we see inscriptions of Seshat measuring Egyptian temples.

Earth Altar

Hierophant
Isis

Air Altar

Hegemon
Ma'at

Stolistes
Neith

Dadouchos
Selket

Water Altar

Fire Altar

Hierus
Nephthys

Sentinel beside door
Renenuet

Illustration 16: Goddess Forms

The elemental altars create the four sides of the temple in Malkuth. From this temple foundation the rituals move up the Tree of Life in the pattern of the path of return, moving from Malkuth to Yesod, Hod, Netzach, and Tiphareth, through each of the connecting paths of the tree.

As in the Golden Dawn tradition, each officer also represents an Egyptian deity. This deity maps onto the powers that the officer administers and represents in the temple. The Dadouchos and Stolistes primarily represent the elemental forces of fire and water. The Hegemon and Hierus also represent elemental forces, but their elemental duties are secondary to their primary function as main officers. The three main officers—Hierophant, Hegemon, and Hierus—represent the powers of the three pillars of the Tree of Life. The Hierophant represents the pillar of mercy, the Hegemon represents the middle pillar, and the Hierus represents the pillar of severity.

Dadouchos

The Dadouchos administers the fire altar, wears red, and sits along the south side of the temple, between the air and fire altars. She takes on the goddess form of Selket. The desert goddess Selket embodies the scorching power of the midday sun, and is portrayed with a scorpion on her head, the scorpion of the sands. She is fiercely protective, and in particular stands over women in childbirth.

Stolistes

The Stolistes administers the water altar, wears blue, and sits along the north side of the temple, between the water and earth altars. She takes on the goddess form of Neith. Neith is one of the oldest goddesses, who created the universe out of the primordial waters.

Hierus

The Hierus administers the earth altar, wears black, and sits along the west side of the temple, between the fire and water altars. She has to walk across the temple to reach her altar—this happens sometimes in Golden Dawn style rituals.

The primary function of the Hierus is to represent the pillar of severity. She takes on the goddess form of Nephthys. The title of Nephthys is "Lady of the Mansion," which appears in hieroglyphic as her headdress. Sister of Isis, she is one of the goddesses of the dead.

Hegemon

The Hegemon administers the air altar and wears yellow. Her primary function is to represent the middle pillar. She sits in the center of the temple, at the center of the energies of the four officers, balancing the Dadouchos and Stolistes, who represent water and fire, and the Hierophant and Hierus, who represent mercy and severity.

She takes on the goddess form of Ma'at. The Egyptian goddess of balance, Ma'at embodies the structured power of the harmonic universe and specifically lawgiving justice.

Hierophant

The Hierophant represents the pillar of mercy. She sits outside the four elemental sides of the temple. She is the officer who oversees the work of all the other officers and makes sure the ritual runs properly.

She takes on the goddess form of Isis, the queen of goddesses. Isis was an old goddess when history first recorded her presence, and grew in power throughout the centuries, absorbing many other deities, and spreading out into the Hellenistic world, to Rome and beyond.

Sentinel

The Sentinel takes on the goddess form of Renenutet, a serpent goddess. She is depicted in conjunction with granaries and the harvest, presumably as protector of the granaries. Egyptian queens acted as priestesses and presided over harvest ceremonies. Lesko points to the ancient association of goddesses, serpents, and priestesses throughout the Mediterranean region, and suspects that this goddess represents a very old substratum of religious practice (Lesko 1999).

TEMPLE RITUAL

Tools

Furniture

Chairs, one for each officer and for other sorors.

Temple tools

Lamens for the goddess forms
A bell
An object which embodies the group egregore
Red cord wound on a spindle (or any other form of cord winder)
First aid kit
Fire extinguisher

Altars

Air altar: small table, yellow altar cloth, yellow candle, spindle with red cord, egregore object, image of Seshat

Fire altar: small table, red altar cloth, red candle, censer and incense, lighter

Water altar: small table, blue altar cloth, blue candle, bowl of water and aspergilum

Earth altar: small table, green altar cloth, green candle

Repast altar: small table, white altar cloth, cups and drink, plate with cakes

Drink can be wine, juice, or water. Cakes can be any cookies or crackers which the sorors prefer to eat.

Preparing the Temple

The temple furniture is set up, then the temple is cleared of all participants except the Hierophant. The Hierophant makes the sign of Seshat. The Hierophant places the group egregore object on the air altar.

The Hierophant establishes the goddesses on each of the thrones. She places the goddess lamen on the throne of the corresponding officer, visualizes the goddess, and vibrates the name of the goddess.

When the Hierophant has established the goddesses on their thrones, she admits the other officers. As each officer enters, she touches the egregore object, goes to her station, puts on the lamen of the goddess form, and centers herself in the power of that form. The Dadouchos then performs the fire functions in the temple, lighting the elemental candles, and lighting the charcoal for the incense.

The Hierophant faces west. The Hierus and the Hegemon both face east. The Stolistes and the Dadouchos face each other. The Sentinel sits by the door, wherever it is. If there is no Sentinel, the Hierus covers the position, performs the actions of the Sentinel, and answers for the Sentinel when the Hierophant calls on her.

Opening the Temple

Hierophant *faces Hierus (west).*
Hegemon *and* **Hierus** *face Hierophant (east).*
Stolistes *and* **Dadouchos** *face each other.*

Hierophant: *(Rings the bell once.)* Sorors of the Order of Seshat, please assist me to construct the temple. Soror Sentinel, please see that the temple is guarded.

Sentinel: *(Checks the door.)* Soror Hierophant, the temple is guarded.

Hierophant: Soror Sentinel, please ensure that all present are sisters of Seshat.

Sentinel: Sorors, please give the sign of Seshat.

All stand and hold out their hands in the sign of Seshat.

Sentinel: Soror Hierophant, all present are sisters of Seshat.

All sit.

Hierophant: Let us establish the officers on their thrones. Soror Hegemon, what are your station and duties?

Hegemon: My station is in the center of the temple in the balance of light and darkness. I sit on the throne of Ma'at, and therefore am I

Earth Altar

Hierophant

Air Altar

Stolistes

Hegemon

Dadouchos

Water Altar

Hierus

Fire Altar

Sentinel beside door

Sorors of the Order

Illustration 17: Temple Ritual

called the Mistress of the Balance. I administer the air altar. I guide and advise the candidate in her introduction to the temple.

Hierophant: Soror Hierus, what are your station and duties?

Hierus: My station is at the edge of the temple where begin the regions of darkness. I sit on the throne of Nephthys, and therefore am I called the Mistress of Darkness. I administer the earth altar. I guard and protect the candidate in her introduction to the temple.

Hierophant: Soror Stolistes, what are your station and duties?

Stolistes: My station is on the cross-balance of the temple. I sit on the throne of Neith. I administer the water altar. I purify with water.

Hierophant: Soror Dadouchos, what are your station and duties?

Dadouchos: My station is on the cross-balance of the temple. I sit on the throne of Selket. I administer the fire altar. I consecrate with fire.

Hierophant: Soror Sentinel, what are your station and duties?

Sentinel: My station is at the doorway to the temple and I sit on the throne of Renenutet. I bar the door to intruders and admit the candidate.

Hierophant: My station is at the edge of the temple where begin the regions of light and therefore am I called the Mistress of Light. I sit on the throne of Isis. I supervise the conduct of the temple, and I receive the candidate into the temple.

Hierophant: Let us prepare the temple. Soror Stolistes, please purify the temple.

Stolistes goes to the water altar. She picks up the bowl and aspergillum, circumambulates the temple once clockwise, asperging as she goes. She places the bowl back on the altar.

Stolistes: Soror Hierophant, the temple is purified. *(She returns to her station and sits.)*

Hierophant: Soror Dadouchos, please consecrate the temple.

Dadouchos goes to the fire altar. She picks up the censer (with lit incense), and circumambulates the temple once clockwise, censing as she goes. She places the censer back on the altar.

Dadouchos: Soror Hierophant, the temple is consecrated. *(She returns to her station and sits.)*

Hierophant: Let us establish the temple. Soror Hegemon, what do you know of the source of our tradition?

Hegemon: It comes to us from all the corners of the globe, from Asia, Africa, Europe, and America.

Hierophant: Soror Hierus, what do you know of the source of our tradition?

Hierus: It comes to us from human knowledge, from religion, philosophy, science, and gnosis.

Hierophant: Soror Hegemon, who preserves our tradition?

Hegemon: Our tradition was bequeathed to us by the ancients and by our foremothers.

Hierophant: Soror Hierus, who created our tradition?

Hierus: Our tradition is created anew every moment in our own hearts.

Hierophant: Let us measure the temple. Let the cord be stretched so that the foundation may be laid.

Hegemon and Hierus stand and go to the air altar. Hegemon picks up the spindle. Hierus takes the end of the red cord and walks to the fire altar while Hegemon holds the spindle so the cord can unspool. Hegemon and Hierus stand holding the red cord.

Hegemon: The temple is measured from the east to the south.

Hegemon walks to Hierus and stands by the fire altar, winding the cord as she goes. Hierus then walks from the fire altar to the water altar while Hegemon remains at the fire altar, holding the spindle so the cord can unspool.

Hierus: The temple is measured from the south to the west.

Hegemon walks to Hierus and stands by the water altar, winding the cord as she goes. Hierus then walks from the water altar to the earth altar while Hegemon remains at the water altar, holding the spindle so the cord can unspool.

Hegemon: The temple is measured from the west to the north.

Hegemon walks to Hierus and stands by the earth altar, winding the cord as she goes. Hierus then walks from the earth altar to the air altar while Hegemon remains at the earth altar, holding the spindle so the cord can unspool.

Hierus: The temple is measured from the north to the east.

Hegemon walks to the air altar. Hierus gives Hegemon the end of the red cord. Hegemon rewinds the cord on the spindle and places the spindle on the air altar.

Hegemon: Soror Hierophant, the walls of the temple have been measured.

Hegemon and Hierus return to their stations and sit.

Hierophant: *(Rings the bell four times: !!!!)* Sorors, the foundation of the temple is laid. Let us invoke the Mistress of the Temple.

All stand.

Hierophant: *(Lifting her hands in the sign of Seshat, she vibrates:)* Seshat! *(She declaims:)* Establish the temple, Mistress of Builders!

All: *(Hands on hearts)* Seshat is the ba in the heart of every magician.

All sit.

Closing the Temple

All sorors return to their stations and sit.

Hierophant: Sorors of the Order of Seshat, please assist me to close the temple. Soror Sentinel, please see that the temple is guarded.

Sentinel: Soror Hierophant, the temple is guarded.

Hierophant: Soror Sentinel, please ensure that all present are sisters of Seshat.

Sentinel: Sorors, please give the sign of Seshat.

All stand and hold out their hands in the sign of Seshat.

Sentinel: Soror Hierophant, all present are sisters of Seshat.

All sit.

Hierophant: Let us prepare the mystic repast.

Sorors place repast altar at center of room. Sorors place cups, drinks, plate, and cakes on altar. All return to their stations and sit.

Hierophant: Let us partake of the mystic repast. Sorors, join me at the altar.

All go to repast altar and stand in a circle. Sorors fill their cups with drink and raise them.

Hierophant: To Seshat!

All: To Seshat!

Sorors drink from cups and eat cakes.

Hierophant: Sorors, our rite has ended. Let us all keep Seshat in our hearts.

All: *(Place hands on heart.)* Seshat is the ba in the heart of every magician.

Grounding the Temple

Each officer takes off the lamen of the goddess form and places it on the throne. She then goes to the air altar to touch the egregore object, grounding any residual deific energy into the object.

The officers leave the temple. The Hierophant picks up the lamens and packs them away, visualizing the goddess forms departing the temple and offering them her thanks. The Hierophant makes sure all energy in the temple is grounded.

THE EARTH INITIATION

EXPLANATORY NOTES

The predecessors of this ritual are the Neophyte and Portal rituals of the Golden Dawn and the Witchcraft first-degree initiation ritual. This ritual aligns the candidate with the structured universe of the operative magician, and specifically establishes Seshat as a magical force dwelling within her heart.

Background reading for this ritual:

- Inanna's Descent to the Underworld (Pritchard 1969).
- The Myth of Demeter and Persephone (Spretnak 1989).
- The Double Goddess (Noble 2003).

Ritual Structure

Opening the temple: The ritual begins with the ritual of establishing the temple, which opens the temple in Malkuth.

Creating the cosmos: The ritual invokes a cosmology based on Egyptian creation myths.

Shadow tree: The temple revolves to evoke the shadow tree.

Seven veils: The officers assist the candidate to trace the route from the outer darkness of the shadow supernals up along the shadow tree to emerge in the underworld. This ritual uses the structure of Inanna's descent into the underworld.

Underworld: When the candidate emerges into the underworld, the mythos shifts to the emergence of Persephone from the underworld. The temple also shifts 180 degrees to realign from the roots of the tree looking downward to the trunk of the tree looking upward.

Earth temple: The officers then re-establish the four pillars of the temple in Malkuth.

Closing the temple: The temple is closed in Malkuth.

The Egyptian Cosmos

Ancient Mediterranean cosmology imagined a three-part structure of the universe: heaven, earth, and underworld.

This ritual invokes a cosmology from the Egyptian creation myths. Before the construction of the Aswan dam, the Nile River flooded each year. As the flood receded, islands of dry land emerged from the waters. Egyptian creation myths imagined a cosmos in which dry land and light emerged from dark waters.

Barbara Lesko points to Mehet-Weret as one of the oldest goddesses of Egypt. This goddess embodied the dark waters that flooded the land with fertile soil and then receded. The goddess also came to represent the darkness of the sky, the land of the dead, in which the sun traveled each night to re-emerge in the daytime. Lesko discusses the ancient goddess Weret-Hekau as the source of magic (Lesko 1999). These two goddesses form the first double-goddess pair invoked in the ritual, that of magic/light and darkness/water.

The temple stands between the regions of limitless light and limitless darkness. The temple of Malkuth is imagined as the earth mound that emerged from the dark waters. This earth mound is the foundation of the Tree of Life.

The Shadow Tree of Life

Egyptian and Babylonian (Semitic) cultures shared the image of a Tree of Life that connected the land of the living and the land of the dead. This Tree of Life imagery migrated into the Jewish mystical system Qabbalah.

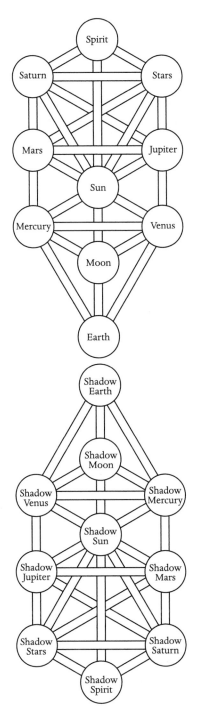

Illustration 18: Tree of Life and Shadow Tree

In this ritual, once the tree is established in the temple, it immediately casts its own shadow, the qliphothic spheres, down into the depths of the surrounding watery darkness. In Qabbalah, the creation of the world progresses through the seven planetary spheres, culminating in the earth. The force that created each sphere spills over into the next one. It also throws off an excess of force in each sphere. The Qlipoth is that shadow, or excessive force. In this ritual, the shadow tree is imagined as a literal reflection.

Mirroring the temple's change, the officers come together in the center of the temple and then trade places. The Hierus takes the Hierophant's station and the Hierophant takes the Hierus's station. The Stolistes and the Dadouchos also trade places. The Hegemon remains in the center of the temple, the anchor point around which this temple shift revolves. In making this move the officers also project the elements they embody down into the depths to provide anchoring pillars for the temple.

The next double-goddess pair is invoked, Inanna and Ereshkigal. The candidate enacts Inanna's descent into the underworld, where the goddess was met at seven gates and relinquished a piece of clothing at each gate. Contemporary dancers in Middle Eastern styles cite this myth as an inspiration for their interpretations of dances of the seven veils.

The movement in the shadow tree is counterclockwise as this temple enacts the mirror image of the tree that the initiation rituals ascend. As the candidate progresses through the ritual, the stations of the shadow tree are made explicitly visible by the ribbons that mark their presence. When the candidate reaches the shadow earth gate, the Hierophant gathers up the ribbons, literally gathering up the shadow temple as she does so. This section of the ritual invokes the third pair of goddesses, Demeter and Persephone. In ancient Greece, the yearly round of winter and summer, withdrawal of life and emergence, found expression in the myth of the mother's loss of her daughter to the underworld and the daughter's re-emergence from the underworld each spring. The earth-maiden was imaged as literally pulled from the ground by her arms. (My sister Kallista first framed the mother-daughter connection to me as the double goddess of life and death, darkness and light.)

While the candidate is hoodwinked, the officers shift the temple again, back into its position as a temple of Malkuth. The officers who have been projecting the elemental pillars into the watery depths of the cosmos now reaffirm the strength of those pillars in the temple.

At this point the temple is created around the candidate just as it is created at the beginning of the ritual. Seshat is then invoked into the candidate's heart as the creator of the temple and the scribe of the Tree of Life.

Ritual Intent

The Golden Dawn Neophyte ritual projects the shadow of the practitioner onto the floor of the temple. At the decisive moment in the ritual, the Hierophant steps on that section of the temple, thus vanquishing the shadow with light.

In 2009, at Pantheacon, the Open Source Order of the Golden Dawn performed a ritual called "In the Shadow of Evil," which reimagined the shadow in the context of contemporary psychology and ethics. Each participant was asked to meditate on the parts of ourselves we wished to release. The audience then participated in a ritual to evoke the shadow in the Neophyte ritual, extract the god-forms which had been merged into it (Set, Apophis, and Anubis), and finally turn the shadow from a rejected part of the psyche into a way to enter into conversation with the higher self.

The Sisters of Seshat earth initiation benefits from this reimagined tradition. The shadow is not rejected, but is acknowledged as a significant force both within the life and character of the magician, and in the injustice and difficulty we experience in the world. The magician's quest is not to vanquish this shadow, as a reflection of the battle between good and evil, but instead to choose appropriate action with each circumstance, to oppose, redirect, or transmute the shadow force.

Recognizing that this is dangerous work, the ritual contains the shadow tree within the reflected elemental pillars. At the end of the ritual, these pillars are reaffirmed as the structural support of the temple in Malkuth. The temple is created in miniature around the magician, literally inviting the magician into her own temple. Finally, Seshat, the creator of the temple and the wielder of magic, is invoked into the magician's own body.

Thus the magician is set on her journey (or reaffirmed on her journey) to transmute herself and her world. She confronts the shadow in herself and in the world, both without and within. She is brought into the temple and energized as a magician. The group has recognized her power to create her own temple and to perform her own magic.

EARTH INITIATION: UNDERWORLD JOURNEY

Tools

Initiatory tools

- **Seven ribbons:** Black, blue, red, gold, green, orange, and silver. A basket to put them in.
- **Hoodwink** of opaque black cloth.

Initiatory token: Small disk painted black on one side, white on the other.

The basket with ribbons and hoodwink are staged beneath the throne of Hegemon. The initiatory tokens are staged beneath the Hierophant throne.

Preparing and Opening the Temple

The officers prepare and open the temple using the temple ritual. The candidate is outside the temple.

Entering the Shadow Tree

Hierophant: Sorors, a candidate seeks admittance to the temple. Is it your will to admit her as a sister of Seshat?

All: It is my will.

Hierophant *extinguishes quarter candles and stands in the center of*
the temple.

Hierophant: Mehet-Weret the vast darkness of the universe filled with
Weret-Hekau the power of limitless light. These twin forces flashed
into existence in the same instant, so that one could not exist without the other, and when one is gone both are gone and the universe
will cease to be.

The vast darkness of the universe spread like water in all directions without limit. This dark water Nun formed the substance of
the universe.

Hierophant *returns to her station and remains standing.*

Hierophant: Sorors, we undertake to bring a candidate from the cha-
otic realms of darkness where the universe is constantly recreated,
through the twisting paths of the shadow tree, to stand with us in
the temple of Malkuth, the temple of the earth. In order to bring her
and ourselves safely through this journey, let us establish the shape
of the universe, and let us invoke the powers of the light to guide
and protect us.

All stand and face east.

Hierophant: *(Vibrates:)* Mehet-Weret! Weret-Hekau! *(Speaking voice:)*
You hold the matrix of existence, from the depths of chaos to the
limitless light. All is equally sacred to you, who are the overflowing
power of magic itself.

All: Mehet-Weret, Weret-Hekau, you are the matrix of the universe.

Hierophant: *(Vibrates:)* Isis! *(Speaking voice:)* You are the power of the
white pillar, the power of light and expansion.

All: Isis, you are the power of life.

Hierus: *(Vibrates:)* Nephthys! *(Speaking voice:)* You are the power of the
black pillar, the power of darkness and contraction.

All: Nephthys, you are the power of death.

Hierophant: Between them they hold the Tree of Life, the ever-regenerating creation.

Hegemon: *(Vibrates:)* Seshat! *(Speaking voice:)* Seshat writes the years of every life on the Tree of Life. The Tree of Life stands on the great mound of the world, rooted in the watery depths and stretching to the heights of the stars.

All remain standing.

Hierophant: Sorors, let us gather around the trunk of the Tree of Life.

All sorors join Hierophant at the center of the temple, facing each other in a circle.

Hegemon: The tree casts a shadow in the dark waters, the imperfect reflection of the manifest universe.

Hierus: Each of us faces the darkness within ourselves and the darkness in the world. We each make the journey through the watery realms to reach the doorway to the temple of the world.

Hierophant: Let Seshat be strong within us and guide us through the watery realms. Let us hold fast to the power which will bring us back to the light of the sun. I hold fast to the power of life. *(Hierophant moves to the Hierus throne between the water and fire altars.)* I stand at the boundary of limitless darkness.

Hierus: I hold fast to the power of earth. *(Hierus moves to the Hierophant throne between the earth and air altars.)* I stand at the boundary between the shadow tree and the temple of Malkuth, the temple of the earth.

Stolistes: I hold fast to the power of water. *(Stolistes moves to the throne of the Dadouchos between the air and fire altars.)*

Dadouchos: I hold fast to the power of fire. *(Dadouchos moves to the throne of the Stolistes between the earth and water altars.)*

Hegemon: *(Turning to face Hierus throne/west)* I hold fast to the power of air. I stand at the center of the temple, the axis around which the temple revolves. I hold fast to the taproot of the tree, I hold fast to the power of Seshat, the one who writes on the leaves of the Tree of Life.

All sit.

Admitting the Candidate
Temple Diagram: The Shadow Tree

Hierus now sits on the Hierophant throne between the earth and air altar.

Hierophant sits on the Hierus throne between the water and fire altars.

Hegemon still sits in the center of the temple but is now facing west.

Dadouchos now sits on the throne of the Stolistes between the earth and water altars.

Stolistes now sits on the throne of the Dadouchos between the fire and air altars.

Hierophant: Sorors, we are now in the shadow tree.

(Pause.)

Hierophant: Soror Hegemon, please bring the candidate to the door. Soror Hierus, please admit her when she gives the proper alarm.

Hegemon leaves the hall and seeks out the candidate in the prepared waiting area. Hegemon checks to make sure the candidate is ready to begin the initiation. Hegemon takes the candidate to the door, instructing her to give four knocks: !!!! Hierus opens the door. Hegemon leads the candidate just inside the door.

Hierophant: *(Stands.)* Soror Hegemon, what stranger do you bring to our temple?

Hegemon: [Candidate name or motto], who seeks to be a sister of Seshat.

Hierophant: Are you willing to vouch for her?

Earth Altar

Hierus

Air Altar

Shadow Moon Gate

Shadow Mercury Gate

Shadow Venus Gate

Dadouchos

Hegemon

Stolistes

Shadow Mars Gate

Shadow Jupiter Gate

Shadow Saturn Gate

Water Altar

Hierophant

Fire Altar

Sentinel beside door

Sorors of the Order

Illustration 19: The Shadow Tree

Hegemon: I am.

*Hierus slams the door, returns to her station and sits. **Hegemon** leads candidate to stand before Hierophant, facing Hierophant on the Hierus throne (west).*

Hierophant: What does she know of the Tree of Life?

Hegemon: She stands in its shadow.

Hierophant: Candidate, in order to enter the temple, you must first walk the path of purification. Are you willing to face the darkness in the world and in yourself?

Candidate: *(Unprompted)* I am.

Hierophant: Soror Hegemon, please provide her with the necessary provisions to successfully complete her journey and advise her how to conduct her way.

Hegemon gives the candidate the seven ribbons to hold loosely in her hand.

Hegemon: These tokens will enable you to pass safely through the realm of darkness. The path you must walk is twisted. There are many shadows along the way, many dangers and difficulties. Yet if you persevere with a courageous heart you will come presently to the gateway that leads you to the light.

The Seven Veils

*Hegemon takes the candidate to stand before Hierus, facing Hierus on Hierophant throne (east). **Hierus** stands.*

Hierophant: *(Speaking from Hierus throne behind the candidate)* Ishtar came to the gates of the underworld seeking an audience with the dread Queen Ereshkigal. Seven gates did she encounter, each guarded by a stern and implacable warder. Seven veils did she surrender, one to each of the gatekeepers.

Hegemon: Then Ishtar said, "Gatekeeper, open the way for me! If you do not open the way I will break the lock, I will smash the door, I will bring down the door posts."

Hierus: Then Ereshkigal said, "Who is it whose heart brings her to the gates of the underworld? Does she wish to eat clay, does she wish to breathe dust? Gatekeeper, open the gate for her, and deal with her according to the ancient covenant."

Hegemon leads the candidate counterclockwise to stand before Hierophant, facing Hierophant on the Hierus throne (west).

Hierophant: (*Stands*) Halt! You stand at the gateway in the shadow of Saturn, the realm of limitation, in which all is concealed and nothing is certain. Are you willing to give up your need to understand?

Candidate: (*Unprompted*) I am.

Hierophant: (*Takes the black ribbon from the candidate and places it on the floor of the temple.*) Pass then through the gate and continue on your way in the realm of the shadows. (*Hierophant sits.*)

Hegemon leads the candidate circumambulating the temple counterclockwise. Stolistes stands and moves to the fire altar. When the candidate reaches the fire altar at the station of the shadow Jupiter, Stolistes bars the way.

Stolistes: Halt! You stand at the gateway in the shadow of Jupiter, the realm of deception, in which authority becomes oppressive and that which should govern instead exploits. Are you willing to give up your need to control?

Candidate: (*Unprompted*) I am.

Stolistes: (*Takes the blue ribbon from the candidate and places it on the floor of the temple.*) Pass then through the gate and continue on your way in the realm of the shadows.

Hegemon leads the candidate circumambulating the temple counterclockwise. Stolistes returns to her station and sits. Dadouchos moves to the water altar. When the candidate reaches the water altar at the station of the shadow Mars, Dadouchos bars the way.

Dadouchos: Halt! You stand at the gateway in the shadow of Mars, the realm of violence, in which cowardice permits brutality to rule. Are you willing to give up your fury?

Candidate: *(Unprompted)* I am.

Dadouchos: *(Takes the red ribbon from the candidate and places it on the floor of the temple.)* Pass then through the gate and continue on your way in the realm of the shadows.

Dadouchos leads the candidate circumambulating counterclockwise around the temple. Hegemon returns to her station and sits. When the candidate reaches the station of the shadow sun (between the throne of Hegemon and the Hierus throne in the west), Hegemon bars the way.

Hegemon: Halt! You stand at the gateway in the shadow of the sun, in which everything withers in the light of condemnation. Are you willing to give up your righteousness?

Candidate: *(Unprompted)* I am.

Hegemon: *(Takes the gold ribbon from the candidate and places it on the floor of the temple.)* Pass then through the gate and continue on your way in the realm of the shadows.

Hegemon leads the candidate circumambulating the temple counterclockwise. Dadouchos returns to her station and sits. Stolistes moves to the air altar. Hegemon continues to lead the candidate circumambulating the temple again. When the candidate reaches the air altar at the station of the shadow Venus, Stolistes bars the way.

Stolistes: Halt! You stand at the gateway in the shadow of Venus, the realm of faithlessness, where the abandoned are led into degradation. Are you willing to give up your compliance?

Candidate: *(Unprompted)* I am.

Stolistes: *(Takes the green ribbon from the candidate and places it on the floor of the temple.)* Pass then through the gate and continue on your way in the realm of the shadows.

Hegemon leads the candidate circumambulating the temple counter-clockwise once. **Stolistes** *returns to her station and sits.* **Dadouchos** *moves to the earth altar. When the candidate reaches the station of the shadow Mercury at the earth altar, Dadouchos bars the way.*

Dadouchos: Halt! You stand at the gateway in the shadow of Mercury, the realm of temptation, in which the wavering succumb to grasping desire and are lost. Are you willing to give up your avarice?

Candidate: *(Unprompted)* I am.

Dadouchos: *(Takes the orange ribbon from the candidate and places it on the floor of the temple.)* Pass then through the gate and continue on your way in the realm of the shadows. *(She returns to her station and sits.)*

Hegemon leads the candidate circumambulating counterclockwise around the temple. When the candidate reaches the station of the shadow moon (between throne of Hegemon and the Hierophant throne in the east), Hierus bars the way.

Hierus: Halt! You stand at the gateway in the shadow of the moon, the realm of nightmares, in which fear overwhelms the mind. Are you willing to give up your despair?

Candidate: *(Unprompted)* I am.

Hierus: *(Takes the silver ribbon from the candidate and places it on the floor of the temple.)* Pass then through the gate and continue on your way in the realm of the shadows.

In the Underworld

Hegemon leads the candidate circumambulating the temple counter-clockwise. **Hierophant** *retrieves the basket from beneath the throne of Hegemon and follows, gathering up the ribbons and putting them back into the basket. Hegemon continues around the temple and stops before Hierus. Hierophant gives basket of ribbons to Hegemon and stands behind Hegemon.*

Hegemon: Then Ishtar, having passed through the seven gates, came to stand before the dread queen Ereshkigal.

Hierus: *(Sternly:)* Who is this who stands before my throne? Why has she come here? Does she wish to eat clay, does she wish to breathe dust?

Hegemon: She has passed through the seven gates, she has made the seven renunciations. ***Hegemon*** *passes the basket of ribbons to Hierus.*

Hierus: Then let her be set down in this place, and let her lose her sight that she may not know, and let her lose her breath that she may not speak, and let her be made as nothing.

*****Stolistes*** and **Dadouchos** *go to the candidate; each take an arm and set the candidate down on the throne of Hegemon facing west.* ***Hegemon*** *covers the candidate with an opaque black cloth reaching to her shoulders. (Note: This hoodwink should be loose and not bound in any way to permit the candidate to breathe.)*

Hierus

Dadouchos

Hegemon

Candidate

Stolistes

Hierophant

Illustration 20: In The Underworld

Hegemon stands to the east of the candidate, facing Hierus (west). *Hierus* returns to the Hierophant throne. *Hierophant* returns to the Hierus throne. *Stolistes* stands to the south of the candidate, and *Dadouchos* stands to the north of the candidate. All remain standing.

Hierophant and *Hierus* revolve one half-circumambulation around the candidate and Hegemon, so that Hierophant, Dadouchos, Stolistes, and Hierus return to their own thrones. While they revolve, Hegemon turns with them to end up facing Hierophant (east). All remain standing.

Stolistes: Is there none who will speak for her? Must she remain as nothing?

Dadouchos: Is there none who will show her the way? Must she remain in this place forever?

Hierus: For as long as she remains in the realms of shadow there is no love, nothing can grow, the sun will not stand.

Hierophant

Stolistes

Hegemon

Candidate

Dadouchos

Hierus

Illustration 21: In the Underworld, Rotated

Hierophant: Let her emerge from the underworld as the Kore emerged from the earth.

Hegemon: As Ishtar you have wandered through the underworld and come to face the dread queen Ereshkigal. As Demeter called her daughter Kore to return to the earth, so you are called to stand up into the temple of the earth. You stand in the gateway of eternity.

As Hierus and Hierophant speak, each takes a step toward the candidate.

Hierus: I am darkness.

Hierophant: I am light.

Hierus: I am death.

Hierophant: I am life.

Hierus: I am Nephthys.

Hierophant: I am Isis.

Hierus: I am the daughter.

Hierophant: I am the mother.

Hierus: I am the sister.

Hierophant: I am the sister.

Hierophant and Hierus: We are the double power of the world.

Hierophant and Hierus put their hands on the candidate's head for a moment.

Hierophant: I call my daughter to light. Come forth from the earth!

Hegemon lifts the cloth from the candidate.

Dadouchos and Stolistes each take an arm of the candidate and lift her to her feet, turning her to face Hierophant and turning the throne of Hegemon to face Hierophant. Dadouchos, Stolistes, and Hierus return to their stations and sit. Hegemon stands beside the candidate.

Purification

Hierophant: Soror Stolistes, purify the candidate.

Stolistes takes the bowl and aspergillum from the water altar, asperges the candidate, and replaces the bowl and aspergillum on the water altar.

Stolistes: Soror Hierophant, the candidate is purified. *(She returns to her station and sits.)*

Hierophant: Soror Dadouchos, consecrate the candidate.

Dadouchos takes the censer from the fire altar, censes the candidate, and replaces the censer on the fire altar.

Dadouchos: Soror Hierophant, the candidate is consecrated. *(She returns to her station and sits.)*

All sorors and officers except Hierophant, Hegemon, and the candidate are sitting. The candidate stands at Hegemon's station facing Hierophant. Hegemon stands behind the candidate facing Hierophant. Hierophant stands at her station facing the candidate.

The Temple of the Earth

Hierophant: You have wandered among the shadows along a twisting path. This path wound between the roots of the great Tree of Life which is anchored in chaos and reaches into the stars. Now you have entered into the temple of the earth at the base of the great trunk of the tree. This temple has four great pillars.

(Pause.)

Soror Hegemon, please establish the pillar of air.

Hegemon retrieves the lighter from the fire altar, moves to the air altar and lights the yellow candle.

Hegemon: Soror Hierophant, the pillar of air is established. *(She returns to stand beside the candidate.)*

Hierophant: Soror Dadouchos, please establish the pillar of fire.

*Hegemon gives the lighter to Dadouchos. **Dadouchos** moves to the fire altar and lights the red candle.*

Dadouchos: Soror Hierophant, the pillar of fire is established. *(She gives the lighter to Stolistes, returns to her station and sits.)*

Hierophant: Soror Stolistes, please establish the pillar of water.

Stolistes moves to the water altar and lights the blue candle.

Stolistes: Soror Hierophant, the pillar of water is established. *(She gives the lighter to Hierus, returns to her station and sits.)*

Hierophant: Soror Hierus, please establish the pillar of earth.

Hierus moves to the earth altar and lights the green candle.

Hierus: Soror Hierophant, the pillar of earth is established. *(She replaces the lighter on the fire altar and returns to stand beside the candidate.)*

Hierophant: Let the candidate be established in the temple.

*Hegemon and **Hierus** retrieve the spindle and red cord from the air altar and arrange the cord on the floor around the candidate in a square. Hierus returns to her station and sits. Hegemon returns to stand beside the candidate.*

Hierophant moves to stand before the candidate, lifts her hands in the sign of Seshat and vibrates:

Seshat!

She declaims:

Establish the temple, Mistress of Builders!

She places her hand near the candidate's heart. She says:

Seshat is the builder of the temple. She is the soul of magic that ensouls every magician.

She visualizes Seshat's crown in the candidate's heart. She then picks up the candidate's hand and moves it so that it presses against the candidate's heart. She says:

Seshat is the ba in the heart of every magician.

All: *(Place hands over hearts.)* Seshat is the ba in the heart of every magician.

Hierophant: *(Gives the candidate the initiatory token.)* This token is black on one side and white on the other. It has three meanings. First, it is a tile of the floor of the temple of the earth, so that with this token you can always return directly to the temple of the earth from any other place you might journey. Second, it is a symbol of the double goddess—Isis and Nephthys, Demeter and Kore, mother/daughter and sister/sister, who guided you today. Third and lastly, this token is a reminder that ours is the magic of light and darkness.

Soror of Seshat, initiate of the temple of the earth, be seated with your sister magicians.

Hierophant picks up the cord, places it on the air altar, returns to her station and sits.

Hierophant: Soror [candidate name or motto], you have passed through the depths where the shadow of the Tree of Life shimmers in the dark waters to emerge in the temple of the earth where the tree roots and reaches to the heights. Each of us confronts the shadows within ourselves and finds our own way along the tree to the stars.

If you decide to proceed in our company, there are further journeys we may take together. Should you desire to move further along this path, you may come to the temple and say to us, "I seek to enter the gate of mystery." In the meantime, we enjoin you to aid your sisters in their journeys as they have aided you in yours. Welcome to the temple, sister of Seshat!

Applause.

Closing and Grounding the Temple

The officers close and ground the temple using the temple ritual.

THE MOON INITIATION

THE MOON INITIATION
EXPLANATORY NOTES

As the number of the moon is nine, this ritual is built on the powers of three times three. The ritual begins in the temple of the earth and then shifts to encompass the 32nd path.

The first part of the ritual explains the Tree of Life as a Qabbalistic symbol system in the present day as well as the specific symbology of the Order of the Sisters of Seshat. The ritual explains the roots of the Tree of Life in the ancient world and the role priestesses played in developing the sacred tree as a metaphor for the universe and a connection to the powers of creation. This section is guided by a representative of Ariadne, whom Minoan texts call the Mistress of the Labyrinth.

The second part of the ritual takes the candidate through the base of the tree and into the world of Yetzirah. Traveling in the world of faerie enacts this journey. The Child ballads record the stories of Tam Lin and Thomas the Rhymer, who were taken by the queen of Elfland to her realm. These ballads depict the three roads that lead into that realm and how to travel within them safely (Child 1886). Writers give different names to the queen of Elfland. This ritual uses Aine, Patricia Monaghan's name for the spring goddess or goddess of the bright half of the year (Monaghan 1994).

In Qabbalistic terms, the realm of Yesod is associated with sexuality. The moon connects to the physical fertility of women. This ritual does not assume that women will choose to manifest physical fertility, and does not assume that this is the source of women's power. However, this ritual does include sexuality and fertility as part of women's experience as a matter of choice.

The third part of the ritual explores the imagery around the source of the Tree of Life, which is nourished by a sacred spring. The imagery moves from the wildest, the pool in the woods, to the most domestic, the well in the field. As the moon is the mirror of the sun, and water is the mirror of the moon, the spring imagery invokes the image of the mirror. This section of the ritual explores the sources of women's creativity, both the spiritual inspiration to create and the power to renew and transform both self and others.

This section of the ritual is guided by a representative of the Celtic goddess Brigid. Brigid's well still exists, and her flame is tended by priestesses around the world. This goddess provides poetic inspiration and also grants healing.

The goddess Hekate takes many forms. She was associated with the moon late in her development among the Greeks and with Saturn in Qabbalistic imagery. The image used here is that of the Hellenistic Hekate, a threefold goddess who bore three torches. She forms a transitional figure connecting the ritual of mystery, leading to the temple of Yesod or the moon, with the ritual of knowledge, leading to the temple of Hod or Mercury.

This ritual also acknowledges the four levels of the Tree of Life: Atziluth, the world of spirit; Briah, the world of image; Yetzirah, the astral world; and Assiah, the material world. In what is called the composite tree, Malkuth corresponds with Assiah, Yesod corresponds with Yetzirah, Tiphareth corresponds with Briah, and Kether corresponds with Atziluth. The candidate's introduction to the temple of the moon moves her from the world of Assiah into the world of Yetzirah.

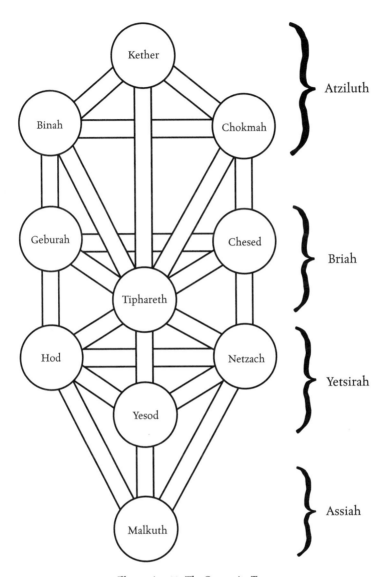

Illustration 22: The Composite Tree

MOON INITIATION: THE GATE OF MYSTERY

Tools

Initiatory tools

- Mirror

- Bell

- Nine white candles (can be tea lights)

Initiatory token: small disk painted black on both sides with a crescent moon on the obverse.

Initiatory tools and token are staged beneath the Hierophant throne until needed.

Diagrams

See List A, at the end of this section. Page 324

Altars

Altar of the Tree: Small table, white altar cloth, Diagrams One through Three

Altar of the Journey: Small table, white altar cloth, Diagrams Four through Six

Altar of the Spring: Small table, white altar cloth, Diagrams Seven through Nine

Altar of the Moon: Small table, white altar cloth, nine white candles in a circle, mirror

Repast altar: Small table, white altar cloth, cups and drink, plate with cakes

Diagrams: One through Nine

Preparing and Opening the Temple

The officers prepare and open the temple using the temple ritual. The candidate is within the temple.

The Petition

Hierophant: Sorors, do we have business today?

Hegemon: Soror Hierophant, a sister of Seshat brings a petition before us.

Hegemon brings the candidate to center of temple, facing Hierophant.

Hegemon: Soror [name], please state your petition.

Candidate: I seek to enter the gate of mystery.

Hierophant: Have you faced the darkness in the world and in yourself?

Hegemon: She bears the token of the temple of Malkuth, the temple of the earth.

Candidate displays the token.

Hierophant: Have you visited that temple again on your own? Are you conversant with its power and familiar with its ways?

Candidate: *[Answers as she wishes.]*

Hierophant: Sisters of Seshat, is it your will to assist this candidate to enter the gate of mystery?

All: It is my will.

Hierophant: Soror [name], please leave the temple for a short time and make yourself ready for the journey.

Hegemon escorts the candidate to the designated waiting area and returns to the temple.

Establishing the Temple of Mystery
Temple Diagram

Sorors break down the altars of earth, fire, and water, leaving the air altar with the image of Seshat and the group egregore object, and set up the Altars of the Tree, the Journey, and the Spring.

Hierophant faces Hierus (west).

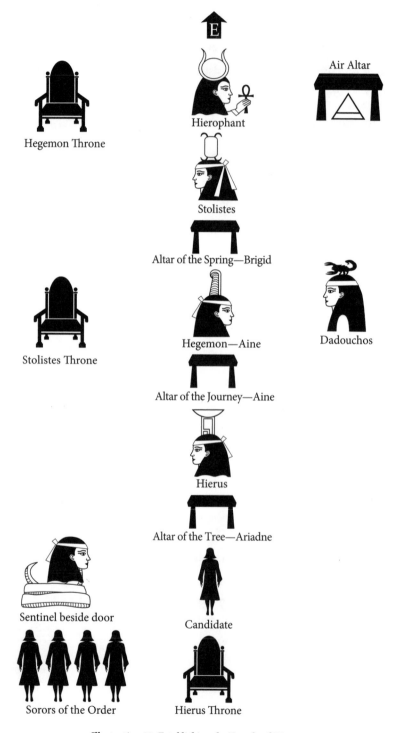

Illustration 23: Establishing the Temple of Mystery

Stolistes stands east of the Altar of the Spring, facing Hierophant (east).

Hegemon stands east of the Altar of the Journey, facing Hierophant (east).

Hierus stands east of the Altar of the Tree, facing Hierophant (east).

Hierophant: Sorors of the Order of Seshat, please assist me to construct the temple of mystery. Soror Hierus, what is the foundation of this temple?

Hierus: The foundation of this temple is in the temple of the earth.

Hierophant: Soror Hegemon, what is the journey of this temple?

Hegemon: The journey of this temple is along the 32nd path from the temple of Malkuth, the temple of the earth, to the temple of Yesod, the temple of the moon.

Hierophant: Soror Stolistes, what sign governs this path?

Stolistes: The path is governed by Saturn, the gatekeeper to the great mystery.

Hierophant: Let us establish the officers on their thrones. Soror Hierus, what are your station and duties?

Hierus: I guard the Altar of the Tree, and I represent Ariadne, Mistress of the Labyrinth.

Hierophant: Soror Hegemon, what are your station and duties?

Hegemon: I guard the Altar of the Journey, and I represent Aine, the queen of Elfland.

Hierophant: Soror Stolistes, what are your station and duties?

Stolistes: I guard the Altar of the Spring, and I represent Brigid, the keeper of the spring.

Hierophant: I guard the Altar of the Moon, and I represent Hekate, the manifestation of Saturn, which rules the 32nd path. Sorors, we have opened the hall of mystery.

Seeking the Gate of Mystery
The Labyrinth

Hierophant: Soror Hegemon, please bring the candidate to the door. Soror Hierus, please admit her when she gives the proper alarm.

Hegemon leaves the hall and seeks out the candidate in the prepared waiting area. Hegemon checks to make sure the candidate is ready to begin the initiation. Hegemon takes the candidate to the door, instructing her to give nine knocks: !!! !!! !!! Hierus opens the door, admits the candidate. Hegemon closes the door and leads the candidate to stand before Hierophant. Hegemon returns to her station and sits.

Hierophant: Candidate, do you pledge to persevere in your quest to experience mystery?

Candidate: *(Unprompted)* I do.

Hierophant: Then say, "Let the triple powers witness my pledge."

Candidate: Let the triple powers witness my pledge.

Hierophant: *(Strikes bell three times.)* Soror Hierus, please provide the candidate with the necessary instructions to successfully complete her journey.

Hierus: I represent Ariadne, the Mistress of the Labyrinth. Follow me as I guide you through the maze before you.

Hierus leads the candidate circumambulating the temple clockwise until the candidate reaches the Altar of the Tree. Hierus places the candidate west of the altar facing Hierophant (east). Hierus moves to the other side of the altar to face the candidate (west). Hierus turns over Diagram One.

Hierus: You stand at the foot of the Tree of Life. This tree has three main trunks: the black pillar, the white pillar, and the middle pillar. In the temple of this order, these pillars are represented by Nephthys, Isis, and Seshat.

Hierus leads the candidate circumambulating the temple clockwise until the candidate reaches the Altar of the Tree. Hierus places the candidate west of the altar facing Hierophant (east). Hierus moves to the other side of the altar to face the candidate (west). Hierus turns over Diagram Two.

Hierus: This tree is rooted in an older tree, the Tree of Life we see in the images of the civilizations of the river valleys. Ariadne's people are among the oldest of these. Minoan priestesses danced before the tree, and desert priestesses honored the green branches. These priestesses built shrines beneath trees, on the mountain peaks, at the seashore, in the deep caves, all the beautiful and sacred places of the earth. We remember those priestesses and honor those places. This reverence is the second key, the knowledge of the true sources of the Tree of Life.

Hierus leads the candidate circumambulating the temple clockwise until the candidate reaches the Altar of the Tree. Hierus places the candidate west of the altar facing Hierophant (east). Hierus moves to the other side of the altar to face the candidate (west). Hierus turns over Diagram Three.

Hierus: As you walk the path from the temple of Malkuth to the temple of Yesod, you enter the world of Yetzirah, where forms shift, where the real casts shadows and is masked by illusion. I give you the third and final key, the key of three. Each power you meet on this journey manifests in three forms.

You have known the tree of Nephthys, Isis, and Seshat. You have seen the source of this tree in the sacred trees of the ancient priestesses. This tree before you now is the third three, the Eildon Tree, that marks the boundary between the human world and the realm of faerie.

The Journey

Hierophant strikes bell three times.

Hegemon goes to the Altar of the Tree to stand beside the candidate.

Hegemon: Why have you come to the Eildon Tree, child of the human world?

Candidate: *(Prompted by Hierus)* I seek to enter the gate of mystery.

Hegemon: Many who wander these ways are lost. Do you bring keys to guide your way?

Hierus: She brings three keys: the token of light and darkness, the knowledge of the sources of the tree of life, and the knowledge of the key of three.

Hegemon: Pass then through the open door into the world of faerie.

Hierus returns to her station and sits. Hegemon leads the candidate circumambulating the temple clockwise until the candidate reaches the Altar of the Journey. Hegemon places the candidate west of the altar facing Hierophant (east). Hegemon moves to the other side of the altar to face the candidate (west). Hegemon turns over Diagram Four.

Hegemon: I represent Aine, the faerie queen. I will show you three wonders. Here is the first: before you stretch three roads. The black road leads to the black court—the blasted ground, the fearful torment, the deceiving guide. The white road leads to the bright court: the flowering meadows, the dancing rings, the healing aid. The middle road leads between these ways to the temple of the moon. This is the path you and I will walk.

Hegemon leads the candidate circumambulating the temple clockwise until the candidate reaches the Altar of the Journey. Hegemon places the candidate west of the altar facing Hierophant (east). Hegemon moves to the other side of the altar to face the candidate (west). Hegemon turns over Diagram Five.

Hegemon: The path which leads from the temple of the earth to the temple of the moon falls under the shadow of Saturn. This sign indicates the discipline of embodiment. This is the second wonder, that of our physical manifestation on earth. Child of the earth, you know your body is sustained by three elements: food which you must eat daily, water which you must drink hourly, air which you must breath every minute.

Hegemon leads the candidate circumambulating the temple clockwise until the candidate reaches the Altar of the Journey. Hegemon places the candidate west of the altar facing Hierophant (east). Hegemon moves to the other side of the altar to face the candidate (west). Hegemon turns over Diagram Six.

Hegemon: The third wonder is the power of sexuality. All human women choose an expression of the body: the way of the virgin, the way of the lover, the way of the mother. The virgin holds her body apart from others, contained and whole in itself. The lover shares her body with others. The mother brings other bodies forth from her own.

(Pause.)

This far and no farther may I guide you on this road.

The Spring

Hierophant strikes the bell three times.

Stolistes goes to the Altar of the Journey and stands beside the candidate.

Stolistes: Why do you approach the spring, traveler on the faerie road?

Candidate: *(Prompted by Hegemon)* I seek to enter the gate of mystery.

Stolistes: Have you seen the wonders that prepare you to enter the gate?

Hegemon: She has seen the wonder of the three faerie roads, the wonder of the discipline of embodiment, and the wonder of sexuality.

Stolistes: I represent Brigid, the keeper of the spring. You have reached the source of mystery, that place where the Tree of Life draws on the water of the universe. This source reveals itself to us in three forms: the pool in the woods, the spring in the rocks, the well in the field.

Hegemon returns to her station and sits. **Stolistes** leads the candidate circumambulating the temple clockwise until the candidate reaches the Altar of the Spring. Stolistes places the candidate west of the altar facing Hierophant (east). Stolistes moves to the other side of the altar to face the candidate (west). Stolistes turns over Diagram Seven.

Stolistes: The pool in the woods is the pool where Hera bathed to renew herself. You have seen the wonder of embodiment and the three paths each of us may take—the path of the virgin, the path of the lover, and the path of the mother. This spring grants the power to move from one state to another. The virgin may open her heart and her body to others, and become the lover. The lover may step into the stream of life and become the mother. The mother may renew her commitment to the sharing of the body and reaffirm her journey as the lover. And the lover may withdraw into herself, becoming again lone and inviolate, the virgin.

Stolistes leads the candidate circumambulating the temple clockwise until the candidate reaches the Altar of the Spring. Stolistes places the candidate west of the altar facing Hierophant (east). Stolistes moves to the other side of the altar to face the candidate (west). Stolistes turns over Diagram Eight.

Stolistes: The spring in the rocks is the source of inspiration. The source of mystery may inspire us to birth, suckle, nourish, the making of the body. It may inspire us in our crafts, the making of the hands. It may spark our most artistic and spiritual creations, the making of the spirit.

Stolistes leads the candidate circumambulating the temple clockwise until the candidate reaches the Altar of the Tree. Stolistes places the candidate west of the altar facing Hierophant (east). Stolistes moves to the other side of the altar to face the candidate (west). Stolistes turns over Diagram Nine.

Stolistes: The well in the fields is the mirror of the tree. As the moon catches the light of the sun, so the well catches the reflection of the tree. Looking into the well as into a scrying bowl we may catch a glimpse of the future. The well captures a snapshot of our souls and shows us to ourselves in truth, or a possibility of becoming what we most wish to be, or experiencing that which we most deeply desire.

Hierophant: You will now leave the temple for a short time to prepare to enter the temple of mystery.

Stolistes leads the candidate out of the temple and returns to the temple.

The Moon Temple
Temple Diagram

The sorors set aside the Altars of the Tree, the Journey, and the Spring. The Altar of the Moon is placed in the center of the temple. The nine candles are arranged in a circle on the altar, with the mirror in the center of the circle of candles.

Hierophant, Hegemon, and Hierus stand to the east of the Altar of the Moon, facing west.

Stolistes and Dadouchos face each other.

Hierophant: Soror Hegemon, please bring the candidate to the door. Soror Hierus, please admit her when she gives the proper alarm.

Hegemon leaves the hall and seeks out the candidate in the prepared waiting area. Hegemon brings the candidate to the door, instructing her to give nine knocks: !!! !!! !!! Hierus opens the door, admits the candidate and Hegemon, closes the door, returns to her station and remains standing.

Hierophant: Approach now the gate of mystery.

Hegemon conducts the candidate to the west of the Altar of the Moon, facing Hierophant (east).

Hierophant: *(Stands.)* Candidate, why do you approach the temple of the moon?

Candidate: *(Prompted by Hegemon)* I seek to enter the gate of mystery.

Hegemon returns to her station and remains standing. Hierophant, Hegemon, and Hierus join hands.

Illustration 24: The Moon Temple

Hierophant, Hegemon, and **Hierus:** *(Together)* We represent Hekate, the triple goddess.

Hierus: Goddess of Saturn, which governs the path you have walked.

Hegemon: Goddess of the moon, whose hall you have entered.

Hierophant: Goddess of creation, the torchbearer of light.

Hegemon and Hierus drop hands and sit.

Hierophant: *(Moves to the Altar of the Moon.)* Three figures have you met in this temple, and each has shown you three marvels. Three times three unlocks the gate to mystery.

Venturing beyond the temple of Malkuth to the temple of Yesod, you move beyond the world of Assiah, where the material is manifest, into the world of Yetzirah which infuses the material world with its energy. Here forms shift and change as they are not yet fixed in manifestation. Here is the stuff of dreams and visions, the source of the fertility which sustains the human race physically and spiritually. We come here to be renewed, to be inspired, to be transformed.

Hierophant indicates mirror.

Hierophant: Look here into the mirror of the moon to see what may be revealed to you.

The candidate looks into the mirror. Hierophant waits until the candidate looks up and indicates she is finished.

Hierophant: *(Gives the candidate the initiatory token.)* This is the token of the temple of Yesod, the temple of the moon. With this token you can always return to the temple of the moon from any other place you might journey. We walk through the gate of mystery many times in our lives.

Sister of Seshat, initiate of mystery, be seated with your sister magicians.

Hierophant: *(Returns to her station and sits.)* Soror [candidate name or motto], you have now passed through the gate of mystery in your journey with us. Should you desire to move further along this path, you may come to the temple and say to us, "I seek to walk the path of knowledge." As before, we enjoin you to aid your sisters in their journeys as they have aided you in yours.

Closing and Grounding the Temple

The officers close and ground the temple using the Temple Ritual.

THE MERCURY INITIATION

THE MERCURY INITIATION
EXPLANATORY NOTES

Path of Fire

The Golden Dawn 31st path imagery invokes male Greek fire deities, the cabiri or kabiri, to embody the power of volcanic fire. However, native peoples speak about volcanoes around the world as embodying female powers as well as male. Many of us are familiar with Pele, the Hawaiian goddess of Mt. Kilauea. In the Pacific Northwest, the Cascade mountain volcanoes which now bear the male names explorers gave them—Baker, Adams, Rainier, St. Helens, Hood—were known by some native tribes by female names—Kulshan, Pahto, Tahoma, Loowik, Wasco. The description of a volcanic eruption in this initiation is based on the 1981 eruption of Loowik, Mt. St. Helens.

The speeches read while the candidate is standing inside the circle of fire paraphrase references to fire from Ruth Majercik's translations of the Chaldean Oracles (Majercik 1989). There are four exact quotes:

Fragment 63: "From there, all things extend wonderful rays down below."

Fragment 10: "All things have been generated from the one fire."

Fragment 128: "Extend your mind, illumined by fire."

Fragment 148: "Then listen to the voice of fire."

The phrase "And when after all the phantoms have vanished, thou shalt see that holy and formless fire" appears in the original Golden Dawn Practicus ritual and in the redaction of that ritual by the Open Source Order of the Golden Dawn.

Although the Golden Dawn emphasizes the Father as source of fire, I have here chosen to emphasize Hekate as the voice of fire. To explore the Chaldean Hekate, see the essay in *The Goddess Hekate* (Ronan 1992).

Path of the Sun

The path of the sun narrates similar stories from around the globe. From Europe we have the story of Demeter and Persephone. This story is not about the sun and her daughter, but is similar in structure to the story of the withdrawal of Amaterasu-omikami from the earth. In both stories, the source of life withdraws from the earth, leaving the earth cast in darkness and cold. Some scholars believe these stories encode a memory of the earth's last ice age.

Scholars studying goddesses of the Mediterranean point to their solar aspects. These goddesses include Hathor, Sekhmet, and Aphrodite. Indo-European dawn goddesses include the Sanskrit Ushas and the Greek Eos. In the Balkans, the sun and her daughter spin and weave.

We see from the telling of stories from around the globe and from the human past that the sun has been comprehended as the life-giving power, echoing on earth through the life-giving power of the female, and in particular the human woman. These are literal truths as well as magical metaphors.

City of Ladies

The temple of Hod or Mercury builds on the work begun by Christine de Pizan in the fifteenth century. With the help of the Ladies Reason, Rectitude, and Justice, she created the walls of the city that shelters the women of history (de Pizan 1405, 1982).

The women in this version of the city fall into eight categories reflecting the structure of the temple of Mercury. Each of us maintains the city by remembering women's names and their contributions to humanity.

MERCURY INITIATION:
THE PATH OF KNOWLEGE

Tools

Initiatory tools

Eight red candles (these can be tea lights).

Initiatory token: small disk painted white on both sides with the symbol of Mercury in orange on the obverse.

Initiatory tools and token can be staged beneath the Hierophant throne or anywhere convenient until needed.

Altars

Altar of the Sun: Small table, yellow candle

Altar of Mercury: Small table, white, yellow or orange altar cloth, Diagram Nine

Diagrams: One through Nine, see List A.

Preparing and Opening the Temple

The officers prepare and open the temple using the Temple Ritual. The candidate is within the temple.

The Petition

Hierophant: Sorors, do we have business today?

Hegemon: Soror Hierophant, a sister of Seshat brings a petition before us.

Hegemon brings the candidate to center of temple, facing Hierophant.

Hegemon: Soror [name], please state your petition.

Candidate: I seek to walk the path of knowledge.

Hierophant: Have you passed through the gate of mystery?

Hegemon: She bears the token of the temple of Yesod, the temple of the moon.

Candidate displays the token.

Hierophant: Have you visited that temple again on your own? Are you conversant with its power and familiar with its ways?

Candidate: [Answers as she wishes.]

Hierophant: Sisters of Seshat, is it your will to assist this candidate to walk the path of knowledge?

All: It is my will.

Hierophant: Soror [name], please leave the temple for a short time and make yourself ready for the journey.

Hegemon escorts the candidate to the designated waiting area and returns to the temple.

Establishing the Temple of Knowledge
Temple Diagram

Hierophant faces Hierus (west).

Hegemon and Hierus face Hierophant (east).

Stolistes and Dadouchos face each other.

Sorors break down the altars of earth, fire, and water, leaving the air altar with the image of Seshat and the group egregore object, and set up red candles in a circle.

Hierophant: Sorors of the Order of Seshat, please assist me to construct the temple of knowledge. Soror Hegemon, what is the journey of this temple?

Hegemon: Along the 31st path from the temple of Malkuth, the temple of the earth; and along the 30th path from the temple of Yesod, the temple of the moon; to the temple of Hod, the temple of Mercury.

Hierophant: Soror Hierus, what signs govern these paths?

Hierus: The sign of fire, and the sign of the sun, the great fire.

Hierophant: Let us establish the officers on their thrones. Soror Hegemon, what are your station and duties?

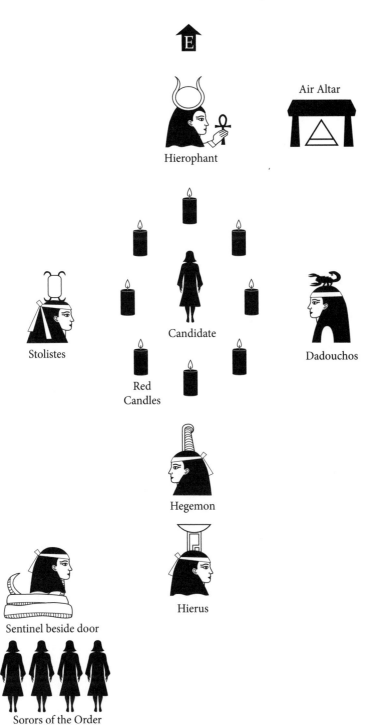

Illustration 25: Establishing the Temple of Knowledge

Hegemon: I guide the candidate on her journey along the path of the sun, and I am a guardian of knowledge.

Hierophant: Soror Hierus, what are your station and duties?

Hierus: I guide the candidate on her journey through fire, and I am a guardian of knowledge.

Hierophant: Soror Dadouchos, what are your station and duties?

Dadouchos: I administer the element of fire in the temple, and I am a guardian of knowledge.

Hierophant: Soror Stolistes, what are your station and duties?

Stolistes: I administer the element of water in the temple, and I am a guardian of knowledge.

Hierophant: I represent Hekate, I supervise the conduct of the ritual, and I am a guardian of knowledge. Sorors, we have opened the path of knowledge.

The Path of Fire

Hierophant: Soror Dadouchos, please take your station in the ring of fire. Soror Hegemon, please bring the candidate to the door. Soror Hierus, please admit her when she gives the proper alarm.

Dadouchos stands in the center of the candle ring, facing the Hierus throne (west). Hegemon leaves the hall and seeks out the candidate in the prepared waiting area. Hegemon checks to make sure the candidate is ready to begin the initiation. Hegemon takes the candidate to the door, instructing her to give eight knocks: !!!! !!!! Hierus opens the door, admits Hegemon and the candidate, closes the door, returns to her station and sits. Hegemon leads the candidate to face Hierophant and remains with the candidate.

Hierophant: Candidate, are you willing to pass through fire to walk the path of knowledge?

Candidate: *(Unprompted)* I am.

Hierophant: Then say, "Let the powers of knowledge witness my pledge."

Candidate: Let the powers of knowledge witness my pledge.

Hierophant: *(Strikes bell four times.)* Let the candidate walk the ring of fire.

> *Hegemon guides the candidate in four clockwise circumambulations outside the ring of fire while Dadouchos speaks. Hegemon should remain on the outside of the candidate during the circumambulations.*

Dadouchos: The earth lives and our lives are spent within the body of a living thing. The currents of the air swirl around and above us while the molten fire swells beneath our feet. The ring of fire surrounds us, the white breasts of the mountains, the sisters of chaos and creation. Our closest sisters are [closest volcano name or names].

> *(Example for the Pacific Northwest:* **Kulshan** *(Baker),* **Tahoma** *(Rainier),* **Loowik** *(St. Helens),* **Pahto** *(Adams),* **Wasco** *(Hood).)*

Dadouchos: When Volcano Woman moves, the living earth changes. The molten fire seeps through cracks in the earth and gently moves over the ground and into the sea. When the earth quakes it starts with a rumble, a thundering rush of sound, and then the earth trembles, moves violently, splits open. When the volcano erupts, the side of a mountain falls away. Glaciers melt and spill walls of water into the valleys, a stone wind blasts the forest for many miles, clouds of ash billow into the air, blanket the ground for hundreds of miles, and encircle the earth.

> *Hegemon stops the candidate at the west of the candle circle, facing east.*

Dadouchos: *(Faces the candidate.)* Do you dare to brave the heart of fire?

Candidate: *(Unprompted)* I do.

Dadouchos: Then cross through the ring of fire.

> *Dadouchos steps out of the circle.* **Dadouchos** *and* **Hegemon** *assist the candidate to step over the circle of candles to stand in the center of the circle, making sure the candidate faces Hierophant (east). Hegemon*

stands on the west side of the circle, facing Hierophant (east). Dadouchos circumambulates clockwise once around the ring of candles while Hegemon reads:

Hegemon: From the source of sources, matter springs forth, a lightning bolt leaping into the hollows of the worlds. From there, all things extend wonderful rays down below.

Dadouchos comes to a stop next to Hegemon. **Hegemon** *and* **Dadouchos** *say together:*

Hegemon and **Dadouchos:** All things extend wonderful rays down below.

Dadouchos circumambulates clockwise a second time around the ring of candles while Hegemon reads:

Hegemon: The first course is the sacred course. The middle course is the course of air. The third course heats the earth with fire. All things have been generated from the one fire.

Dadouchos comes to a stop next to Hierus. **Hegemon** *and* **Dadouchos** *say together:*

Hegemon and **Dadouchos:** All things have been generated from the one fire.

Dadouchos circumambulates clockwise a third time around the ring of candles while Hegemon reads:

Hegemon: The soul descended in a certain order to serve the body. Seek out the channel of the soul. Seek how you will raise it up again by combining sacred ritual with sacred word. For the soul is an immortal fire. Rise up and onward to the center of the light. Let the immortal depth of your soul be opened. Let your eyes reach up, making your soul bright with fire. Extend your mind, illumined by fire.

Dadouchos comes to a stop next to Hegemon. **Hegemon** *and* **Dadouchos** *say together:*

Hegemon and **Dadouchos:** Extend your mind, illumined by fire.

Dadouchos circumambulates clockwise a fourth time around the ring of candles while Hegemon reads:

Hegemon: After the invocation, you may see many forms. You may see a child, or a horse, or a lion-form. You may perceive billows of air, or darkness where the stars do not shine, or darkness where the moon's light is hidden. You may see a place where everything is illuminated by lightning flashes. You may see a sumptuous spiraling light. But when at last the phantoms have vanished, you will see the holy and formless fire shining throughout the world. Then listen to the voice of fire.

Dadouchos comes to a stop next to Hegemon. **Hegemon** *and* **Dadouchos** *say together:*

Hegemon and **Dadouchos:** Listen to the voice of fire!

Hierophant: The voice of the fire is Hekate, the torch-bearer of the universe. Nature is suspended on the back of this goddess. Because of her the sky spins every night in its eternal rounds, the sun keeps its eternal course. From Hekate the great stream of soul flows, en-souling light, fire, aether, worlds. Her shimmering hair appears in dazzling light, she has faces on all sides, she sends forth the channels of mortal life, she contains within herself the procession of all beings. Her voice reveals to us the order of the universe and guides our souls, kindling the fires that lead us upwards.

You will now leave the temple for a short time to prepare to receive the knowledge of this temple.

Hegemon leads the candidate out of the temple.

The Path of the Sun
Temple Diagram

Sorors set up the Altar of the Sun.

Hierophant faces Hierus (west).

Hierophant

Air Altar

Altar of the Sun

Candidate

Stolistes

Dadouchos

Hegemon

Hierus

Sentinel beside door

Sorors of the Order

Illustration 26: The Path of the Sun

*Hegemon and **Hierus** face Hierophant (east).*

*Stolistes and **Dadouchos** face each other.*

Hierophant: Soror Hegemon, please bring the candidate to the door. Soror Hierus, please admit her when she gives the proper alarm.

*Hegemon leaves the hall and seeks out the candidate in the prepared waiting area, takes the candidate to the door, and instructs her to give eight knocks: !!!! !!!! **Hierus** opens the door, admits Hegemon and the candidate, closes the door, returns to her station and sits. Hegemon leads the candidate to face Hierophant and remains with the candidate.*

Hierophant: Candidate, you have passed through fire on your journey along the path of knowledge. You must now receive instruction so that you may enter the company of those who preserve and add to knowledge.

*Hegemon leads the candidate in the first circumambulation clockwise around the temple. When they reach **Hierus**, she blocks the candidate's path.*

Hierus: You cannot pass by me unless you can tell me the knowledge I keep.

Candidate: *(Prompted by Hegemon)* You are the guardian of the sources of our tradition and the teller of the story that comes to us from Europe.

Hierus: Europe knows the sun goddess as Sul and her daughter Sunna, and Saule and her daughter Saules Meita. We do not have their stories, but we do have the story of the mother and daughter Demeter and Persephone. When Persephone the daughter withdrew from the world to travel to the underworld and bring light to the souls in darkness there, her mother Demeter grieved for her absence. She locked herself into the earth and would not show her face. Cold winds blew, snow fell, all green things died, and the creatures of the earth struggled to survive. The people of the earth knew they would die if Demeter did not return and the cold went on forever. They sent the woman Baubo to bring Demeter out of her cave. Baubo called to Demeter, "My lady, look!" and danced for her, lifting her skirts like a bawdy clown. Demeter laughed and came forth from her cave, the cold lifted, and green things grew again. Persephone came back from the underworld and promised to remain with her mother through most of the year, returning only for a third of the year to bring comfort to the souls of the underworld.

Hierus sits. Hegemon leads the candidate in the second circumambulation clockwise around the temple. When they reach Dadouchos, she stands to block the candidate's path.

Dadouchos: You cannot pass by me unless you can tell me the knowledge I keep.

Candidate: *(Prompted by Hegemon)* You are the guardian of the sources of our tradition and the teller of the story that comes to us from Africa.

Dadouchos: In Egypt there are many stories of the goddess who is the eye of the sun, Sekhmet, Bast, Hathor, Mut. The story is told of this goddess that she wandered away and left the black fertile land. Then the world grew cold, the skies opened and fierce rains filled the sky, and all living things shivered and suffered. With dancing, singing, and offering beautiful jewels, the sun goddess was enticed to return and bring light and warmth to the black earth again.

Hegemon leads the candidate on the third circumambulation clockwise around the temple. When Hegemon and the candidate reach the station of Stolistes, she stands to block the candidate's path.

Stolistes: You cannot pass by me unless you can tell me the knowledge I keep.

Candidate: *(Prompted by Hegemon)* You are the guardian of the sources of our tradition and the teller of the story that comes to us from Asia.

Stolistes: Here is the story of Amaterasu-omikami, the Great Shining One of Heaven. It happened that Amaterasu-omikami flinched from the violence and impurity of the world and hid herself in a cave. The *kami* knew that the world would not survive without her light. They held a great party before the cave. At the height of the party Ame-no-uzume-no-mikoto danced for the *kami*, spinning on the head of her giant drum. The *kami* clapped and shouted. Amaterasu-omikami peeked out from the cave and saw her own beautiful reflection in the mirror. She was drawn to emerge from the cave, which was quickly shut behind her. So light came back into the world and life was saved.

Hegemon returns to her station and sits. **Stolistes** *leads the candidate on the fourth circumambulation clockwise around the temple. When Stolistes and the candidate reach the station of Hegemon, she stands to block the candidate's path.*

Hegemon: You cannot pass by me unless you can tell me the knowledge I keep.

Candidate: *(Prompted by Stolistes)* You are the guardian of the sources of our tradition and the teller of the story that comes to us from America.

Hegemon: Here is the story of Grandmother Sun. It happened that she became angry with the people of the earth and shone down on them so brightly that they feared they would all die. They decided that they had to kill Grandmother Sun so they could survive. They sent the rattlesnake to kill her. He knocked on the door of the house of the sun. The door opened and the rattlesnake struck. Alas, it was only the sun's daughter, who fell on the doorstep dead. The rattlesnake ran away in fear and grief.

When the sun returned, she found her daughter dead. Then she sent up a great lamentation. She locked herself in her house and refused to emerge. Then the earth grew cold, the ice came, and the green things died. The people realized they could not survive without the sun. They gathered at the sun's house and danced and sang for her to show her that they needed her and loved her. The sun

Hierophant

Air Altar

Altar of Mercury

Candidate

Stolistes

Dadouchos

Hegemon

Hierus

Sentinel beside door

Sorors of the Order

Illustration 27: The Temple of Knowledge

E: Diagram 1

NE: Diagram 8   SE: Diagram 2

Hierophant

Hegemon

Altar of Mercury

N: S:
Diagram 7   Diagram 3

Stolistes   Dadouchos

NW: Diagram 6   SW: Diagram 4

Hierus

W: Diagram 5

Sentinel beside door

Sorors of the Order

Illustration 28: Temple of Knowledge Diagrams

heard their singing and emerged to watch their joyful dancing. Her grief lifted, she smiled, and she resumed her daily courses. The ice melted, green things grew, and life was saved.

Stolistes returns to her station and sits. Hegemon leads the candidate directly to the west of the Altar of the Sun, facing Hierophant (east). Hegemon returns to her station and sits. Hierophant descends from her station to the east of the Altar of the Sun.

Hierophant: You have heard the stories that come to us from the four quarters of the earth, the sources of our tradition. These ancient stories encode the memories and wisdom of our ancestors. The sun is the great fire, the source of all life on earth. This is a profound insight and a fundamental truth. Look here into the candle flame, a small spark of the great fire, and meditate upon this knowledge.

The candidate looks at the flame. Hierophant waits until the candidate looks up and indicates she is finished.

Hierophant: You will now leave the temple for a short time. When you return you will be admitted to the company of those who preserve and add to knowledge.

Hegemon takes the candidate back out to the waiting area. Hegemon ensures that the candidate is well and able to be left alone before returning to the temple.

The Temple of Knowledge
Temple Diagram

Sorors set up the Altar of Mercury and place diagrams in their positions.

Hierophant faces Hierus (west).

Hegemon and Hierus face Hierophant (east).

Stolistes and Dadouchos face each other.

E—Diagram One, Creatives

SE—Diagram Two, Explorers

S—Diagram Three, Athletes

SW—Diagram Four, Magicians

W—Diagram Five, Religious

NW—Diagram Six, Philosophers

N—Diagram Seven, Makers

NE—Diagram Eight, Politicians

Hierophant: *(Rings bell eight times: !!!! !!!!)* Soror Hegemon, please bring the candidate to the door, and knock once. Soror Hierus, please admit the candidate.

*Hegemon leaves the hall and seeks out the candidate in the prepared waiting area. When Hegemon knocks, **Hierus** opens the door, admits Hegemon and the candidate, closes the door, returns to her station and sits. Hegemon leads the candidate to face Hierophant, returns to her station and sits.*

Hierophant: *(Stands)* Soror [name], welcome to the temple of Mercury, the City of Ladies. You have passed through fire and stand on the wings of the sun to achieve admittance to this temple.

Hierophant points to Diagram One in the east.

Hierophant: Let me begin your tour of the city. Its foundations were laid by Christine de Pizan, a Frenchwoman whose father was the court astrologer to Charles the Fifth. Growing up at court with a doting father, she received an education that was extraordinary in its time. When Charles the Fifth died, Christine's father fell from grace at court and died himself. A few years later Christine's husband also died, leaving her, at 25, with three young children and a mother to support.

Christine parlayed her education and political acumen into a living. She came to be known as Christina Magistra Ludi, Mistress of the Game. An accomplished lyric poet and writer, she was the official biographer of Charles the Fifth and wrote many works on commission.

Most importantly, she was a fierce champion for women. Her great work, *The Book of the City of Ladies*, was published in 1405. It begins with a lament: "Why do so many learned men slander women?" Christine defended the character of women and recorded the lives of notable women, inviting them into the city.

Here is Christine in her study. She is a true sister of Seshat. The names arrayed below her are the names of other notable creative women, artists, musicians, writers, dancers, actors: Hildegard the musician-composer, Isabella Andreini the actress, Mary Wollstonecraft the writer, Isadora Duncan the dancer, Emily Carr the painter, Lillian Hellman the playwright, and many others. We admire and remember them.

Hegemon leads the candidate to Diagram Two in the southeast, returns to her station and sits. Narrator Two joins them at the diagram.

Narrator Two: Here you see the explorers in the city, travelers, scientists, seekers of knowledge and of adventure. *(Narrates life of the featured woman and repeats the additional names on the diagram.)*

Narrator Two leads the candidate to Diagram Three in the south, returns to her station and sits. Narrator Three joins the candidate at the diagram.

Narrator Three: Here you see the athletes in the city. Among these are counted the warriors who fought in or led their people's armies. *(Narrates life of the featured woman and repeats the additional names on the diagram.)*

Narrator Three leads the candidate to Diagram Four in the southwest, returns to her station and sits. Narrator Four joins the candidate at the diagram.

Narrator Four: Here you see the magicians in the city. These women are our closest sisters, and we continue the work they began, even as other women will continue our work *(Narrates life of the featured woman and repeats the additional names on the diagram.)*

Narrator Four leads the candidate to Diagram Five in the west, returns to her station and sits. Narrator Five joins the candidate at the diagram.

Narrator Five: Here you see the religious in the city. These include the thinkers and religious practitioners of the religions of humanity, all the theologians, ritualists, priestesses, nuns, mystics, and householders who have centered their lives on the works of the spirit. *(Narrates life of the featured woman and repeats the additional names on the diagram.)*

Narrator Five leads the candidate to Diagram Six in the northwest, returns to her station and sits. Narrator Six joins the candidate at the diagram.

Narrator Six: Here you see the philosophers. There are fewer names here because of the fierce opposition these women faced in their calling. Especially we remember Hypatia, the fourth-century philosopher mathematician who taught privately and in the streets of Alexandria and was killed by a mob of assassins. *(Narrates life of the featured woman and repeats the additional names on the diagram.)*

Narrator Six leads the candidate to Diagram Seven in the north, returns to her station and sits. Narrator Seven joins the candidate at the diagram.

Narrator Seven: Here you see the makers in the city, all the architects, farmers, weavers, potters, designers. *(Narrates life of the featured woman and repeats the additional names on the diagram.)*

Narrator Seven leads the candidate to Diagram Eight in the northeast, returns to her station and sits. Narrator Eight joins the candidate at the diagram.

Narrator Eight: Here you see all the politicians in the city, all the women who have ruled, led, and taught, the queens, empresses, pharaohs, presidents, who have devoted their lives to leadership. *(Narrates life of the featured woman and repeats the additional names on the diagram.)*

Narrator Eight leads the candidate to the west of the Altar of Mercury, facing Hierophant (east). Narrator Eight returns to her station and sits.

Hierophant: *(Stands in the east, facing Hierus/west.)* Sorors, please stand.

All stand, facing the Altar of Mercury.

Hierophant: Christine invited the mother of her god into her city. Sorors, let us invite into the temple our sister Seshat, Mistress of Builders, She who is Foremost in the House of Books.

All place hands in the sign of Seshat and vibrate:

All: Seshat!

All: *(Place hands over hearts.)* Seshat is the ba in the heart of every magician.

Hierophant: Sorors, please be seated.

All return to their stations, except the candidate, who remains west of the Altar of Mercury, facing Hierophant (east).

Hierophant: *(Gives the candidate the initiatory token.)* This token bears the symbol of Mercury. It indicates the trials you have undergone and the powers you have made your own in achieving the City of Ladies. With this token you can always return to the temple of Mercury from any other place you might journey. We encourage you to visit the City of Ladies as often as you can, to remember the citizens of that city, and to bring other women into the city.

Sister of Seshat, citizen of the City of Ladies, be seated with your sister magicians.

Hierophant returns to her station and sits.

Hierophant: Soror [candidate name or motto], now you have walked the path of knowledge in your journey with us. Should you desire to move further along this path, you may come to the temple and say to us, "I seek the charm of beauty." As before, we enjoin you to aid your sisters in their journeys as they have aided you in yours.

Closing and Grounding the Temple

The officers close and ground the temple using the temple ritual.

THE VENUS INITIATION

THE VENUS INITIATION
EXPLANATORY NOTES

Path of Pisces

The goddesses associated with the planet Venus in the Near East and Mediterranean connect with one another. In addition to Inanna, Ishtar, Aphrodite, and Anat, there are also Hathor, Asherah, Qadesh, Astarte, Anahita, and many others. Atargatis is one of these goddesses. The description of her temple comes from the Latin writer Lucian's *Syrian Goddess*.

The constellation Pisces was connected to Atargatis and her lake by many stories. Atargatis fell into the lake and was saved by a fish; threw herself into the lake for love and was turned into a half-fish; fell into the lake as an egg and hatched as a half-fish. Ovid tells the story of Dione fleeing from a monster by jumping into a river and being saved by a fish. In each case the shape of the constellation commemorates the relationship of the fish and the goddess.

Path of Aquarius

Any of the goddesses of love could exemplify the traditionally feminine qualities invoked by the path from the moon to Venus. The goddess Juno Covella was proclaimed at the nones of the month, the first quarter of the moon and the early part of the month, linking her to the calendar, appropriate for the sign that begins the astrological calendar. As

Juno bears both maidenly and matronly aspects, she is also an exemplar of the double goddess and the double nature of women's physical life, which divides into fertile and mature phases.

In the Iliad, Hera asks Aphrodite for a love charm. Aphrodite loans her the *kestos himas*, a band of cloth that contains three powers: *himeros*, the desire of love; *philotes*, probably sexual desire; and *oaristys paraphasis*, sweet beguilement (Brenk 1998).

Path of Mars

Although modern mythology types deities with a function, like "god of war" and "goddess of love," in their original cultural contexts deities are often more complex. Ancient Greek and Roman deities bear many epithets relating to their extended functions and personalities. The Qabbalistic classification system encourages us to think about deities as relating to a single sphere, but many deities can fill the entire tree. Each of the Mediterranean goddesses of love also bear warrior aspects and act as goddesses of war.

The path of the warrior refers to physical combat. The war memorial here commemorates all women who have walked that path, with examples from around the world and many time periods.

The path of war encompasses more than armed combat. Any woman or man who acts to protect others steps into the warrior role. The memorial here commemorates those women who lose their lives because they are women and the targets of physical and cultural violence. The path of the warrior enjoins us to protect ourselves and those less able than us.

The goddess Anat appears throughout the Mediterranean region. Her story is told as a European one, although it is more accurately Near Eastern. This story derives from the Ugaritic myths (Pritchard 1958). Numerous writers reference the story about Sekhmet's rage being tamed by red beer. The story of Durga and Kali comes from the eighth chapter of the Devi Mahatmya (*Sivananda nd*). The Incan goddess Mama Huaco is a complex deity who acts to nurture and protect her people. This story is the most aggressive story told about her and the most aggressive story in the collection.

The stories illustrate both the admirable and execrable aspects of war-rage. They serve as reminders of the cruelty and bravery of human conduct in war. It is also a reminder that although the cultural expectation of women is that of peacemakers, women are as capable of cruelty and bravery as men.

The Charm of Beauty

The temple itself plays on the inside-outside tropes of war and gender with the warrior outside protecting the vulnerable inside. In this temple, the sisters themselves act to protect the temple space. The warrior stands outside to protect the community, the house, or the circle; inside, the inhabitants are free to relax and participate in all the pleasures of sensual and spiritual delights.

VENUS INITIATION: THE CHARM OF BEAUTY

Tools

All tools of the Temple Ritual.

Initiatory tools

- Seven blue vases.
- Girdle (cord to tie around candidate's waist).
- Sword.

Initiatory token: a disk painted white on both sides with the Venus sign in green on the obverse.

Initiatory tools and token can be staged beneath the Hierophant throne or anywhere convenient until needed.

Altars

Altar of Pisces: Small table, decorative altar cloth, Diagram One

Altar of Aquarius: Small table, white cloth, bowl of water and aspergillum, girdle

Altar of Mars: Small table, red cloth, Diagram Two, personal images brought by sorors

Altar of Venus: Small table, white or green altar cloth, roses

Diagrams: Diagrams One and Two, see List A.

Preparing and Opening the Temple

The officers prepare and open the temple using the Temple Ritual. The candidate is within the temple.

The Petition

Hierophant: Sorors, do we have business today?

Hegemon: Soror Hierophant, a sister of Seshat brings a petition before us.

Hegemon brings the candidate to center of temple, facing Hierophant.

Hegemon: Soror [name], please state your petition.

Candidate: I seek the charm of beauty.

Hierophant: Have you walked the path of knowledge?

Hegemon: She bears the token of the temple of Hod, the temple of Mercury.

Candidate displays the token.

Hierophant: Have you visited that temple again on your own? Are you conversant with its power and familiar with its ways?

Candidate: [*Answers as she wishes.*]

Hierophant: Sisters of Seshat, is it your will to assist this candidate to obtain the charm of beauty?

All: It is my will.

Hierophant: Soror [name], please leave the temple for a short time and make yourself ready for the journey.

Hegemon escorts the candidate to the designated waiting area and returns to the temple.

Establishing the Temple of Beauty
Temple Diagram

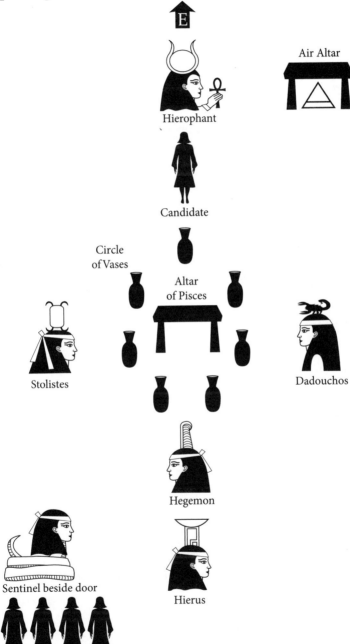

Illustration 29: The Temple of Beauty

Hierophant faces Hierus (west).

Hegemon and Hierus face Hierophant (east).

Stolistes and Dadouchos face each other.

Sorors break down the altars of earth, fire, and water, leaving the air altar with the image of Seshat and the group egregore object, and set up circle of vases to surround the Altar of Pisces.

Hierophant: Sorors of the Order of Seshat, please assist me to construct the temple of beauty. Soror Hegemon, what is the journey of this temple?

Hegemon: Along the 29th path from the temple of Malkuth, the temple of the earth; the 28th path from the temple of Yesod, the temple of the moon; and the 27th path from the temple of Hod, the temple of Mercury; to the temple of Netzach, the temple of Venus.

Hierophant: Soror Hierus, what signs govern these paths?

Hierus: The sign of Pisces, the sign of Aquarius, and the sign of Mars.

Hierophant: Let us establish the officers on their thrones. Soror Hegemon, what are your station and duties?

Hegemon: I guide the candidate on her journey, and I am a soldier of beauty.

Hierophant: Soror Hierus, what are your station and duties?

Hierus: I guide the candidate on her journey, and I am a soldier of beauty.

Hierophant: Soror Dadouchos, what are your station and duties?

Dadouchos: I administer the element of fire in the temple, and I am a soldier of beauty.

Hierophant: Soror Stolistes, what are your station and duties?

Stolistes: I administer the element of water in the temple, and I am a soldier of beauty.

Hierophant: I guide the candidate in the temple, I supervise the conduct of the ritual, and I am a soldier of beauty. Sorors, we have invoked the charm of beauty.

The Path of Pisces

Hierophant: Soror Stolistes, please take your station at the gate of water. Soror Hegemon, please bring the candidate to the door. Soror Hierus, please admit her when she gives the proper alarm.

Hierophant stands, removes the flower from Altar of Pisces and holds it, remaining standing. Stolistes stands west of the circle of vases, facing Hierophant (east). Hegemon leaves the hall and seeks out the candidate in the prepared waiting area. Hegemon checks to make sure the candidate is ready to begin the initiation. Hegemon takes the candidate to the door, instructing her to give seven knocks: !!!! !!! Hierus opens the door, admits Hegemon and the candidate, closes the door, returns to her station and sits. Hegemon leads the candidate to stand before Hierophant, and remains standing.

Hierophant: Candidate, are you willing to pass through water to obtain the charm of beauty?

Candidate: *(Unprompted)* I am.

Hierophant: Then say, "Let the powers of beauty witness my pledge."

Candidate: Let the powers of beauty witness my pledge.

Hierophant: *(Declaims:)* The priestess who governs the works of fire must first sprinkle with the lustral water of the loud resounding sea.

(Speaking tone:) We grasp fire as a tool. We wield fire to create our work in the world. Poised on the knife-edge of discipline we bring all the power of intellect to bear on the works of fire to contain and direct it, control and master it.

We give ourselves to water. Relaxing, surrendering, we release control, borne away on the currents which carry us to an unknown destination. The boundaries of our soul blur and we open ourselves to dreams and visions. The boundaries of our body blur and we open ourselves to desire, touch, merging with another, allowing another to emerge from us.

When we slip into water we risk pain, loss, drowning. Yet water nourishes us, cleans us, bears us up, brings to us what we need, brings us to the temple of fulfillment of desire.

(Pause.)

Hierophant *gives the candidate the flower.*

Hierophant: Circumambulate clockwise outside the circle of water four times.

> *Hierophant sits.* **Hegemon** *escorts the candidate as she circumambulates.*

Stolistes: *(While the candidate circumambulates)* The priestess of Askalon plunged into the sacred lake. As she swam the fishes of the lake surrounded her. These fishes were all decorated with jewels and sparkled in the water. The priestess swam through her fear, swam until she grew tired and feared she would slip below the surface. Then the fishes bore her up, supporting her, bringing her to the island. She pulled herself up onto the shore.

> *When the candidate has completed four circumambulations, she stops before Hierophant.* **Hegemon** *assists her to step inside the circle of vases.*

Hierophant: Circumambulate clockwise inside the circle of water three times.

Stolistes: *(While the candidate circumambulates)* The priestess walked toward the altar at the center of the island. There before her loomed a great statue of Atargatis, with the body of a woman and the tail of a fish, decked with jewels, wearing a crown like the tower of a city, smiling down on her.

An altar of solid gold strewn with flowers sheltered beneath sacred trees. The priestess laid her flower down on the altar. She thought her prayer, that she would enter into the dissolving power of water to receive its blessings and be brought safely back to herself again.

Hierophant: Lay the flower on the altar.

Stolistes: *(When the candidate has laid the flower on the altar)* When she had given her offering and spoken her prayer, the priestess returned to the shore where a boat awaited to bring her effortlessly out from the lake again while the shining fishes swam alongside in celebration.

Hegemon assists the candidate to step outside the circle of vases.

Hierophant: You will now leave the temple for a short time. When you return you will be prepared to obtain the charm of beauty.

Hegemon leads the candidate out of the temple.

The Path of Aquarius
Temple Diagram

Hierophant faces Hierus (west).

Hegemon and Hierus face Hierophant (east).

Stolistes and Dadouchos stand east of Altar of Aquarius, side by side, facing Hierus (west).

Hierophant: Soror Hegemon, please bring the candidate to the door. Soror Hierus, please admit her when she gives the proper alarm.

Hegemon leaves the hall and seeks out the candidate in the prepared waiting area, takes the candidate to the door, and instructs her to give seven knocks: !!!! !!! Hierus opens the door, admits Hegemon and the candidate, closes the door, and returns to her station and sits. Hegemon leads the candidate to face Hierophant and remains with the candidate.

Hierophant: Candidate, you have passed through water on your quest to obtain the charm of beauty. You will now be prepared to receive that charm. You stand now on the glittering path that leads from Hod to Nezach, the moon to Venus. It is the path which opens the

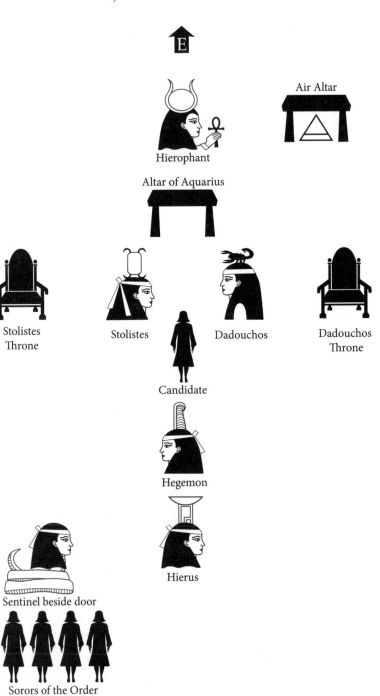

Illustration 30: The Path of Aquarius

gate to the powers of the feminine. This path is governed by a goddess who wears two aspects.

Hegemon leads the candidate to stand before Stolistes and Dadouchos, facing them. Hegemon returns to her station and sits.

Dadouchos: I represent Juno Covella, the Maiden. She rules the time when the sign of Aries rules again and springtime touches the lands of the northern hemisphere. The first day of each month, the calends, are sacred to her. She governs beginnings.

Stolistes: I represent Juno Pronuba, the Matron. She rules the months when the fruiting harvest is gathered in. Marriage and childbirth are sacred to her. She governs fulfillment.

Dadouchos: She is intuitive.

Stolistes: She is forgiving.

Dadouchos: She is desirable.

Stolistes: She is nurturing.

Dadouchos: She is receptive.

Stolistes: She grants life.

(Pause.)

Stolistes: Her lesson is to be grounded in the body.

Stolistes takes the bowl and aspergillum from the altar and sprinkles the candidate.

Stolistes: Cleansing and renewal are her blessing.

Dadouchos: Her lesson is to be grounded in the heart.

Dadouchos takes the girdle from the altar and ties around the candidate's waist.

Dadouchos: Joy and abundance are her blessings.

(Pause.)

Dadouchos: To be desired is a form of power, wielded when we with-hold or grant what is desired.

Stolistes: To desire and fulfill that desire is also a form of power, to exercise the will.

Hierophant: You have received the blessing of water from Juno Cov-ella and have received the girdle from Juno Pronuba. This girdle you wear is the girdle of Aphrodite, that grants the wearer to be loved and desired by everyone who looks upon her.

Hierophant steps around altar to stand between Stolistes and Dadouchos, who move to let her join them and then close so all officers are standing in a line.

Hierophant: There is another face to Juno. She is Juno Sospita, the war-rior, wearing the goatskin and the buckler and bearing the lance.

Hierophant, Stolistes, and **Dadouchos** together: She is Juno Regina, the Queen!

Hierophant: You will now quit the temple for a short time to prepare yourself for the ordeal of beauty.

Hierus leads the candidate out of the temple.

The Path of Mars
Temple Diagram

The sorors set up the Altar of Mars. The base of the altar has three vases with flowers in them. The sorors may also place images of women who have been victims of violence who are known to the group. On top of the altar is Diagram Two, standing up as if it is a war memorial. The sword is placed behind the diagrams on the altar or on the floor behind the altar.

Hierophant faces Hierus (west).

Hegemon and Hierus face Hierophant (east).

Stolistes and Dadouchos face each other.

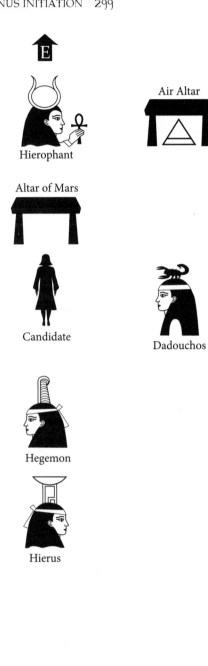

Illustration 31: The Path of Mars

Hierophant: Soror Hegemon, please bring the candidate to the door. Soror Hierus, please admit her when she gives the proper alarm.

*Hegemon leaves the hall and seeks out the candidate in the prepared waiting area, takes the candidate to the door, and instructs her to give seven knocks: !!!! !!! **Hierus** opens the door, admits Hegemon and the candidate, closes the door, returns to her station and sits. Hegemon leads the candidate to face Hierophant and remains with the candidate.*

Hierophant: Candidate, you have obtained the charm of beauty. You are entering into the path of Mars, which leads from the temple of Mercury, the temple of knowledge, to the temple of Venus, the temple of beauty. You will now be instructed how to defend that charm. Soror Hegemon, conduct the candidate to the Altar of Mars.

Hegemon conducts the candidate to Altar of Mars and places her on the west side of the altar facing Hierophant (east). Hierophant moves to the east side of the altar facing west. The officers and sorors of the temple stand around the altar.

Hierophant: The charm of beauty, to be desired, opens the vulnerable woman to the danger of violence. At the base of the altar is a memorial to all the women who have suffered because they were women. We mourn the women who have lost their health, power, children, lives to those who treated them as prey. Women who have been beaten, raped, kidnapped, enslaved, murdered. Women who were made pregnant against their will, whose children were taken from them, who were killed while pregnant because they were pregnant.

Any soror, officer in the ritual or not, may speak a story. If the group has set up images of women in the memorial, they may speak of the women pictured. The sorors may also choose to leave the pictures as silent testimony.

Hierophant: We remember them and mourn them.

(Moment of silence)

Hierophant: Atop the altar is a memorial to women soldiers who have come before us. You see the names of women and tributes to women soldiers in history and around the world. They served as soldiers and led as generals and queens. They served in groups of women, as lone women among men, disguised as men. They acted to defend their homes, attacked their enemies, or simply sought to make their way in the world as adventurers. They marched, rode, fought hand to hand, drew bows, threw lances, crossed swords, shot guns, fired cannons. They lost, they won, they died in battle, they died at home among friends. We remember them and honor them.

(Moment of silence)

Hierophant *picks up the sword, comes around the altar to the candidate, and ties the sword onto the girdle.*

Hierophant: You have received the girdle of Aphrodite. To defend the charm of beauty you also need the sword of Athena. With this sword you can defend yourself, your family, your land, and your people.

Soror Hegemon, please escort the candidate on her tour of duty.

Officers and sorors return to their stations.

Hegemon *leads the candidate clockwise to the station of Hierus.*

Hierus: *(Stands)* I salute you, soldier of beauty. Hear the story that comes to us from Europe. The Goddess Anat offered to trade eternal life to the archer Aqhat for his bow. Aqhat laughed at her and said, "The bow is for men, not women!" Anat struck him on his head, three times above the ear, pouring his lifeblood like sap, letting his life breath escape from his nostrils. Beware Anat when she is angry, as she rages among her enemies, exuberant, knee-deep in blood, covered with gore to her thighs.

Hegemon *leads the candidate clockwise to the station of Dadouchos.*

Dadouchos: *(Stands)* I salute you, soldier of beauty. Hear the story that comes to us from Africa. The goddess Sekhmet saw that humans had stood up against the gods to defy them. The lion-goddess came like the desert wind, raging, slaying humans, spilling their blood on the sand, until she had killed so many it seemed that humanity itself would be lost. The humans who remained collected all their beer and colored it red and left it as an offering. Thinking the beer was blood, Sekhmet drank, and fell over in a sleep. Thus was her rage finally broken and humanity was saved.

Hegemon leads the candidate clockwise to the station of Stolistes.

Stolistes: *(Stands)* I salute you, soldier of beauty. Hear the story that comes to us from Asia. The demon Raktabija had been granted the boon that from each drop of his blood would spring another demon. He made war against the gods, leading an army of demons. The goddess Durga rode forth on her tiger to battle with him. She slew every demon until she reached Raktabija. She struck him with her sword, his blood fell on the ground, and more demons sprang forth, attacking her by thousands, riding chariots and elephants, shouting and laughing as she strove to defend herself.

Then the goddess became enraged. She rose up and transformed into Kali, the terrible one, the skeleton hag with red eyes and wild hair, bearing the sword of vengeance. The universe shook with the power of her shout. She fell upon the demons with a furious howl, shoving them into her mouth with the claws of her hands. As the demons turned to run, she opened her mouth and licked them up with her tongue. When she had eaten all the demons, she turned back to Raktabija himself. She skewered the demon with her sword and lapped up his blood. When she had drained him of all his blood, she threw away his lifeless corpse.

Then, drunk on the blood of the demon, Kali laughed and danced. As she danced, she destroyed everything she touched. She trampled the living things under her feet. The gods called to Shiva that Kali would destroy the world. He loved her dance and refused to intervene. Then the thunder of her dancing shook him down onto the ground. He understood then that the world was near an end, and to stop her rage, he threw himself beneath her feet. Kali danced on the body of Shiva until she had flattened it entirely. Finally she realized that Shiva himself lay beneath her feet. That realization brought her calm again, and she stopped her dancing, and the world was saved.

*Hegemon returns to her station and sits. **Stolistes** leads the candidate to the station of Hegemon, returns to her station and sits.*

Hegemon: *(Stands)* I salute you, soldier of beauty. Hear the story that comes to us from America. The goddess Mama Huaco wanted the land of the Huallas for her people. She attacked a Hualla man and ripped him apart, carrying his heart and lungs in her mouth. When the people saw this they were terrified and ran from her, but she followed them and killed them, warriors and families, children and babies in the womb, so that no Hualla remained alive on the earth.

Hegemon leads the candidate to Hierophant, returns to her station and sits.

Hierophant: Candidate, you have completed your tour of duty as a soldier of beauty. As protectors of women, we may be called upon to fight in many ways. Anger is that surge of energy that gives us the strength to perform physically and emotionally difficult work. It is also true that our anger at the injustice and cruelty women endure can overwhelm us and we may lose ourselves in vengeance as the goddesses whose stories you heard lost themselves in battle lust.

You have heard the stories that come to us from the four quarters of the globe about the bloody fury of the vengeful goddess. There may come a time when you need to invoke their dread power. This is why the sword you bear is Athena's sword. When we wield her sword, her cool intellect and courage guide and sustain us, ensuring that our blows cut only as deeply as necessary to accomplish our goals. Whatever anger we unleash we must in the end ground out to calm again.

You will now quit the temple for a short time to prepare yourself to enter the temple of beauty.

Hegemon leads the candidate out of the temple.

The Temple of Venus
Temple Diagram

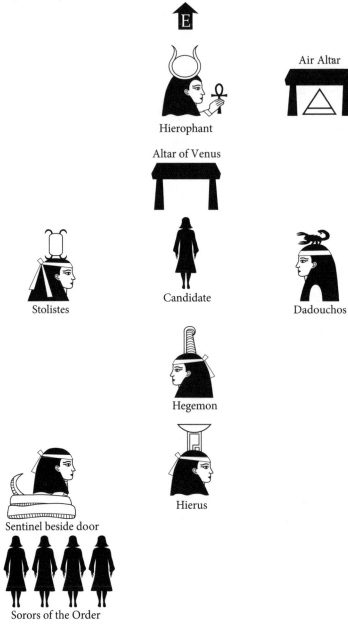

Illustration 32: The Temple of Venus

The sorors should create as luxurious a temple as possible, with cushions, fabric, decorations, candles, scent, music. The Altar of Venus can have any lovely decorations the sorors devise. Rose petals can be sprinkled on the floor. The sorors can also have glasses and drinks, and plates of food.

Hierophant *faces Hierus (west).*

Hegemon *and* **Hierus** *face Hierophant (east).*

Stolistes *and* **Dadouchos** *face each other.*

Hierophant: Soror Hegemon, please bring the candidate to the door. Soror Hierus, please admit her when she gives the proper alarm.

Hegemon leaves the hall and seeks out the candidate in the prepared waiting area, takes the candidate to the door, and instructs her to give seven knocks: !!!! !!! Hierus opens the door, admits Hegemon and the candidate, and closes the door.

Hierus: Welcome, soldier of beauty to the temple of beauty. *(Takes sword from the candidate.)* At ease, soldier. In this temple, we leave our swords at the door and enter the delights of the temple.

The sorors of the temple wander freely in the temple, eating and drinking. Hierophant meets the candidate with a welcome, for example, handing her a champagne flute with a drink.

Hierophant: *(Gives the candidate the token.)* This is the token of the temple of Netzach, the temple of Venus. With this token you can always return to the temple of Venus from any other place you might journey.

Here you have entered the precinct of the great goddesses Inanna, Ishtar, Aphrodite. Each is known as a goddess of beauty, charm, and love. Each also bears the sword, acting to protect herself and those in her charge, and support warriors who call on her. In this temple, guarded by the soldiers of beauty, we are free to relax, surrender, and explore our sensual natures.

The temple of beauty is the garden of earthly delights. Here we celebrate all the pleasures of the body, the lusciousness of color and texture, the deliciousness of scent and food. Here we celebrate the pleasures of love given and returned. Here we celebrate the pleasures of the spirit, the sweet inspiration of music, and most especially the company of our sisters.

Soror [candidate name or motto], now you have obtained the charm of beauty in your journey with us. Should you desire to move further along this path, you may come to the temple and say to us, "I seek to ascend to the sun." As before, we enjoin you to aid your sisters in their journeys as they have aided you in yours.

Closing and Grounding the Temple

The officers close and ground the temple using the Temple Ritual.

THE SUN INITIATION

THE SUN INITIATION
EXPLANATORY NOTES

The Ascent

This rite is an enactment of the central theurgic ritual of ascending in the sun as described by Gregory Shaw (Shaw 1989). The ritual calls for purification using synthema, physical objects associated with the power of the planets, as I discussed in *Practical Magic for Beginners* (Williams 2005). Here I have specified synthema traditionally associated with the sun, yellow stones, and frankincense. Any synthema also associated with the sun can be substituted for these, although the second purification should be of solar incense.

The vocables are the classic Greek vowels that were specified for chanting in magic texts of the period (Miller 1989).

The Temple of the Sun

As with many orders of operative magicians, the initiation of the sun marks the end of one set of magical workings and the beginning of another. The sorors of the order may choose to create new rituals to work as a group. The magician who bears the serpent crown wields the power to create her own magic.

SUN INITIATION: ASCENT TO THE SUN

All Tools of the Temple Ritual

Initiatory tools

- Eight red candles

- Seven blue vases

- Solar synthema: solar stone (any yellow stone, especially quartz) and solar incense (frankincense, sandlewood)

- Hekate wheel (whirligig toy)

- Serpent crown

Initiatory token: small disk painted white on both sides with a sun disk in yellow on one side.

Initiatory tools and token can be staged beneath the Hierophant throne or anywhere convenient until needed.

Preparing and Opening the Temple

The officers prepare and open the temple using the Temple Ritual. The candidate is within the temple.

The Petition

Hierophant: Sorors, do we have business today?

Hegemon: Soror Hierophant, a sister of Seshat brings a petition before us.

Hegemon brings the candidate to the center of the temple, facing Hierophant.

Hegemon: Soror [name], please state your petition.

Candidate: I seek to ascend to the sun.

Hierophant: Have you obtained the charm of beauty?

Hegemon: She bears the token of the temple of Netzach, the temple of Venus.

Candidate displays the token.

Hierophant: Have you visited that temple again on your own? Are you conversant with its power and familiar with its ways?

Candidate: [*Answers as she wishes.*]

Hierophant: Sisters of Seshat, is it your will to assist this candidate to ascend to the sun?

All: It is my will.

Hierophant: Soror [name], please leave the temple for a short time and make yourself ready for the journey.

Hegemon escorts the candidate to the designated waiting area and returns to the temple.

Establishing the Temple of the Sun
Temple Diagram

Elemental altars remain. Officers move thrones to their altars.

Hierophant faces water and fire altars (west).

Hierus and Hegemon face water and fire altars (west).

Stolistes and Dadouchos face Hierophant (east).

Hierophant: *Sorors of the Order of Seshat, please assist me to construct the temple of the sun. Soror Hegemon, what is the journey of this temple?*

Hegemon: Along the 26th path from the temple of Hod, the temple of Mercury; the 25th path from the temple of Yesod, the temple of the moon; and the 24th path from the temple of Netzach, the temple of Venus, to the temple of Tiphareth, the temple of the sun.

Hierophant: Soror Hierus, what signs govern these paths?

Hierus: The sign of Capricorn, the sign of Sagittarius, and the sign of Scorpio.

Hierophant: Let us establish the officers on their thrones. Soror Hegemon, what are your station and duties?

Hierophant

Earth Altar

Air Altar

Hierus

Hegemon

Stolistes

Dadouchos

Water Altar

Fire Altar

Sentinel beside door

Sorors of the Order

Illustration 33: The Temple of the Sun

Hegemon: I administer the air altar, I represent the temple of the moon, and I guard the candidate on the white road.

Hierophant: Soror Hierus, what are your station and duties?

Hierus: I administer the earth altar, I represent the temple of the earth, and I guard the candidate on the black road.

Hierophant: Soror Dadouchos, what are your station and duties?

Dadouchos: I administer the fire altar, I represent the temple of Mercury, and I guard the candidate on the ascent.

Hierophant: Soror Stolistes, what are your station and duties?

Stolistes: I administer the water altar, I represent the temple of Venus, and I guard the candidate on the ascent.

Hierophant: I guide the candidate in the temple, and I supervise the conduct of the ritual. Sorors, we have established the temple of the sun.

Ascending to the Sun

Hierophant: Soror Hegemon, please bring the candidate to the door. Soror Hierus, please admit her when she gives the proper alarm.

Hegemon leaves the hall and seeks out the candidate in the prepared waiting area. Hegemon checks to make sure the candidate is ready to begin the initiation. Hegemon takes the candidate to the door, instructing her to give six knocks: !!! !!! Hierus opens the door, admits Hegemon and the candidate, closes the door, returns to her station and sits. Hegemon leads the candidate to face Hierophant, returns to her station and sits.

Hierophant: Candidate, you stand at the portal of that temple which leads you to the knowledge of yourself. Are you ready to face the ordeals that await you, both within the temple and as a consequence of taking this most serious step on your path?

Candidate: *(Unprompted)* I am.

Hierophant: Then say, "Let the powers of the sun witness my pledge."

Candidate: Let the powers of the sun witness my pledge.

Hierophant: Then measure the temple you have created in your journeys with us.

*The candidate circumambulates the temple unescorted. At the earth altar **Hierus** stands to bar her path.*

Hierus: Why do you pass by the temple of the earth, traveler in the underworld?

Candidate: *(May be prompted by Hierophant)* I seek the path of ascent.

Hierus: That way is not here, you must travel onward to find it. Yet remember that you have faced the darkness in the world and in yourself and have emerged from the underworld and the dark waters of Nun. Pass on in your quest for the way of ascent.

***Hierus** sits. The candidate continues circumambulation. When she reaches the air altar **Hegemon** stands to bar her path.*

Hegemon: Why do you pass by the temple of the moon, traveler on the faerie roads?

Candidate: I seek the path of ascent.

Hegemon: That way is not here, you must travel onward to find it. Yet remember you bear with you the key of light and darkness, the key of the tree, and the key of three. You have seen three wonders, the wonder of the three faerie roads, the wonder of the discipline of embodiment, and the wonder of sexuality. You have visited the pool in the woods, the spring in the rocks, and the well in the fields. You have passed through the gate of mystery. Pass on in your quest for the way of ascent.

***Hegemon** sits. The candidate continues circumambulation. When she reaches the fire altar **Dadouchos** stands to bar her path.*

Dadouchos: Why do you pass by the temple of Mercury, traveler on the path of knowledge?

Candidate: I seek the path of ascent.

Dadouchos: That way is not here, you must travel onward to find it. Yet remember you are a citizen of the City of Ladies and your accomplishments build on the achievements of the women who have come before you. Pass on in your quest for the way of ascent.

Dadouchos sits. The candidate continues circumambulation. When she reaches the water altar Stolistes stands to bar her path.

Stolistes: Why do you pass by the temple of Venus, traveler on the path of the warrior?

Candidate: I seek the path of ascent.

Stolistes: That way is not here, you must travel onward to find it. Yet remember that you wear the girdle of Aphrodite and the sword of Athena, you have obtained the charm of beauty and you are enjoined to defend it. Soror Hierophant, the candidate has measured the temple.

Hierophant: You will now leave the temple for a short time. When you return you will be prepared for the ascent.

Stolistes leads the candidate out of the temple.

The Ascent

Hierophant faces water and fire altars (west).

Hierus and Hegemon face water and fire altars (west).

Hierophant: Soror Hegemon, please bring the candidate to the door. Soror Hierus, please admit her when she gives the proper alarm.

Hegemon leaves the hall and seeks out the candidate in the prepared waiting area, takes the candidate to the door, and instructs her to give six knocks: !!! !!! Hierus opens the door, admits Hegemon and the candidate, closes the door, returns to her station and sits. Hegemon leads the candidate to the end of corridor facing Hierophant (east), returns to her station and sits.

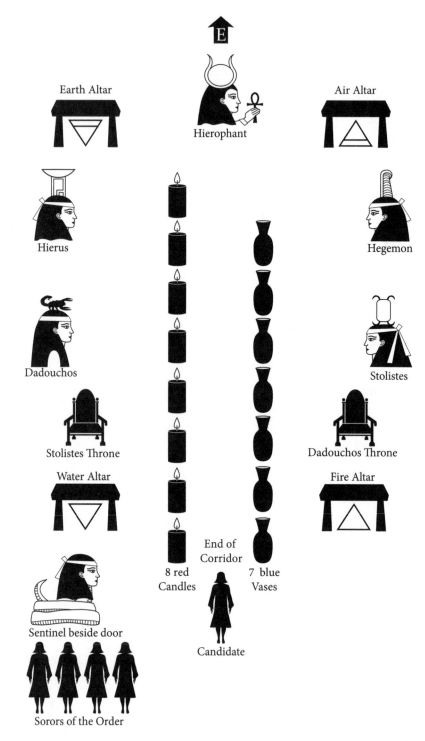

Illustration 34: The Ascent

Hierophant: Candidate, you have measured the temple which you created in your journeys with us. There are three roads before you. Your sisters will guide you on your journey along these roads.

The Path of Capricorn

Hierus stands and conducts the candidate along the north side of the temple, walking alongside the line of candles. Hierus keeps her hand on the candidate's shoulder to stop her walking when she reaches about the midpoint of the corridor.

Hierus: The path you venture upon now is the black road. It is the path of Capricornus, the very ancient goat-fish constellation whose image is called the Devil among those who reject the lessons of the body. One of the images of this constellation is Amalthea, the nursing goat whose horn is the horn of plenty. Once the sun was nourished in this sign before turning in the sky back toward springtime. We too must turn back on this road, for this is not the path of ascent.

Hierus conducts the candidate back to the end of the corridor of candles and vases, returns to her station and sits.

The Path of Scorpio

Hegemon stands and conducts the candidate about halfway along the south side of the temple, walking alongside the line of vases.

Hegemon: The path you venture upon now is the white road. It is the path of Scorpio, the stinging scorpion who guards the path to the sun. Scorpio reminds us that if we approach the ascent without preparation or too quickly we risk burning up or plunging out of the ascent to the depths.

Hegemon stands and conducts the candidate along the north side of the temple, walking alongside the line of candles. Hegemon keeps her hand on the candidate's shoulder to stop her walking when she reaches about the midpoint of the corridor.

The Path of Sagittarius

Hierophant: *(Strikes bell six times.)* Prepare the candidate for the ascent.

> *Stolistes and Dadouchos stand. Dadouchos takes the censer and stands outside the line of candles. Stolistes takes the solar stone and stands outside the line of vases.*

Stolistes: This stone embodies the virtue of the sun. Take it and hold it in your hand. *(Gives the candidate the solar stone.)*

Hierus: The personal daimon guides the soul on the descent through the multifaceted life and multiform body of the cosmos into generation and binds the soul into the body. When the daimon appears to the soul she reveals her name and the manner of invoking her. To recognize the daimon requires discriminating among the phasmata of all other entities: gods, archangels, angels, daimons, souls.

Dadouchos: *(Censes the candidate with solar incense.)* By the scent of the sun are you further purified to withstand the height of your ascent.

Hegemon: The soul draws strength from the divine light which is seen in the operation called *photos agoge*, drawing in the light. The eyes of the soul drink this light, the soul breathes in this light, it heats the soul and causes it to stand. The soul thus strengthened becomes the *augoeides ochema*, the luminous vehicle, which can comprehend the true earth, the true heaven, the true light, and directly contact those sacred forces which the daimon apprehends.

Stolistes: Give back to me now the stone of the sun so that it does not weigh you down for the ascent. *(Takes the stone from the candidate.)*

Hierophant: You have held the stone of the sun and breathed in the scent of the sun. With this protection the soul hastens toward the streams of light, is drawn upward, mingles with the solar channels or rays, and is ultimately established in the sun itself.

> *Dadouchos stands outside the candles and lays a guiding hand on the candidate's left shoulder. Stolistes stands outside the vases and lays a hand on the candidate's right shoulder.*

Hierophant: When I tell you to do so, close your eyes and walk between the water and the fire, guided by your sisters. When they stop, keep your eyes closed and take three breaths, drawing in light from the rays of the sun.

All lights in the temple are extinguished, leaving only enough light to make sure that Hierophant can see the candidate.

Hierophant: Close your eyes.

Dadouchos and Stolistes guide the candidate walking along the corridor. Hierophant spins the Hekate wheel to make it whistle. All the sorors, including all officers, chant the voces mysticae:

All: A, E, H, I, O, Υ, Ω (see pronunciations on page 329)

As the candidate approaches Hierophant, the chanting speeds up and becomes louder. Hierus moves to the light switch. Hierophant stops spinning the Hekate wheel and makes cut-off gesture to the temple. All chanting stops abruptly. At the same time, Hierus turns all the lights up to full brightness.

Hierophant: Take three deep breaths!

Hierophant watches the candidate closely to make sure the candidate has time to take three full breaths.

Hierophant: All life partakes of the life of the sun.

Hierus brings lights back down to a dim level.

Hierophant: Open your eyes now and return to the temple and the company of your sisters.

Sorors give the candidate a few moments to recenter.

Hierophant moves to stand in front of the candidate, holding the serpent crown.

Hierophant: *(Gives the candidate the token.)* This is the token of the temple of Tiphareth, the temple of the sun. With this token you can always return to the temple of the sun from any other place you might journey.

The priestesses, queens, and goddesses of Egypt wore many crowns. One of these was the crown associated with the power of the sun, the serpent or cobra crown. It reminds us of the serpent goddesses of desert and mountain. Having ascended to the sun you have earned the right to wear that crown.

Hierophant places the serpent crown on the candidate's head.

Hierophant: Soror [magical name or motto], I crown you with the power of the sun.

Hierophant turns the candidate to face the sorors of the temple.

Hierophant: Sisters of Seshat, I present to you Soror [magical name or motto], who has achieved the fulfillment of the temple of the sun!

Sorors applaud.

Hierophant: Soror [magical name or motto], be seated on the Hierophant throne.

The candidate is seated at the station of Hierophant. Hierophant remains in front of the corridor of candles and vases, facing Hierus (west).

Hierophant: Soror Stolistes, please collect the power of water in the temple. Soror Dadouchos, please collect the power of fire in the temple and see that it is safely grounded.

Stolistes collects the vases and sets them aside, Dadouchos collects the candles and sets them aside.

Hierophant: In our work with Soror [magical name or motto] we have traveled many paths and seen many wonders. We have invoked many goddesses: Isis, Ma'at, Nephthys, Neith, Selket, Renenuet, Mehet-

Weret, Weret-Hekau, Ishtar, Ereshkigal, Demeter, Persephone, Ariadne, Aine, Brigid, Hekate, Sul and Sunna, Saule and Saules Meita, Sekhmet, Bast, Hathor, Mut, Amaterasu-omikami, Grandmother Sun, Atargatis, Juno Covella, Juno Pronuba, Juno Sospita, Juno Regina, Aphrodite, Athena, Anat, Durga, Kali, Mama Huaco, Inanna, Hathor. Yet always it is Seshat who remains within our hearts.

We have honored the double goddess, as mother and daughter, sister and sister, the two stages of every woman's life. We have passed from darkness to light, understanding these as the double power of magic.

Closing and Grounding the Temple
The officers close and ground the temple using the Temple Ritual.

PLANETARY TEMPLE WORKINGS

At the conclusion of each initiation in the group ritual section, the initiate is given a token that acts as a key to the temple of the initiation. Before moving on to the next initiation the magician should enter into the temple on her own to continue learning about the powers of the planetary sphere.

These rituals can be performed in any space where a small altar can be set up. This space, and preferably the entire room, should be clean and neat. The magician herself should also be clean and neat. She should wear the robe of a Sister of Seshat.

The Temple of the Earth
Tools

- Small altar, green altar cloth, censer, bowl and aspergilum
- Yellow, red, blue and green candles, containers for candles

Establishing the Temple of Earth

The magician asperges the temple and says:
I purify the temple with water.
The magician censes the temple and says:
I consecrate the temple with fire.
The magician lights the yellow candle and says:
I establish the pillar of air.
The magician lights the red candle and says:
I establish the pillar of fire.
The magician lights the blue candle and says:
I establish the pillar of water.
The magician lights the green candle and says:
I establish the pillar of earth.

Returning to the center of the temple, facing east, the magician places the temple of the earth initiatory token on the altar, knocks four times (!!!!) and says:

I invoke the temple of Malkuth, the temple of the earth.

The magician visualizes a temple with four walls. The east wall is yel-low, the south red, the west blue, and the north green. The floor is laid with black and white tiles, the ceiling is painted as a night sky with thousands of stars.

Working

The magician can then conduct personal work in the temple of the earth. This work can include all elemental workings and rituals with a health or financial focus. The magician can also invoke the goddesses she encountered during her journey through the underworld to further understand their nature.

Closing the Temple

The magician extinguishes the lamps, picks up the temple of the earth initia-tory token, and says:

The temple is closed.

Temple of the Moon
Tools

Small altar, white altar cloth, white or silver candle, bowl of water, bell, glass cup with an appropriate drink

Establishing the Temple

The magician lights the candle(s), places the initiatory token on the altar, rings the bell nine times (!!! !!! !!!) and says:

I invoke the temple of the moon.

The magician visualizes a temple of crystal or glass. The clear floor is as shimmering as a pool of water. From the ceiling hang nine silver lamps.

Working

The magician can then conduct personal work in the moon temple. This work can include dreamwork, divination, rituals with a fertility or sexuality focus, and meditation on the Tarot card the World or the Universe. The magician can also invoke the goddesses she encountered during her journey through the gate of mystery to further understand their nature. It is also appropriate to continue to use a mirror as a scrying device.

Closing the Temple
The magician extinguishes the candle(s), picks up the initiatory token, and says:

The temple of the moon is closed.

The Temple of Mercury
Tools

Small table, white altar cloth, orange candle, bell

Establishing the Temple of Mercury
The magician lights the candle(s), places the initiatory token on the altar, rings the bell eight times (!!!! !!!!) and says:

I invoke the temple of Mercury.

The magician visualizes a temple with eight walls. Each wall bears images and names of women in the City of Ladies. The floor is lapis blue, the ceiling is a vault of lapis.

Working
The magician can then conduct personal work in the temple. This work can include any intellectual work, including works of memorization, learning and speaking sacred alphabets, and studying the lives of women. This work can also include works of healing, such as visualizing the person to be healed and sending energy, and creating healing potions and talismans. The magician can study the Tarot cards Judgment and the Sun. It is also appropriate to continue to use a candle as a scrying device.

Closing the Temple

The magician extinguishes the candle(s), picks up the initiatory token, and says:

The temple of Mercury is closed.

The Temple of Venus
Tools

Small altar, decorative altar cloth, green candle, bell, rose, and incense

Establishing the Temple of Venus

The magician lights the candle(s), places the initiatory token on the altar, rings the bell seven times (!!!! !!!) and says:

I invoke the temple of Venus.

The magician visualizes a temple with seven walls hung with rich wall coverings. The floor is deep emerald, the ceiling is a vault of amber.

Working

The magician can then conduct personal work in the temple of Venus. This work can include work to give or receive love from lovers, friends, and family; invocations for artistic inspiration; and work with the goddesses of the temple in any of their aspects. She may meditate on the Tarot cards the Moon, the Star, and the Tower. It is also appropriate to continue to use a bowl of water as a scrying device.

Closing the Temple

The magician extinguishes the candle(s), picks up the silver initiatory token, and says:

The temple of Venus is closed.

The Temple of the Sun
Tools

Solar stone, solar incense, Hekate wheel, serpent crown

Establishing the Temple
The magician lights the candle(s), places the initiatory token on the altar, rings the bell six times (!!! !!!) and says:

> I invoke the temple of the sun.
>
> *The magician chants the voces magicae.*
>
> *The magician visualizes a temple with walls of yellow glass, translucent and glowing. The floor is solid amber. The ceiling is lost in a blaze of white light.*

Working
The magician can then conduct personal work in the sun temple. This work can include meditation on the Tarot cards the Devil, Temperance, and Death. The magician can engage in the practice of photogogia, ascending to the sun.

Closing the Temple
The magician extinguishes the candle(s), picks up the initiatory token, and says:

> The temple of the sun is closed.

LIST A: DIAGRAMS

These diagrams are created by the sisters themselves as part of the preparation for the rituals and reflect the taste and preferences of each individual or group. They can be elaborate, involving drawings or photographs, or can be very simple, collages created from graphics or photographs found online.

Diagrams for the Moon Initiation
Diagram One: The Tree of Life
This diagram shows the three pillars—white on the left, black on the right, and the middle pillar, which does not have a color.

Diagram Two: The Minoan Tree
This diagram is an image of one of the Minoan seals depicting priestesses standing beneath trees. These are widely available in books about Minoan religion and on the Internet.

Diagram Three: The Eildon Tree
Any image of a large tree will do. The Eildon Tree has a door which leads to the world of faerie.

Diagram Four: The Three Roads
This diagram includes three images: on the left a black road, on the right a white road, and in the middle a forest road.

Diagram Five: Earthly Sustenance
This diagram includes three images: bread, water in a cup, and wind.

Diagram Six: Sexuality
This diagram includes three images: a young woman in white, a woman in red, and a pregnant woman, preferably with a green element.

Diagram Seven: The Pool in the Woods
This drawing or photo shows a lake surrounded by trees.

Diagram Eight: the Spring in the Rocks
This drawing or photo shows a body of water surrounded by rocks.

Diagram Nine: the Well in the Field
This drawing or photo shows a well in a grassy field.

Diagrams for the Mercury Initiation

The sisters of each temple create their own diagrams. Each diagram features the image of one woman whose story is described by the soror who explains the diagram to the candidate. The diagram also includes a list of names of other notable women of that category. This list should be reasonably long to indicate that a great many women inhabit the City of Ladies. Photos or drawings of these women can also be included in the diagram, although the featured lady's image should be largest and central.

Note: Except for Diagrams One and Nine, which should be narrated by Hierophant, any of the sisters of the temple can narrate any of the diagrams. It is especially appropriate for the sister or sisters who created a particular diagram to narrate it to the candidate.

Diagram One: Creatives (East)
Christine de Pisan, artists, writers, poets, musicians, actors.

Diagram Two: Explorers (Southeast)
Travelers, scientists

Diagram Three: Athletes (South)
Sportswomen, warriors

Diagram Four: Magicians (Southwest)
Magicians, alchemists, metaphysicians

Diagram Five: Religious (West)
Theologians, priestesses, worthies

Diagram Six: Philosophers (Northwest)
Thinkers, writers, academics

Diagram Seven: Makers (North)
Architects, farmers, weavers, potters, designers

Diagram Eight: Politicians (Northeast)
Leaders and rulers, elected and hereditary

Diagram Nine: City of Ladies
City, book

Diagrams for the Venus Initiation
Diagram One: Atargatis
There are a few extant statues of Atargatis whose photographs are possible to find online.

Diagram Two: Warriors

Ahotep	Vishpla	Penthisilea
Antiope	Scathach	Mavia
Artemisia	Tomyris	Boadicea
Aoife	Medb	Zabibi
Samsi	Cartimandua	Gaita
Hethna	Visna	Stikla
Kahula bint Azwar	Waferia	Trung Trac
Trung Nhi	Tomoe Gozen	Gautrekssonar
A'ishah Bint Abi Bakr	Septima Zenobia	Salaym Bint Malham
Dihya al-Kahina	Hippolyta	Thyra
Himiko	Jingo Kogo	Saimei
Hua Mu Lan	Vebiorg	Rusilla
Sela	Urraca	Jeanne de Danpierre
Alvid	Gurath	Hervor
Freydis Eiriksdottir	Thordis	Matilda
Alrude	Petronilla	Tamara
Isobel	Lady Bruce	Black Agnes
Maria of Pozzuoli	Margaret of Denmark	Isabella I
Maroula of Limnos	Caterina Sforza	Catalina de Erauso
Queen Margaret	Ameliane du Puget	Graine Ni Maille
Mother Ross	Phoebe Hessel	Ann Mills
Anne Macintosh	Mary Lacy	Virginie Ghesquiere

Lady Lude	Hannah Snell	Hannah Whitney
Maria Theresa	Margaret Catchpole	Catherine the Great
Mme Arno	Flora Sanders	Zoya Smirnow
Elena Haas	Mary Hagidorn	Mary Anne Talbot
Anna Dosa	Deborah Samson	Margaret Corbin
Jemima Warner	Rachel Martin	Grace Martin
Frances Clayton	Jennie Hodges	Sarah Emma Edmonds
Loreta Velazquez	Cathay Williams	

LIST B: PRONOUNCIATIONS

A frequently asked question about these rituals is: how do you pronounce that name? Any way you are pronouncing a name is correct for
the purposes of the ritual. If you understand how to pronounce Latin,
Greek, Japanese, ancient Egyptian, or any other language represented
here, you may correct these pronunciations for yourself and your
group. This is a working version of the pronunciations to give ritualists
a way to speak the names.

(In the phonetic columns below, g is a hard g as in go, while a soft g
as in gem is represented with a j.)

Officer Names

Hierophant	HIE-ro-fant
Hegemon	HEH-ge-mon
Hierus	HIE-roose
Dadouchos	Da-DOO-kose
Stolistes	Stoh-LIS-tees

Goddess Names

Aine	AY-na
Amaterasu-omikami	Ah-ma-TER-ah-soo oh-mee-KA-mee
Anat	Ah-NAT
Aphrodite	Af-ro-DYE-tee
Ariadne	Ah-ree-AD-nee
Atargatis	Ah-tar-GA-tis
Athena	Ah-THEE-na

Bast	BAHST
Brigid	BRIH-jid
Demeter	DEH-meh-tur
Durga	DER-ga
Ereshkigal	Eh-RESH-ki-gal
Grandmother Sun	Grandmother Sun
Hathor	HAH-thor
Hekate	He-KAH-teh
Ishtar	IHSH-tar
Isis	EYEsis
Juno Covella	JOO-no Koh-VEH-la
Juno Pronuba	JOO-no Pro-NOO-ba
Juno Regina	JOO-no Reh-GEE-na
Juno Sospita	JOO-no Soh-SPEE-ta
Kali	KAH-lee
Ma'at	Mah-AHT
Mama Huaco	Mama WHA-ko
Mehet-Weret	Meh-HET Whe-RET
Mut	MOOT
Neith	NEETH
Nephthys	NEF-this
Persephone	Per-SEF-uh-nee
Renenutet	Re-NEN-you-tet
Saule	SALL
Saules Meita	SALL-es MAY-ta
Sekhmet	SEHK-met
Selket	Sell-KET
Sul	SOOL
Sunna	SOO-na
Weret-Hekau	Whe-RET Heh-KOW

Voces Magicae

The voces magicae in the sun initiation are the vowels in classical Greek: Alpha, Epsilon, Eta, Iota, Omicron, Upsilon, Omega. They are pronounced as follows:

A (Alpha) as in *father*
E (Epsilon) as in *bet*
H (Eta) as in *late*
I (Iota) as in *beet*
O (Omicron) as in *cough*
Y (Upsilon) as in *boot*
Ω (Omega) as in *boat*

Saying these vowels together, it is "Ah Eh Ay Ee Aw You Oh."

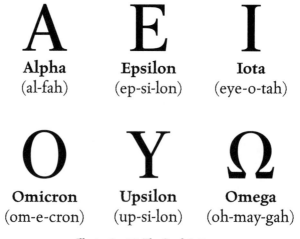

Alpha
(al-fah)

Epsilon
(ep-si-lon)

Iota
(eye-o-tah)

Omicron
(om-e-cron)

Upsilon
(up-si-lon)

Omega
(oh-may-gah)

Illustration 35: The Greek Letters

PART THREE

THE HEART OF THE TRADITION

ENCLOSURE,
TRANSFORMATION, EMERGENCE

The three-step movement of women's initiation that Carol Lee Flinders describes has played itself out in the structure of this book. Part One, Magia Femina, worked its way toward enclosure. Part Two, Sisters of Seshat, mapped out a series of ritual transformations. Every withdrawal requires an eventual emergence, bringing the gifts of the transformation to the world. What will emergence mean to us in this work?

The process of withdrawal, transformation, and emergence pulses through our lives. Every night we lay our bodies down, pass into dream, and awaken. Illness takes us into this place as well, the place where we must pay attention to the needs both of body and of spirit, and confront the change required of us. The processes of pregnancy and birth and of sexual experience blur the boundaries of our bodies which share in other bodies in a literal and concrete way. Entering into these states as forms of transformation enables us to spiritualize these experiences.

Another way to read the process of enclosure, transformation, and emergence is as a tool to strengthen us to face the challenges of being embodied as women in a world in which being embodied as women places us at risk. The great lesson the women's spirituality movement brings to the magical traditions is that the personal is political. Transformation begins with the self, but does not end with the self, unfolding in ripples from the individual to everyone around us.

Directions in Transformation

Emergence does not mean that women's magic is a phase that must be temporarily experienced on our way to somewhere else. Magia Femina is a lifetime of work in its own right. Some women will choose to spend their entire magical lives only in the company of other women, or working only with their families.

Magia Femina is also an essential precondition for Magia Humana. Only through including people of all genders in the full definition of human can magic equip itself to address the challenges of the new millennia. This work will require the input of men, women, people of all genders, as well as people of all ages, races, and ability. The next form magic will take will emerge from our collective contributions.

At the end of the sun initiation we sit on the Hierophant's throne wearing the serpent's crown, surrounded by our sisters, and supported by a universe of magic shaped in a female form. Now that we possess this temple, the Sisters of Seshat may choose to write other woman-only rituals to be performed within this temple. We may instead, or in addition, choose to create a new temple and this time invite men to join us in it.

In Witchcraft, the third-degree initiation empowers us to initiate other Witches, and to create and manage our own covens. In the Ceremonial traditions, when we complete the work of the first order, we stand at a crossroads.

The initiate of the outer order is positioned to move into the second or inner order. The work of the second order is usually based on Rosicrucian symbology. Women working within Magia Femina may choose to create an inner order and to work with the Rosicrucian mythos to reshape and revalorize that system for women's interests and concerns.

In Western Traditional Magic, the sun initiation also prepares us to invoke the angel/Genius/daimon, to work out our own unique magical path. Those of us who choose to engage in that operation may find ourselves entering into another cycle of enclosure.

Each of us will decide for ourselves where we will go from here: out into the world to work with our siblings of all genders, continuing to explore woman-centered magic, or embarking on the great solo adventure of the Knowledge and Conversation of the Holy Guardian Angel.

RE-ENGAGING THE TRADITION

My choice is to re-engage Western Traditional Magic, to assess what I have learned, and place the work of a Sister of Seshat within the tradition.

It is spring again. I have retreated to another house in a woods on an island. This time the island is Bainbridge, and I am staying in a wooden yurt, called the Moon Yurt by the women who own and run this retreat. Inside, the wood trim is painted white and blue, and it is furnished with blue rugs and white lace doilies and paintings of flowers. The windows look out on a garden, cleared from the surrounding woods and circled around by a deer netting, making the yurt an enclosure within an enclosure. This is a fine place for an esoteric anchorite.

I am wearing a new blue linen shirtdress, the habit of my time in retreat. The book is nearly done, I have only this section to finish. I have felt many emotions as I wrote, from fear to anger to humility to pride to joy. As I complete this work I am profoundly, deeply, grateful that I have been able to attain peace.

I have retreated this last time to invoke Lady Tradition again. I want to renew my understanding of the tradition with the insights I have gained through my experiences as a Sister of Seshat.

Confidently I say, *Come to me, Lady Tradition...*

She appears before I finish the invocation, straight and stiff in her high-necked blouse and floor-length skirt, her head with its tight bun held very high. She is decidedly affronted. Her steely eyes glitter with anger.

I have been fighting with Lady Tradition as a daughter fights with her mother. I am fully ready to stand up to her now. I say to her, "Your time was then, my time is now. I lived with the tradition for many years before I was driven to analyze and contest it and add to it. The world has changed and the tradition must change with it."

In a clipped precise voice, she says, "Without my patient caretaking there would have been no tradition for you to analyze and contest."

Looking more closely at her, I recognize that her eyes are glittering, not with anger, but with tears. I realize that I have upset her, wounded her, as only a daughter can wound. How sharper than a serpent's tooth is the ungrateful child.

She is hurt, and I am hurting as well. I don't want to fight with her. I don't want her to be angry with me or pained by my actions. I realize that, like any daughter, I want her approval.

I say gently, "I have always loved your formality, your discipline, and your courage. Through you the Magician's Body of Knowledge passes to the generations that come after us. Whatever I have said, whatever I have created, builds on what you have given me. It is all within the tradition. I have not left you. I am still here."

Her lips soften, and she holds herself a little less stiffly. "What did you call me here to ask me?" she says.

I started my invocation filled with pride. I have undertaken a journey of discovery, of questioning and learning. I have undergone a further journey of transformation, passing through a series of tests and revelations. It seemed like a great accomplishment, but looking at Lady Tradition, it suddenly doesn't seem so impressive. I realize how many women over how many decades have added to her store of knowledge. Am I so sure that I cannot learn from her? I say quietly, "Would you show me what I have missed?"

I find myself in a dark tiled room, warm and steamy. It is a woman-only bathhouse, with a sauna, a hot pool, benches. Lady Tradition reaches up and loosens her hair. She slips out of her skirt and her blouse, revealing a thin athletic frame, and lowers herself into the hot pool. I drop my clothes on the bench and join her, sliding into the pool. Other women move around the edges of the room, emerging from the steam and vanishing again. It always amazes me in places like this one what a great variety of bodies women have, how different they are from the ideals presented to us.

Lady Tradition says quietly, "However many genders there are, two or a thousand, you yourself are a woman. Women know women. Women's bodies bring life into the world. You have bled just as your sisters have bled, bearing the fertility that brings forth human life. Through that ability you are connected to every other woman alive, to every other woman that ever lived or ever will."

I say, "Some men say that this is women's meaning and purpose. Some men say that when I claim the power of the womb I am proving that point."

Her eyes are closed. "It doesn't matter what the men say," she says serenely.

By that jujitsu mothers possess she has sidestepped my challenge, becoming not my adversary but my ally—and she is way cooler than I ever suspected.

I love that she has brought us both here, but I am also aware that we are both naked and vulnerable. I say to her, "Who is watching the door?"

Holding the Circle

I passionately long for a world in which every child is cradled, fed, and encouraged to grow strong, creative, and gentle. I passionately long for a world in which every woman is safe walking anywhere at any time, where every man is a potential friend, and brutality is a reviled and fading memory.

That world is a dream and a possible future, but it is not the present. Carol Lee Flinders was moved to write *At the Root of this Longing* by the abduction and murder of a girl in her community. In our world, every child and every woman is at risk every moment, not only of physical violence, but also of being exploited, wounded, silenced.

Those who withdraw to enclosure require protection. Sometimes that protection can take a very physical form. In the 1970s, Z Budapest organized men to stand outside women's circles to act as their protectors. This is a great function for the men who wish to support our magic, to protect our ability to withdraw into woman-only and solitary space, and to respect that space and not press us to permit them to enter into it with us.

Ultimately, though, it is up to us to remember the lesson of the warrior, to defend ourselves and defend our sisters, speaking up for each other, backing each other up, magically and physically.

In the bathhouse, Lady Tradition says to me, "There is a strong and armed sentinel at the door. We are safe here for as long as we wish to remain."

I came to this place to close out the work and prepare myself to emerge again into the world. I say to Lady Tradition, "Just when I was about to move on, you have taken me deeper into enclosure."

The sound of dripping water is everywhere around us, and women's laughter echoing softly off the tiles. "There is still work you have to do," she says.

DAUGHTER

Our foremother Moina Mathers wrote:

> The whole aim and object of the teaching is to bring a man to the knowledge of his higher self, to purify himself, to strengthen himself, to develop all qualities and powers of the being, that he may ultimately regain union with the Divine Man latent in himself, that Adam Kadmon, whom God hath made in His Own Image (Mathers 1926).

We have recast her words to read:

> The whole aim and object of the teaching is to bring a woman to the knowledge of her higher self, to purify herself, to strengthen herself, to develop all qualities and powers of the being, that she may ultimately regain union with the Divine Woman latent in herself, that Eve Kadmon, whom Goddess hath made in Her Own Image.

The series of ritual initiations in the Sisters of Seshat system reshaped the tradition to build a development system which would fulfill that idea. All these thoughts, meditations, rituals, transformations, have brought us to the place where we can begin the real work of creating ourselves.

Our foremother Doreen Valiente wrote:

. . . thy seeking and yearning shall avail thee not unless thou knowest the Mystery: that if that which thou seekest, thou findest not within thee, thou shalt never find it without thee. For behold, I have been with thee from the beginning, and I am that which is attained at the end of desire (Valiente 2000).

On December 22, 1923, Jane Wolfe wrote:

. . . I realized that in order to fully complete herself Woman had to achieve something in which Man has no part, i.e., Woman may give up her entire life to helping Man achieve his Will; it is not sufficient for her (Wolfe 2008).

Lady Tradition approves this sentiment: "Achieve something in which Man has no part. Tell me, that formula you were interested in, what was it again?"

I said, "The father becomes the son through the holy spirit."

"Not that formula," she said. "The other one."

Is this what she means? "The mother becomes the daughter through the holy spirit."

"It took you long enough to get there," she says tartly.

It turns out that this too is in the tradition.

The Mother Becomes the Daughter

Crowley's Gnostic Mass culminates in the moment when the priest declares, "O pater estin ho huious dia to pneuma hagion," or, "The father becomes the son through the holy spirit."

What happens when we say, "He meter estin he thugater dia to pneuma hagion," or, "The mother becomes the daughter through the holy spirit"?

The journey of the male magician resonates with the entire mythological infrastructure of father-mother-son, all the male-centered triads of deity: Osiris-Isis-Horus, God-Mary-Jesus, Mother Goddess-Consort-Son. There are fewer images that place the female child at the third point of that triad, but they do exist. In modern times, Leland gave us Lucifer-Diana-Aradia. In ancient Egypt, there is a marvelous triad at Aswan, that juncture between Egyptian and Nubian culture, which holds great hope for a new vision of the divine family. The water god and potter Khnum makes the ka, the physical side of the double being ka-ba, and places this ka in the womb of the mother. His blessing is health. His wife Satet, the warrior goddess, employs her arrows both to protect the pharaoh and to release the waters of the Nile in the annual flood. The flood itself is their daughter, Anukis, the life-giving Nile.

Western magic has asked women to read ourselves into the triad as the bride of the magician and the mother of the magician. These mythological images offer a way to read ourselves into the triad as the daughter, the beneficiary of the working. Through the magical formula we remake ourselves.

But in this formula—the mother becomes the daughter through the holy spirit—who or what is the holy spirit?

Human and Divine

For many centuries, Western metaphysics have focused on the union of opposites, and in particular the union of male and female, as its driving force. Women in the monastic traditions worked a different polarity, the union between the human and the divine.

Sister Prudence Allen briefly summarizes the theological writings of four women, Beatrice of Nazareth, Hadewijch, Mechtild of Magdeburg, and Marguerite Porete. These women viewed the mystical path through the lens of love. Beatrice discussed stages of love, Hadewijch used pregnancy and birth as metaphors for the development of love, Mechtild developed bridal metaphors, and Marguerite left a record of her solitary relationship with the divine (Allen 2002).

The bridal metaphor was commonplace in the monastic tradition. Women responded passionately to the call to become brides of Christ. They interpreted the Song of Songs as a love poem describing the relationship between Christ and themselves.

The Song of Songs is worth reviewing. At first glance it doesn't seem to belong in the Bible, emerging from the sensual Near Eastern love poem tradition. Some academics believe it was so well known and deeply loved that it had to be included in the canon. Hebrew commentary read the poem as a spiritual metaphor describing God's love for his people. Medieval Christian theology also treated the poem as a metaphor describing the union of Christ and his church.

The poem describes the love between a man and a woman, the Shulamite. It begins with the woman's voice: "Let him kiss me with the kisses of his mouth: for thy love is better than wine." Its language is at once physical and ecstatic.

Many musicians have been inspired by this poem through the millennia. Medieval monastic musicians wrote melodies to excerpts of the text. In the fourteenth century, Katherina von Tirs set to music a part of the poem where the woman describes her lover's seduction, "My beloved one spoke to me: Arise, make haste, my love, my dove, my beautiful one, and come" (Tindemans 2010).

Dorothy Donnelly described the physicality women mystics have brought to their devotions. Hadewijch, Catherine of Siena, the mystic Theresa of Avila all wrote of the love of God as deeply felt, sensually experienced, a physical eros. The title of her essay, "The Sexual Mystic, Embodied Spirituality," brings us to the fulfillment of the promise of the union between body, mind, and spirit, the joy that arises when we experience spirituality through our physicality (Donnelly 1987).

The medieval musician and theologian Hildegard de Bingen directed a woman's monastery where she dressed the women in bridal gowns. Her music often spoke of love; in *Karitas* she sang, "Love lives in everything, from the deepest depths to the highest stars, and most lovely over all, Because she gave the highest King the kiss of peace" (Tindemans 2010).

In the monastic tradition that treated each woman as the bride of Christ, I see a resonance of the Krishna Lila. In this Hindu story Krishna danced with the gopis (milkmaids) who loved him, multiplying himself so that each woman in the dance was able to dance with him.

Medieval monastic theology also focused on the image of Mary as separate from the world of human sexuality, as the bride of God and mother of Christ. Although some women theologians today valorize Mary as a form of Goddess, it was important in the medieval context that Mary remain human, as an exemplar and example of the lives the women monastics sought to lead, apart from the world of men, and turned entirely toward relationship with the divine.

There were many reasons women entered monasteries, as many stories as there were women. Some were forced to enter, like Heloise and Hildegard. Some women must have chafed at the confinement, but others surely fled to the monasteries as a retreat. Women's lot varied with time and place, but women worked very hard everywhere and were often victims of brutality. The monastery provided shelter, and also provided education, the company of women, and the ability to focus on the internal and spiritual life. The image of the human Mary as the mother of God provided an authorizing example for dedication to the spiritual life.

Women and Angels

Mary was visited by an angel. Dr. Amy Hale explores the work of Ithell Colquhoun, the Celtic mystic whose journals and especially whose images hint at union (both physical and spiritual) with spiritual beings (Hale 2009).

My brother in the O.T.O., Vere Chappell, champions the work of Ida Craddock (Chappell 1999). This early modern Theosophist, feminist teacher, and writer advocated sexual education for women. She explored the esoteric ramifications of sexuality. In *Heavenly Bridegrooms* she wrote: "It has been my high privilege to have some practical experience as the earthly wife of an angel from the unseen world" (Craddock 1894).

This type of operation is intensely personal. In Western Traditional Magic, this falls into the category of adept's work, a form of the Knowledge and Conversation of the Holy Guardian Angel. As we have seen, this operation summons the magician's personal daimon, angel, Genius to directly connect with the divine. This operation is arguably the central mystery of Western Traditional Magic, the mystery of the direct contact with the divine, a divinity which is not only the universe, but which manifests in a spirit that has a unique connection to one individual human and no other. Marriage is one metaphor for this; sexuality is another, with the caveat that this sexuality is emphatically not heterosexual—it is not a sexuality that connects woman to man, but instead connects woman to the divine, through the agency of her own unique angel, Genius, daimon.

The formula, the mother becomes the daughter through the holy spirit, is an invitation, the possibility of blending self with spirit to create a new way of being. In this formula I am pregnant through an infusion of spirit, pregnant with myself.

THE END AND THE BEGINNING

I invoked Lady Tradition to teach her a new form to her magic. In response she has led me more deeply into enclosure, to an ancient inmost sanctuary of women's magic.

"Are you ready to dare to face yourself?" she asks me.

I follow her eyes to the small room beyond the pool. I know it will be completely bare, simply a room, but luminous, and when I walk into it, I will be completely naked. The magic I can make with no tools, no clothes, entirely alone, that magic is the secret heart of the women's magical tradition. In that room I can effect the transformation of myself that transforms the world.

Protected by my sisters and deeply grateful to them, supported by Lady Tradition and profoundly grateful to her, driven by that love for spirit that has given the deepest meaning to my life, I step into the room and close the door.

WORKS CITED

Ackerman, Robert (1991). *The Myth and Ritual School: J.G. Frazer and the Cambridge Ritualists*. New York: Routledge.

Ackerman, Susan (1992). *Under Every Green Tree: Popular Religion in Sixth-Century Judah*. Atlanta: Harvard Semitic Monographs.

Adams, T., B. Edwards, G. Nutting (producers), and B. Edwards (director). *Victor Victoria* [Motion picture]. United States: Metro-Goldwyn-Mayer, 1982.

Allen, Sister Prudence (1985). *The Concept of Woman: The Aristotelian Revolution, 750 B.C. – A.D. 1250*. Grand Rapids: William B. Eerdmans Publishing Company.

———— (2002). *The Concept of Woman, Volume II: The Early Humanist Reformation, 1250–1500, Part 1 and Part 2*. Grand Rapids: William B. Eerdmans Publishing Company, 2002.

Ashcroft-Nowicki, Dolores (1983). *The Shining Paths*. Wellingborough, Northhamptonshire: Aquarian Press.

———— (1986). *The Ritual Magic Workbook, A Practical Course of Self-Initiation*. Wellingborough, Northhamptonshire: Aquarian Press.

Assiter, Alison (1996). *Enlightened Women, Modernist Feminism in a Postmodern Age*. London: Routledge.

Bachofen, J. J. (1967). *Myth, Religion, and Mother-Right*. New York: Princeton University Press.

Battersby, Christine (1989). *Gender and Genius: Towards a Feminist Aesthetics*. Indianapolis: Indianapolis University Press.

———— (1998). *The Phenomenal Woman: Feminist Metaphysics and the Patterns of Identity*. New York: Routledge.

Belenky, Mary Field, Blythe McVicker Clinchy, Nancy Rule Goldberger, and Jill Mattuck Tarule (1986). *Women's Ways of Knowing: The Development of Self, Voice and Mind*. New York: Basic Books.

Bell, Lanny (1997), "The New Kingdom 'Divine' Temple—The Example of Luxor." In *Temples of Ancient Egypt*, Byron E. Shafer, editor. Cornell: Cornell University Press.

Bell, Susan Groag (2008). "Christine de Pizan in her study." Cahiers de Recherches Medievales, Études Christiniennes, 10 June 2008. Retrieved December 22, 2009. Website: http://crm.revues.org/index3212.html.

Bem, Sandra (nd). *Bem Sex Role Inventory*. Retrieved June 12, 2010. Website: www.neiu.edu/~tschuepf/bsri.html.

Berkenwald, Leah (2010). "Happy 90th Birthday, Gerda Lerner!" Retrieved August 14, 2010. Website: http://jwablog.jwa.org/happy-90th-gerda-lerner.

Bernal, Martin (2006). *Black Athena: The Afroasiatic Roots of Classical Civilization*. New York: Rutgers University Press.

Bilefsky, Daniel (2008). "Albanian Custom Fades: Woman as Family Man." *New York Times*, June 28, 2008. www.nytimes.com/2008/06/25/world/europe/25virgins.html.

Bishop Athanasius (367). *Letter XXIX. Of the particular books and their number, which are accepted by the Church. From the thirty-ninth Letter of Holy Athanasius, Bishop of Alexandria, on the Paschal festival; wherein he defines canonically what are the divine books which are accepted by the Church*. Retrieved November 5, 2009, from Christian Classics Ethereal Library. Website: www.ccel.org/ccel/schaff/npnf204.xxv.iii.iii.xxv.html.

Bleir, Ruth (1984). *Science and Gender: A Critique of Biology and Its Theories on Women*. Oxford: Pergamon Press.

Bolen, Jean Shinoda (1985). *Goddesses in Everywoman*. New York: Harper Collins.

Brenk, Frederick (1998). "Aphrodite's Girdle: No Way to Treat a Lady." In *Relighting the Souls: Studies in Plutarch, in Greek Literature, Religion, and Philosophy, and in the New Testament Background*. Stuttgart: Steiner.

Budapest, Zsuzsanna (2007). *The Holy Book of Women's Mysteries*. York Beach, ME: Red Wheel/Weiser.

Burke, Edmund (1790). *Reflections on the Revolution in France*. Retrieved June 12, 2010, from the Archive for the History of Economic Thought. Website: http://socserv.socsci.mcmaster.ca/oldecon/ugcm/3ll3/burke/revfrance.pdf.

Butler, Judith (1990). *Gender Trouble*. New York: Routledge.

Campbell, Joseph (1949, 1968, 2008). *The Hero with a Thousand Faces*. Novato, California: New World Library.

Chappell, Vere (1999). "Ida Craddock: Sexual Mystic and Martyr for Freedom." Retrieved June 9, 2010, from O.T.O. USA. Website: www.idacraddock.org.

Child, Francis James (1886). *The English and Scottish Popular Ballads*. Boston: Houghton, Mifflin.

Christ, Carol P., with Judith Plaskow, editors (1992). *Womanspirit Rising: A Feminist Reader in Religion*. San Francisco: Harper and Row.

Christ, Carol P. (2003). *She Who Changes, Re-Imagining the Divine in the World*. New York: Palgrave MacMillan.

Colquhoun, Ithell (1961, 2003). *Goose of Hermogenes*. London: Peter Owen.

Copenhaver, Brian (1995). *Hermetica: The Greek Corpus Hermeticum and the Latin Asclepius in a New English Translation, with Notes and Introduction*. Cambridge: Cambridge University Press.

Craddock, Ida (1894). *Heavenly Bridegrooms*. Retrieved June 9, 2010, from O.T.O. USA. Website: www.idacraddock.org.

Crowley, Aleister (1904). *Liber Al Vel Legis (The Book of the Law)*. Retrieved June 12, 2010, from O.T.O. USA. Website: http://lib.oto-usa.org/libri/liber0220.html.

———— (1911). *Liber Resh vel Helios*. Retrieved June 12, 2010, from O.T.O. USA. Website: http://lib.oto-usa.org/libri/liber0200.html.

———— (1941). *Liber Oz*. Retrieved June 12, 2010, from O.T.O. USA. Website: http://lib.oto-usa.org/libri/liber0077.html.

Crowley, Vivianne (1996, 2003). *Wicca, A Comprehensive Guide to the Old Religion in the Modern World*. London: Harper Collins.

Daly, Mary (1971). "After the Death of God the Father: Women's Liberation and the Transformation of Christian Consciousness." *Commonweal*, March 12, 1971. Retrieved June 12, 2010, from Duke University Libraries. Website: http://scriptorium.lib.duke.edu/wlm/after.

———— (1973). *Beyond God the Father, Toward a Philosophy of Women's Liberation*. Boston: Beacon Press.

Dashu, Max (2000). "Knocking Down Straw Dolls: A Critique of Cynthia Eller's *The Myth of Matriarchal Prehistory: Why an Invented Past Won't Give Women a Future*." The Suppressed Histories Archives. Website: www.suppressedhistories.net/articles/eller.html.

Davis, Phillip (1998). *Goddess Unmasked: The Rise of Neopagan Feminist Spirituality*. Dallas: Spence Publishing Company.

Dean, Rev. Dave (nd). "The Rosette." Retrieved June 12, 2010, from Seshat. org. Website: www.seshat.org/seshat/page3.html.

de Gouge, Olympe. *Declaration of the Rights of Woman and the Female Citizen*. Retrieved June 12, 2010, from Sunshine for Women. Website: www. pinn.net/~sunshine/book-sum/gouges.html.

de Pizan, Christine (1405, 1982). *The Book of the City of Ladies*. New York: Persea Books.

Devor, Holly (1989). *Gender Blending, Confronting the Limits of Duality*. Bloomington: Indiana University Press.

Dickinson, Gloria Harper (nd). "Ancient Kemet." Retrieved September 26, 2010, from website: http://dickinsg.intrasun.tcnj.edu/diaspora/kemet. html.

Donnelly, Dorothy (1987). "The Sexual Mystic: Embodied Spirituality." In *The Feminist Mystic*, Mary Giles, editor. New York: Crossroad.

Downing, Christine (1981). *The Goddess: Mythological Images of the Feminine*. Lincoln, NE: Author's Choice Press.

Dreger, Alice Domurat (1998). *Hermaphrodites and the Medical Invention of Sex*. Cambridge: Harvard University Press.

Dreger, Alice (2010). "Intersex and Sports: Back to the Same Old Game." *Bioethics Forum, Diverse Commentary on Issues in Bioethics*. January 22, 2010. Website: www.thehastingscenter.org/Bioethicsforum/Post. aspx?id=4426&blogid=140.

Dreger, Alice, and Ellen K. Feder (2010). "Bad Vibrations." *Bioethics Forum, Diverse Commentary on Issues in Bioethics*. June 16, 2010. Website: www. thehastingscenter.org/Bioethicsforum/Post.aspx?id=4730&blogid=140.

Dworkin, Andrea (1974). *Woman Hating: A Radical Look at Sexuality*. New York: Dutton Press.

Ehrenberg, Margaret (1989). *Women in Prehistory*. Norman, OK: University of Oklahoma Press.

Eller, Cynthia (2000). *The Myth of Matriarchal Prehistory: Why an Invented Past Won't Give Women a Future*. Boston: Beacon Press.

Eisler, Riane (1987). *The Chalice and the Blade: Our History, Our Future*. New York: Harper Collins.

Farr, Florence (1894). *The Dancing Faun*. BiblioBazaar.

———— (1901, 1996). *The Enochian Experiments of the Golden Dawn*. Edmonds: Holmes Publishing.

———— (1896, 1982). *Egyptian Magic*. Wellingborough, Northamptonshire: Aquarian Press.

Farrar, Janet and Stewart (1989). *The Witches' Goddess*. Custer, WA: Phoenix Publishing.

———— (1989). *The Witches' God*. Custer, WA: Phoenix Publishing.

Faulkner, R. O. (2007). *The Ancient Egyptian Pyramid Texts*. Stillwell, KS: Digireads.

Flax, Jane (1990). *Thinking Fragments, Psychoanalysis, Feminism, and Post-Modernism in the Contemporary West*. Berkeley: University of California Press.

Flinders, Carol Lee (1998). *At the Root of This Longing, Reconciling a Spiritual Hunger and a Feminist Thirst*. San Francisco: Harper and Row.

Fortune, Dion (1935). *The Sea Priestess*. London: Inner Light Publishing.

———— (1935, 1998). *The Mystical Qabbalah*. San Francisco: Red Wheel/Weiser.

Frazer, James George (1922). *The Golden Bough*. Retrieved June 12, 2010, from Project Gutenberg. Website: http://onlinebooks.library.upenn.edu/webbin/gutbook/lookup?num=3623.

Frye, Marilyn (1996). "The Necessity of Differences: Constructing a Positive Category of Women." *Signs*, Vol. 21, No. 4. Chicago: University of Chicago Press.

Frymer-Kensky, Tikva (1992). *In the Wake of the Goddesses: Women, Culture and the Biblical Transformation of Pagan Myth*. New York: Fawcett Columbine.

Fulbrook, Mary (2003). *Historical Theory*. New York: Routledge.

Gardner, Gerald (1949). *High Magic's Aid*. London: Michael Houghton.

Giles, Mary, editor (1989). *The Feminist Mystic and Other Essays on Women and Spirituality*. New York: Crossroad.

Gimbutas, Marija (1974). *The Goddesses and Gods of Old Europe, 6500–3500 BC, Myths and Cult Images*. Berkeley: University of California Press.

———— (1999). *The Living Goddesses*. Berkeley: University of California Press.

Goldberger, Nancy, Jill Tarule, Blythe Clinchy, and Mary Belenky (1996). *Knowledge, Difference, and Power*. New York: Basic Books.

Goldstein, Joshua (2001). *War and Gender: How Gender Shapes the War System and Vice Versa*. Cambridge: Cambridge University Press.

Goldstein, Rabbi Elyse (1998). *ReVisions: Seeing Torah Through a Feminist Lens*. Woodstock, VT: Jewish Lights Publishing.

Goodrich, Normal Lorre (1989). *Priestesses*. New York: Franklin Watts.

Gottleib, Lynn (1995). *She Who Dwells Within: A Feminist Vision of a Renewed Judaism*. New York: Harper Collins.

Graves, Robert (1948). *The White Goddess: A Historical Grammar of Poetic Myth*. London: Faber and Faber.

Greer, Mary K. (1995). *Women of the Golden Dawn: Rebels And Priestesses*. Rochester, VT: Park Street Press.

Gross, Rita (1996). *Feminism and Religion, An Introduction*. Boston: Beacon Press.

Hale, Amy (2009). "The Bride of the Snake: A Brief Introduction to the Magic of Ithell Colquhoun." In *Women's Voices in Magic*, Brandy Williams, editor. London: Megalithica.

Hammer, Olav (2004). *Claiming Knowledge: Strategies of Epistemology from Theosophy to the New Age*. Leiden, the Netherlands: Koninklijke Brill, 2004.

Heselton, Phillip (2001). *Gerald Gardner Witchcraft Revival*. Thame, England: Essex House.

Hirshey, Gerry (2005). "The Butterflies and Banshees of L-O-V-E: When Girls Ruled the Airwaves." *One Kiss Can Lead to Another: Girl Groups Lost and Found*. Rhino Entertainment, Warner Music 601993_cd 081227464523.

Hutton, Ronald (1999). *The Triumph of the Moon: A History of Modern Witchcraft*. Oxford: Oxford University Press.

Johnson, Allan G. (2006). *Privilege, Power and Difference*. New York: McGraw-Hill.

Johnson, Captain Charles (1724). *A General History of the Robberies and Murders of the Most Notorious Pyrates*. Eastern North Carolina Digital Library. Website: http://digital.lib.ecu.edu/historyfiction/item.aspx?id=joh.

Kaplan, Aryeh (1997). *Sepher Yetzirah, the Book of Creation*. York Beach, ME: Red Wheel/Weiser.

Keuls, Eva C. (1985). *The Reign of the Phallus: Sexual Politics in Ancient Greece*. Berkeley: University of California Press.

King James Bible. Retrieved August 14, 2010. Website: www.kingjamesbibleonline.org/.

Kingsford, Anna Bonus, and Edward Maitland (1890). *The Perfect Way: or, the Finding of Christ*. London: Field and Tuer, the Leadenhall Press.

Kingsford, Anna (Bonus) (1937). *Clothed with the Sun*. Edward Maitland, editor. London: John Watckins.

Kittay, Eva (1984). "Womb Envy as an Explanatory Concept." *Mothering: Essays in Feminist Theory*. Joyce Trebilcot, editor. New Jersey: Rowman and Allanheld.

Kindlon, Daniel, and Michael Thompson (1999). *Raising Cain: Protecting the Emotional Life of Boys*. New York: Random House.

Kuntz, Darcy (1996). *The Complete Golden Dawn Cipher Manuscript*. Edmonds: Holmes Publishing Group.

Kunzig, Robert (1999). "A Tale of Two Archaeologists." *Discover: Science, Technology and the Future*, May 1 1999. http://discovermagazine.com/1999/may/archeologist.

Lakoff, Robin Tolmach (2004). *Language and Women's Place, Text and Commentaries*. New York: Oxford University Press.

Lang, Sabine (1998). *Men as Women, Women as Men: Changing Gender in Native American Cultures*. Austin: University of Texas Press.

Laquer, Thomas (1990). *Making Sex: Body and Gender from the Greeks to Freud*. Cambridge: Harvard University Press.

Laura, Judith (1997, 2008). *Goddess Spirituality for the 21st Century: From Kabbalah to Quantum Physics*. Banger, ME: Open Sea Press.

Leland, Charles G. (1899). *Aradia: Gospel of the Witches*. New York: Samuel Weiser, 1974. First publication David Nutt, London.

Lesko, Barbara (1999). *The Great Goddesses of Egypt*. Norman, OK: University of Oklahoma Press.

Levi, Eliphas (1999). *Transcendental Magic*. Tr. A. E. Waite. York Beach, ME: Samuel Weiser, 1999. First publication Rider & Co., England, 1896.

Levy, Ariel (2009). "Either/Or: Sports, Gender, and Caster Semenya." *New Yorker*, November 30, 2009: 46.

Long, Asphodel (1992). "Goddess Figures in Czechoslovakia." *Wood and Water 40*, Autumn 1992, www.asphodel-long.com/html/czech.html.

Louis, Margot K (2009). *Persephone Rises, 1860–1927, Mythography, Gender, and the Creation of a New Spirituality*. Burlington, VT: Ashgate Publishing.

Lucian, *The Syrian Goddess*. Herbert A. Strong and John Garstang, transators (1913). Retrieved June 12, 2010, from Sacred Texts. Website: www.sacred-texts.com/cla/luc/tsg/tsg07.htm.

Magee, Bryan (1998). *The Story of Philosophy: A Concise Introduction to the World's Greatest Thinkers and Their Ideas*. New York: DK Publishing.

Majercik, Ruth (1989). *The Chaldean Oracles, Texts, Translations, and Commentary*. Leiden: E. J. Brill.

Marler, Joan (1997). *From the Realm of the Ancestors: An Anthology in Honor of Marija Gimbutas*. San Diego: Paradigm Publishing Company.

———— (2003). "The Myth of Universal Patriarchy: A Critical Response to Cynthia Eller's *Myth of Matriarchal Prehistory*." Belili Productions. Website: www.belili.org/marija/eller_response.html.

———— (2003). "The Myth of Universal Patriarchy: A Critical Response to Cynthia Eller's *Myth of Matriarchal Prehistory*". Belili Productions. Web site: http://www.belili.org/marija/eller_response.html.

Mathers, S. L. MacGregor (1889, 1999). *The Key of Solomon the King*. York Beach, ME: Samuel Weiser, 1999. First publication George Redway, London, 1889.

———— (1900). *The Book of Sacred Magic of Abramelin the Mage*. New York: Dover.

———— (1926). *The Kabbalah Unveiled*. England: Arkana, 1991.

Meador, Betty de Shong (2000). *Inanna, Lady of Largest Heart: Poems of the Sumerian High Priestess Enheduanna*. Austin: University of Texas Press.

Mellaart, James (1967). *Catal Huyuk, A Neolithic Town in Anatolia*. New York: McGraw-Hill.

Middlebrook, Diane Wood (1998). *Suits Me: The Double Life of Billy Tipton*. New York: Houghton Mifflin, 1998.

Miller, Casey, and Kate Swift (1980). *The Handbook of Nonsexist Writing*. New York: Harper and Row.

Monaghan, Patricia (1994). *O Mother Sun, A New View of the Cosmic Feminine*. Freedom, CA: Crossing Press.

Miller, Patricia Cox (1989). "In Praise of Nonsense." A. H. Armstrong, editor, *Classical Mediterranean Spirituality, World Spirituality 15*. New York: Crossroad.

Moore, Keith (2010). "Semenya Wins Comeback Race in Finland." Retrieved August 14, 2010, from NBC Sports. Website: http://nbcsports.msnbc.com/id/38264595/ns/sports/.

Moore, Keith. and R. V. N. Persaud (1998). *The Developing Human, Clinically Oriented Embryology*. Philadelphia: Harcourt Brace.

Murray, Margaret Alice (1921). *The Witch-Cult in Western Europe*. London: Oxford University Press.

Nataf, Zachary I. (1998). "Whatever I Feel." *New Interntionalist*, Issue 300, April 1990. Retrieved June 12, 2010, from the New Internationalist. Website: www.newint.org/issue300/trans.html.

Noble, Vicki (1983). *Motherpeace: A Way to the Goddess through Myth, Art, and Tarot*. New York: Harper and Row.

———— (2003). *The Double Goddess: Women Sharing Power*. Rochester, VT: Bear and Company.

Norton, Rosaleen (2009). *Thorn in the Flesh*. York Beach, ME: Teitan Press.

Nye, Andrea (1990). *Words of Power: A Feminist Reading of the History of Logic*. London: Routledge.

Owen, Alex (1989). *The Darkened Room: Women, Power and Spiritualisim in Late Victorian England*. Chicago: University of Chicago Press.

———— (2004). *The Place of Enchantment, British Occultism and the Culture of the Modern*. Chicago: University of Chicago Press.

Open Source Order of the Golden Dawn. www.osogd.org.

Pagels, Elaine (1979). *The Gnostic Gospels*. New York: Random House.

Paine, Thomas (1791). *The Rights of Man*. Retrieved June 12, 2010, from USHistory.org. Website: www.ushistory.org/paine/rights/.

Paris, Ginette (1990). *Pagan Grace*. Trans. Joanna Mott. Dallas, TX: Spring Publications.

———— (1986). *Pagan Meditations: The Worlds of Aphrodite, Artemis and Hestia*. Trans. Gwendolyn Moore. Dallas, TX: Spring Publications.

Parker, Roszika, and Griselda Pollock (1981). *Old Mistresses: Women, Art and Ideology*. London: Harper Collins.

Patai, Raphael (1967). *The Hebrew Goddess*. Detroit: Wayne State University Press.

Phillips, Julia (2004). *History of Witchcraft in England, 1939 to the Present Day*. Website: www.geraldgardner.com/History_of_Wicca_Revised.pdf.

Phillips, Osbourne (2001). *The Aurum Solis Initiation Ceremonies and Inner Magical Techniques*. Loughborough, England: Thoth Publications.

Pike, Albert (1992). *Masonry of Adoption: Masonic Rituals for Women*. Whitefish, MT: Kessinger.

———— (2005). *Secret Masonic Rituals for Women*. Whitefish, MT: Kessinger.

Plaskow, Judith, with Carol P. Christ, editors (1989). *Weaving the Visions: New Patterns in Feminist Spirituality*. New York: Harper and Row.

Plaskow, Judith, with Donna Berman, editor (2005). *The Coming of Lilith: Essays on Feminism, Judaism, and Sexual Ethics, 1972-2003*. Boston: Beacon Press.

Pollack, Rachel (2004). *The Kabbalah Tree: A Journey of Balance and Growth*. St. Paul, MN: Llewellyn Publications.

———— (1980) *Seventy-Eight Degrees of Wisdom, A Book of Tarot, Part 1: The Major Arcana*. Wellingborough, Northhamptonshire: Aquarian Press.

————l (1983) *Seventy-Eight Degrees of Wisdom, A Book of Tarot, Part 2: The Minor Arcana and Readings*. Wellingborough, Northhamptonshire: Aquarian Press.

Pritchard, James Bennet, editor (1958). *The Ancient Near East, Volume I, An Anthology of Texts and Pictures*. Princeton: Princeton University Press.

——— (1969). *Ancient Near Eastern Texts Relating to the Old Testament*. Princeton: Princeton University Press.

Reed, Ellen Cannon (1985, 1997). *The Witches' Qabbalah: The Pagan Path and the Tree of Life*. Boston: Red Wheel/Weiser.

Rigoglioso, Marguerite (2003). "Women's Spirituality Scholars Speak Out: A Report on the 7th Annual Gender and Archeology Conference at Sonoma State." Bellili Productions. Website: www.belili.org/marija/rigoglioso.html.

Ritner, Robert (1997). *The Mechanics of Egyptian Magical Practice*. Chicago: The Oriental Institute.

Robinson, James M, editor (1978). *The Nag Hammadi Library*. Leiden: E.J. Brill.

Ronan, Stephen, editor (1992). *The Goddess Hekate*. Great Britain: Antony Rowe.

Rose, Elliot (1962). *A Razor for a Goat: Problems in the History of Witchcraft and Diabolism*. Toronto: University of Toronto Press.

Ruether, Rosemary Radford (1992). *Gaia and God, An Ecofeminist Theology of Earth Healing*. New York: Harper Collins.

——— (2005). *Goddesses and the Divine Feminine: A Western Religious History*. Berkeley: University of California.

Sagan, Carl (1980). *Cosmos*. New York: Random House.

Sabazius X° and AMT IX° (nd). *History of Ordo Templi Orientis*. Retrieved December 11 2009 from O.T.O.-USA. Website: http://oto-usa.org/history.html.

Sanders, Maxine (2007). *Fire Child: The Life and Times of Maxine Sanders 'Witch Queen'*. Oxford: Mandrake.

Seckler, Phyllis (2003). *Jane Wolfe: Her Life with Aleister Crowley, Part 1 and Part 2*. Red Flame.

Serano, Julia (2007). *Whipping Girl: A Transsexual Woman on Sexism and the Scapegoating of Femininity*. Emeryville, CA: Seal Press.

Seraphina, Soror Inde (2009). "Enochian Motherhood." In *Women's Voices in Magic*, Brandy Williams, editor. London: Megalithica.

Shaw, Gregory (1967). *Theurgy and the Soul. The Neoplatonism of Iamblichus*. University Park, PA: Pennsylvania University Press.

Shelley, Mary Wollstonecraft (1818). *Frankenstein*. Retrieved June 12, 2010, from Project Gutenberg. Website: www.gutenberg.org/etext/84.

Sivananda, Sri Swami (nd). Devi Mahatmya. Retrieved June 12, 2010, from the Divine Life Society. Website: www.sivanandaonline.org/graphics/activities/navaratri_04/chapter-8.htm.

Spretnak, Charlene (1989). "The Myth of Demeter and Persephone." In Judith Plaskow and Carol Christ, editors, *Weaving the Visions: New Patterns in Feminist Spirituality.* San Francisco: Harper and Row.

Stanton, Elizabeth Cady (1891). "The Matriarchate and Mother-Age." In *Transactions of the National Council of Women of the United States, Assembled in Washington DC, February 22 to 25, 1891.* Rachel Foster Avery, editor. Philadelphia: J.P. Lippincott Company.

Stanton, Elizabeth Cady, and the Revising Committee (1898). *The Woman's Bible.* Sacred Texts. Website: www.sacred-texts.com/wmn/wb/.

Starhawk (1979, 1999). *The Spiral Dance: A Rebirth of the Ancient Religion of the Great Goddess.* San Francisco: Harper Collins.

Sterling, Anne Fausto (2000). *Sexing the Body: Gender Politics and the Construction of Sexuality.* New York: Basic Books.

Stern, David, and Mark Jay Mirsky (1990). *Rabbinic Fantasies: Imaginative Narratives from Classical Hebrew Literature.* New Haven: Yale University Press, 1990.

Stone, Merlin (1976). *When God Was a Woman.* Barnes and Noble reprint, 1993.

T. Apiryon (1995). *History of the Gnostic Catholic Church.* Website: www.hermetic.com/sabazius/history_egc.htm.

Tannen, Deborah (1990). *You Just Don't Understand: Women and Men in Conversation.* New York: Harper Collins.

Tedlock, Barbara (2005). *The Woman in the Shaman's Body: Reclaiming the Feminine in Religion and Medicine.* New York: Bantam Dell.

Tindemans, Margriet (2010). "Song of Songs," Medieval Womens Choir concert program.

Trucan, Robert (2001). *The Gods of Ancient Rome: Religion in Everyday Life from Archaic to Imperial.* New York: Routledge.

Tully, Caroline (2009). "Florence and the Mummy." In *Women's Voices in Magic,* Brandy Williams, editor. London: Megalithica.

Turnbull, H. (producer), and J. von Sternberg, (director). *Morocco* [Motion Picture]. United States: Paramount Pictures, 1930.

Valiente, Doreen (2000). *Charge of the Goddess.* Brighton: Hexagon Hoopix.

———— (1989, 2008). *The Rebirth of Witchcraft.* London: Robert Hale.

———— (1978, 1993). *Witchcraft for Tomorrow.* London: Robert Hale.

Velasco, Sherry (2000). *The Lieutenant Nun: Transgenderism, Lesbian Desire, and Cataline de Erauso*. Austin: University of Texas Press.

Vincent, Norah (2006). *Self-Made Man, One Woman's Year Disguised as a Man*. London: Penguin Books.

Whyte, Lesa (2009). "Magic and Pregnancy." In *Women's Voices in Magic*, Brandy Williams, editor. London: Megalithica.

Wilkinson, Richard (2003). *The Complete Gods and Goddesses of Ancient Egypt*. London: Thames and Hudson.

Williams, Brandy (2009). "Feminist Thelema." *Beauty and Strength, Proceedings of the Sixth Biennial National Ordo Templi Orientis Conference, Salem, Massachussetts, August 10–12, 2007 EV*. Riverside, CA: Ordo Templi Orientis U.S.A.

——— (1998). "The Woman's Phallus: Possession and Power in the Worship of Dionysos." *Think! The Best in Pagan Thought*, Volume 3 Issue 2, Beltaine/Summer 1998.

——— (2005). *Practical Magic for Beginners: Techniques and Rituals to Focus Magical Energy*. St. Paul, MN: Llewellyn.

Wolfe, Jane (2008). *Jane Wolfe: The Cefalu Diaries 1920–1923*. Sacramento, CA: College of Thelema.

Wollstonecraft, Mary (1787). *Thoughts on the Education of Daughters, with Reflections on Female Conduct, and the more important Duties of Life*. London: J. Johnson.

——— (1790). *A Vindication of the Rights of Men, in a Letter to the Right Honourable Edmund Burke, occasioned by his Reflections on the Revolution in France*. Retrieved June 12, 2010, from the Online Library of Liberty. Website: http://oll.libertyfund.org.

——— (1792). *A Vindication of the Rights of Woman*. Retrieved June 12, 2010, from the Modern History Sourcebook. Website: www.fordham. edu/halsall/mod/mw-vind.html.

Yates, Frances (1964). *Giordano Bruno and the Hermetic Tradition*. Chicago: University of Chicago Press.

——— (1966, 2001). *The Art of Memory*. Chicago: University of Chicago Press.

——— (1979). *The Occult Philosophy in the Elizabethan Age*. London: Routledge and Kegan Paul.

——— (1973). *The Rosicrucian Enlightenment*. London: Routledge.

——— (1969, 2009). *Theater of the World*. New York: Barnes and Noble.

MUSIC

While on retreat, I listened to many musical women's voices. Their work is never explicitly called out in the text, but their sensibility is woven into everything I write. Much of the music I listen to is created and recorded by Northwest musicians. I know some of them personally, and I even get to perform with them now and again.

EASTERN EUROPEAN
The oldest music I know is kept alive by Balkan and Slavic choirs.

Volya
The CD *Queen Earth* from the group Volya captures what they think are the oldest known unaltered songs, from Belarus. Group leader Volya Dzemka lists only an email contact, volyadzemka@gmail.com.

Juliana and PAVA
Juliana and PAVA's CD *Let the Bird Fly* reproduces village songs from Russia. Website: www.ethnorussia.com.

Dunava
The Seattle group Dunava recorded Balkan favorites on their self-titled CD. Website: www.dunava.org.

MEDIEVAL

Medieval Womens Choir

Mine is one of 60 voices captured on the two Medieval Women's choir CDs, *River of Red* and *Laude Novella*. Website: www.medievalwomenschoir. org.

Catherine Bott

Her lovely CD, *Sweet Is the Song, Music of the Troubadours and Trouveres*, has my favorite version of the woman troubador's song "A chantar m'er de so qu'ieu non volria" (I must sing of that which I would rather not).

Sinfonye

The group's anthology *Bella Domna, The Medieval Woman Lover, Poet, Patroness and Saint* records some of the cantigas de amiga, haunting and beautiful songs of women waiting for fishermen to return home from sea.

Heliotrope

This group features one of my favorite woman musicians, Shira Kammen. Their CD *The Romance of the Rose, Feminine Voices from Medieval France* covers many medieval musical styles and is on my frequent rotation pile.

MODERN

Laura Love

I've clapped at Laura Love concerts for decades. She is a powerful activist with a strong heart and amazing musical skills. My favorite CD for this journey was *Shum Ticky*. Website: www.lauralove.net.

Carrie Akre

Another Northwest voice whom I first encountered at the Northwest Folklife Festival. Whenever I hit the fear wall while writing this book, I'd pop in her CD *Last the Evening* and play her anthem "Breathe" until I could.

INDEX

TO WRITE TO THE AUTHOR